"Shame is indeed a phenomenon that is ~~both in the~~ ~~in~~ the space between us. Dr DeYoung does a solid job ~~in addressing the chal~~lenges of living with and treating chronic shame using a thoughtful, humane, and scientific approach."

—**Louis Cozolino**, PhD, professor of
psychology at Pepperdine University's Graduate
School of Education and Psychology

"Beginning with diverse clinical vignettes with very dissimilar diagnoses, Patricia DeYoung tackles the unvoiced but powerful presence of shame that so often lies at the unspoken core of what troubles our clients. She beautifully and evocatively gives voice and shape to the annihilating impact of lack of attunement. DeYoung also makes the point that because shame takes root in relationship, we must heal it relationally. Equally important, she reminds us that, to be effective in this work, therapists must engage in their own ongoing internal work. This special book needs to be read by all of us."

—**Patricia L. Papernow**, EdD,
instructor in psychology at Harvard Medical
School and author of *Surviving and Thriving in
Stepfamily Relationships*

"Defining shame as first and foremost a relational experience, Patricia DeYoung unpacks the extensive, damaging consequences of feeling chronically shamed while illustrating effective treatment in clear, accessible language. For clinicians who wish to understand and treat shame from the psychodynamic perspective, this book is a vital resource."

—**Martha Sweezy**, PhD,
associate director and director of training
for the dialectical behavioral therapy program
at Harvard Medical School's Cambridge Health Alliance

Understanding and Treating Chronic Shame

Chronic shame is painful, corrosive, and elusive. It resists self-help and undermines even intensive psychoanalysis. Patricia A. DeYoung's cutting-edge book gives chronic shame the serious attention it deserves, integrating new brain science with an inclusive tradition of relational psychotherapy. She looks behind the myriad symptoms of shame to its relational essence. As DeYoung describes how chronic shame is wired into the brain and developed in personality, she clarifies complex concepts and makes them available for everyday therapy practice.

Grounded in clinical experience and alive with case examples, *Understanding and Treating Chronic Shame* is highly readable and immediately helpful. Patricia A. DeYoung's clear, engaging writing helps readers recognize the presence of shame in the therapy room, think through its origins and effects in their clients' lives, and decide how best to work with those clients. Therapists will find that *Understanding and Treating Chronic Shame* enhances the scope of their practice and efficacy with this client group, which comprises a large part of most therapy practices. Challenging, enlightening, and nourishing, this book belongs in the library of every shame-aware therapist.

Patricia A. DeYoung, MSW, PhD, is a relational psychotherapist, clinical supervisor, and a founding faculty member of the Toronto Institute for Relational Psychotherapy.

Understanding and Treating Chronic Shame
A Relational/Neurobiological Approach

Patricia A. DeYoung

NEW YORK AND LONDON

First published 2015
by Routledge
711 Third Avenue, New York, NY 10017

and by Routledge
27 Church Road, Hove, East Sussex BN3 2FA

Routledge is an imprint of the Taylor & Francis Group, an informa business

Library of Congress Cataloging in Publication Data
DeYoung, Patricia A., 1953–
Understanding and treating chronic shame: a relational/neurobiological
approach/by Patricia A. DeYoung.
pages cm
Includes bibliographical references and index.
1. Shame. 2. Psychotherapist and patient. I. Title.
RC455.4.S53D49 2015
616.89'14—dc23
2014032939

ISBN: 978-1-138-83119-3 (hbk)
ISBN: 978-1-138-83120-9 (pbk)
ISBN: 978-1-315-73441-5 (ebk)

Typeset in Sabon
by Swales & Willis Ltd, Exeter, Devon, UK

MIX
Paper from
responsible sources
FSC
www.fsc.org   FSC® C013056

Printed and bound in Great Britain by
TJ International Ltd, Padstow, Cornwall

To my adult children,
Adriel, Rowan, and Jason,
and to rewriting legacies of shame
with tenacity and love

CONTENTS

ACKNOWLEDGMENTS   x

INTRODUCTION   xii

PART I: UNDERSTANDING CHRONIC SHAME   1

CHAPTER 1   Chronic Shame: An Unspoken Problem   3
CHAPTER 2   Shame Is Relational   18
CHAPTER 3   Shame and the Relational Brain   34
CHAPTER 4   Relational/Neurobiological Narratives
                   of Shame   44
CHAPTER 5   Assessing for Shame   58

PART II: TREATING CHRONIC SHAME   75

CHAPTER 6   Prerequisites for Working with Shame   77
CHAPTER 7   Fostering Right-Brain Connection   87
CHAPTER 8   Narrative as Right-Brain Integration   102
CHAPTER 9   Giving Shame Light and Air   116
CHAPTER 10   The Challenge of Dissociated Shame   136
CHAPTER 11   Lifetime Shame Reduction   162

REFERENCES   178

INDEX   184

ACKNOWLEDGMENTS

This book has been more than a decade in the making, and so I have had time to test its ideas in countless clinical discussions. I owe thanks to all those colleagues, supervisees, and students who through the years have listened to my thoughts on the presence and power of chronic shame in clients' lives and who have offered their ideas in response. It has been my privilege to theorize in a community full of lively talk about the connections between many kinds of clinical theory and the relational practice of psychotherapy.

A few of my colleagues have been closely involved in constructing this particular book. Rozanne Grimard, Jason Winkler, Karen Essex, and Judy Gould, who teach with me at the Toronto Institute for Relational Psychotherapy, read an early version of the text carefully. Their comments were especially useful because of the theory/praxis understanding of relational therapy we share, honed in our joint endeavor to teach an essentially right-brain model of clinical work.

Four other colleagues—Bonnie Simpson, David Schatzky, Susan Marcus, and Pat Archer—brought clinical wisdom and writerly sensitivity to their reading of the text. In the responses of all my Toronto readers, I felt understood in my passion to write about the shame we encounter so often in our work and also in ourselves. No one could offer more depth of support than a group of relational psychotherapists! They took my project seriously, and I welcomed their honest challenge to give it the best articulation possible, to peel back my own verbiage until I could find with clarity "what must be said."

Over the years, I started the book in at least four different ways, looking for a key concept that would bring meaningful coherence to a welter of material on shame. As I explain in the text, the theoretical key fell into my hand just over a year ago at an Allan Schore conference on the practice of right brain therapy. I wrote some new chapters quickly and gave them to my daughter, Adriel Weaver, to read. Though not a therapist, she is an accomplished legal and academic writer, and I am grateful for her help in thinking through opening issues of audience, voice, and tone. I'm also pleased that she made time to edit a final version of the text after all the substantive changes had been made.

Help came from far as well as near: I would like to thank Anna Moore, my editor at Routledge, for her encouragement to write this book ahead of the project she had first requested and for her reliable, reassuring presence just an email click away. I trust her intention to give the book the best life possible out in the world. Routledge review readers were helpful; I would especially like to mention Patricia Papernow, a therapist/writer I have never met but who gifted me with detailed attention to the first half of the text and valuable help in peeling away verbiage.

Clearly, many eyes and hands have been on this book to shape it into something useful. In its pages I also refer to dozens of theorists, past and present, who have influenced the shape and direction of my thought. But although I have benefitted from so much collegial conversation, both actual and virtual, I also need to say that this particular take on understanding and treating chronic shame is mine, and I take responsibility for how it now goes out into the world.

Though I cannot mention them by name, the book could not have been written without the many clients who have allowed me to come close to their emotional experience, the heart and soul of where they live, suffer, and hope. I have been moved by their pain, their courage, and their trust. Most of the client examples in the text are fictionalized and composite stories; only the emotional realities are true. Where a story is thinly disguised, I have asked for permission to use it as it appears in the text, and I deeply appreciate the consents given.

As each chapter of the book came off my printer, I gave it immediately to one person, Mary Greey, my partner for more than twenty years, knowing that my thoughts and words, like all the rest of me, would find a safe home with her. It may be true that "there ain't no cure for shame," but the consistent experience of safe home—knowing that one's being is welcomed with compassion and delight—makes a world of difference. In a sentence, and not so strangely (for we are often drawn to theorize what we know without words), that's also the take-home message of this book.

Patricia A. DeYoung
Toronto
May, 2014

INTRODUCTION

Shame hurts. If our shame is exposed, the pain can be unbearable. To save ourselves, we push shame away as fast as we can, covering for it with more tolerable states of being. These states of being are what we come to know of shame, both in ourselves and others. But they are compensations and collapses, masks and sleights of mind; they are not shame itself. What is shame itself? This book proposes that, despite its many disguises, shame can be understood as a unique, specific kind of interpersonal experience. This understanding of shame helps us see what's behind the camouflage. It also helps us, as therapists, make interpersonal contact with our chronically shamed clients in ways that can ease their suffering.

In the first part of the book, I define the interpersonal experience of shame and I use this relational definition to bring coherence to diverse aspects of existing shame theory. All shame theory seeks to shed light on a shape-shifting phenomenon that lives in the dark. I'm grateful for the snapshots, documents, and storylines that shame theorists have contributed to date. Their theories become part of the new story I offer, one that seeks out shame in its most shadowy origins, before thought can frame it or words can speak it. I try to capture how early, nonverbal shame experience, unrepaired, takes on a furtive but powerful life of its own as chronic shame. I believe that this understanding may begin to do some justice to the havoc such shame wreaks in the lives of psychotherapy clients who have no name for what ails them.

I take a relational, psychodynamic approach to what has been written about the problem of shame, drawing on self-psychological, intersubjective, self-in-relation, interpersonal, and attachment theories. Most recently, relational theorists have linked neuroscience research results with processes of intensive psychotherapy. Affect Regulation Theory (ART) is one notable example of that linking work. I use Allan Schore's ART notion of "right-brain therapy" as a guiding heuristic, a relational/neurobiological interpretation of pathology and therapy that helps me explain chronic shame and its treatment. Regulation theory also merges well with mentalization theory and dynamic systems theory, other aspects of the new science behind the art of relational psychotherapy.

But while I appreciate science-based explanations of how psychotherapy works, I hold them somewhat lightly. For I also believe, along with relational therapists of a more philosophical/hermeneutic bent, that all theory is interpretation. As a psychotherapist, I am not a scientist; I am a partner with clients in searching out the metaphors and meanings that make sense of their lives. I attend to the right-brain relational experiences clients hold in their bodies, emotions, and images. Likewise, I invite readers to join me in a rather right-brain approach to shame theory. Part I of this book defines and describes shame so that we can imagine what shame feels like from within many relational situations. The theory I offer is in service of helping our clients make personal emotional meaning of their unique, subjective shame experiences. It also highlights the vulnerable presence required of us if we are to connect viscerally and compassionately with the shame our clients can't bear to feel.

Our troubled clients protect themselves from feeling chronic shame with a stunning variety of emotional symptoms and behaviors. We therapists have to be just as persistently adept at finding various ways to connect with their underlying trouble. We need to hold in mind many possibilities about how we might best connect with each chronically shamed client. So much depends on the forms and energies of the client's self-protections, which often have become the style of the client's personality. Part II of the book presents different ways we can respond therapeutically to our clients' specific constructions of self around core chronic shame. No single "shame-busting" technique will do; instead, we learn how to move among our multiple therapist selves, all of them shame-savvy, to find the responses best suited to each client.

UNDERSTANDING CHRONIC SHAME

The book begins with stories from the lives of six clients. Their symptoms and life experiences are vastly different, and yet each struggles with shame. Reflecting on their diverse stories, I note the commonalities related to chronic shame. My frame for understanding these clients begins to emerge: Shame seems like a one-person problem, the negative self-feelings a person has because he or she believes "there's something terribly wrong with me." But in fact, shame is a relational problem; it has relational origins and it desperately needs relational attention, even though it is kept out of sight and out of the reach of relational contact.

The second chapter follows up these stories with relational theory about shame. I begin with a definition: *Shame is an experience of one's felt sense of self disintegrating in relation to a dysregulating other.* When we are at our most vulnerable, our experience of being an integrated self depends on the emotional attunement or "regulation" we receive from those closest to us. A "dysregulating other" is someone close to us whose emotional responses leave us feeling fragmented instead.

What happens when a self is fragmented by shame? Forty years of theory about shame and the self offer some answers. Affect theory highlights a sudden shift in a pattern of neural firing. Those who define shame as emotion deepen our visceral sense of what it costs to suffer shame. Self psychologists track how the misattunements that produce chronic shame are transformed into self-objectifying thoughts and faulty self-images. Recent research clarifies the difference between the experience of guilt and the experience of shame.

All these accounts of shame fill out the picture of what it's like for a person to live with shame, but none is a good match for my definition, which locates shame at a basic, early level of relational affective experience. Affect Regulation Theory offers the match I seek. Chapter 3 outlines what I find complementary and instructive in Allan Schore's "right-brain therapy" for relationally traumatized clients. Schore's ideas about shame also add scientific support to the idea that chronic shame has roots in early, repeated, right-brain experiences of affective dysregulation.

Chapter 4 addresses the question of how this early dysregulation becomes the established patterns of shame we see in our adult clients. I return to earlier shame theory, now reading it through an understanding of how affective dysregulation might in specific relational situations generate specific kinds of shame-patterns. The distress/deficit categories of attachment theory and self psychology prove most amenable to this kind of imaginative back-reading—and small wonder, since both bodies of theory are built around the idea that reliable attuned responsiveness creates healthy connection and healthy selves.

Holding in mind all this information about the developmental and relational roots of shame, how do we recognize chronic shame when it comes into the room with a client? Chapter 5 suggests we begin with what we feel. Our right brain attunes to right-brain trouble, and it will give us visceral, emotional signals if we pay attention. We can link what we feel with patterns we recognize from clinical experience and from shame literature; for example, perfectionists, procrastinators, and pleasers are often hiding chronic shame. We notice the aspects of our clients' family-of-origin histories that left them misrecognized and emotionally isolated, and we are alert for signs of trauma, dissociation, and addiction.

The chapter ends with the reminder that above all, chronically shamed clients need right-brain connection with us, and this includes how we do assessment with them. With that note, we move from understanding chronic shame to treating chronic shame.

TREATING CHRONIC SHAME

Chapter 6 outlines prerequisites for doing effective right-brain work with chronically shamed clients. The primary precondition is thorough self-awareness, the kind that usually takes in-depth psychotherapy to achieve. If we provide long-term psychotherapy for relationally traumatized clients and if we have any propensity to shame, our shame and our clients' shame will inevitably become entangled. That's why we must be self-reflective about our own shame, and not just once, but continually.

It also helps to do our homework. We read shame theory. We think about how to create non-shaming protocols for our practice. We reflect on the basic stance we take toward all clients and consider how it fits for shamed clients. We develop our capacities for mentalizing and mindfulness, and we aim for a stance that combines playfulness, acceptance, curiosity, and empathy.

Since shamed clients are quick to feel evaluated or misunderstood, we know that we have to begin gently, attending to shame subliminally. With some of them the word *shame* will never be spoken. But even if we should become able to work explicitly with our clients' shame, we always have to begin with the subtle, implicit work of fostering right-brain connection with them. Chapter 7 tells us how to do that.

In brief, we offer our engaged emotional presence, trusting our clients' right-brain selves to be listening to us long before they can respond. We hold what we know of our clients' minds in our own minds, intuiting the relational/emotional narratives implicit in the limited stories our clients can tell. We nurture tendrils of healthy interpersonal need and trust as they emerge. We respond to clients in ways that link their experiences with their emotions. In all these ways we help clients develop the neural networks they need to connect more consciously with a felt sense of self, including memories, intentions, and emotions.

Chapter 8 begins with the principle that an autobiographical sense of self is a sign of right-brain integration. This felt coherence, grounded in visceral emotion, is not to be confused with a self-history created by left brain logical and linguistic processes. Relational/emotional narratives integrate right-brain neural networks because such stories can be *felt* as part of self, even while words facilitate the feelings and reflections.

We encourage our clients to move from disconnected narratives to felt narratives in many ways: we search with them for words that match feelings; we help them sustain in-the-moment mindful reflection; we spend hours with them inside the details of their attachment histories. What matters more than the story is the storyteller who experiences a more conscious, integrated sense of self while speaking to someone who listens deeply. Such integration is the opposite of shame, for shame is the dis-integration that happens when a self cannot find empathic recognition from an emotionally significant other.

And so it is that we can often do effective, self-integrative work with chronically shamed clients and never speak of shame. But even more often, clients need to speak directly about shame before they can challenge how it governs their lives. The dark emotional convictions of chronic shame will feel like truth until they are brought out into brighter spaces where compassionate acceptance is the rule. Chapter 9 suggests that whenever we can, we should help our clients give their shame the light and air it needs for healing.

A relationship of mutual connectedness may become a safe enough place for clients to speak of shame. Then we can offer clients bits of education about shame, helping them learn the ins and outs of how it works. We might revisit their family-of-origin narratives to understand better the roots of their chronic shame. Some clients find it especially helpful to let their shamed and shaming "parts of self" speak to us and to one another.

But there are always some clients who can't afford to let themselves know about their chronic shame, even though it permeates their lives and relationships. Chapter 10 builds an understanding of how to be with them. I talk about dissociation, trauma, and the unconscious, and I share the story of my work with a highly dissociative client, a story that turns on the mutative power of making direct contact with her shame.

When clients are invested in keeping their shamed, vulnerable selves unknowable, we struggle to make genuine contact with them. We can't touch their shame, but we can notice with them how each part of their carefully divided self-structure functions. We can hope that with sustained, patient understanding, their rigidities will soften, allowing them more real connection with other people and with their own vulnerabilities. Perhaps in time, and with continued connected support, they will even come to know something about the shamed, vulnerable self they have spent a lifetime banishing.

Often a client's dissociated shame comes very close to the surface through its enactment in the therapy relationship. When the enactment is powerful and touches the therapist's vulnerabilities, client and therapist may fall into a mutual enactment, one of the most difficult challenges a relational therapist can face. I end chapter 10 with Donnel Stern's explanation of such enactments and of how they can end—not by insight, but by an unpredictable, unscripted change in affect and relatedness between partners. I note that "realization," the kind of non-verbal knowing Stern believes can lead one out of enactment, is very much like the relational/emotional cognition Schore locates in the right brain. With this coda, I rest my right-brain case.

And yet there's one more chapter. Chapter 11 asks the question, "Is there a cure for chronic shame?" The answer is complex. Therapy cannot erase the effects of childhood relational trauma; nevertheless, in relationship with us, our adult clients may experience profound positive changes in their patterns of implicit relational knowing. Furthermore, once our clients have named and faced their shame, we can work with them to reduce its power, offering them specific guidance as they seek to build shame-resilient lives.

First, they need help learning how to make authentic connections with important others in their lives. We encourage them to share emotions, negotiate needs, stop cycles of shame and blame, and discover the relief of guilt acknowledged and forgiven. Second, they need more authentic connection with themselves. We suggest that they build on the self-compassion and mindful self-awareness they have learned in therapy, and we celebrate with them the surprising new self-initiatives that emerge as the constrictions of their chronic shame ease.

As their dreams of perfection fade, shame-prone clients discover how to risk their hearts and their ambitions in the world. They find strength in being able to acknowledge failure, accept loss, and live with limits. As they end therapy, they accept that shame management will be a lifelong task. On saying good-bye, they may add, "I might need to call you sometime," because they believe now that it's okay to need help and to ask for it. This is a kind of transformation after all, and it is rooted in qualitative changes in our clients' relationships with others, with self, and with their own shame. These are the changes we can hope for when we take a relational/neurobiological approach to understanding and treating chronic shame.

PART I

Understanding Chronic Shame

CHAPTER 1

Chronic Shame: An Unspoken Problem

For three decades I have been asking clients what brings them to psychotherapy, and not one of them has said, "I need help with my chronic shame." Clients come for help with troubled emotions and difficult relationships. They say they have problems with stress, anxiety, depression, or self-esteem. But they don't name shame as a problem. As therapists, we may not ask about shame either, if only because we know it's a frightening word. It can be deeply shaming just to admit to feeling shame. But even if we and our clients tacitly agree not to speak of it, a pervasive sense of shame may well be part of their daily experience, especially for clients who also suffer from other symptoms of relational trauma.

I believe most symptoms of so-called mental illness, from depression and anxiety disorders to personality and dissociative disorders, have something to do with childhood relational trauma. As a relational therapist, I've had ears for the quiet trauma hidden in stories of clients' early relationships with fragile, needy, wounded parents. I have also heard in accounts of cruel, abusive caregivers the deeper story of trauma inflicted on a child's longing for loving attachment.[1]

Once hurt, human beings have remarkably creative ways to repel and avoid further harm, and so relational trauma engenders a wide spectrum of self-protective symptoms. There are common symptoms, too. Clients often tell us about anxiety far stronger than their life situations warrant and about depression that drags them down even when everything seems to be going well. The anxiety and depression seem to come from nowhere. And then there's that other ubiquitous symptom of relational trauma—chronic shame—that clients don't usually mention, though they may speak of problems with self-confidence or self-esteem.

For a while now I have been watching for the silent shame that shadows my clients' experiences of themselves in the world. I have come to believe that shame is a much more powerful and pervasive phenomenon than most of us realize. When I say that, I echo a small chorus of theorists who have been writing about shame and psychoanalytic psychotherapy for the last forty years. Interest in the topic of shame waxes and wanes; recently it seems on the upswing again with Brené Brown's popular self-help books, for example, and with the Dearing and Tangney collection of essays on shame, by and for psychotherapists.[2]

I don't have much new to add about how chronic shame destroys emotional well-being or about what a terrible, life-long affliction it can be. Rather, I will weave together many threads of theory—developmental theory, shame theory, and theory of clinical practice—into a new narrative of how relational psychotherapists can help clients who struggle with the chronic shame that follows on early relational trauma. If shame is a core problem, we need to address it, always subliminally and often directly. To do that, we first need to understand it.

Rather than begin with theory, however, I will begin with some stories from my own practice. The personalities and circumstances are fictionalized, but the essential situations are real, and so is the chronic shame at the heart of them. In their dissimilarity these stories illustrate the range and variety of disguises that chronic shame wears. Nonetheless, although these clients seem vastly different, their stories reveal some important common themes that belong to the experience of chronic shame.

PRODUCING A STELLAR PERFORMANCE

Recently a client returned to me after several years away. I'll call her Clare. I first saw her when she'd just lost an executive position. With a generous severance package, she'd set up a consulting firm of her own. But she couldn't make herself do the work to keep her business running. She found herself spending days drifting to the kitchen and eating too much, evenings drinking too much, and nights sleeping badly.

Clare came to me because, as she put it, "I need somebody to kick my butt." We found, instead, that she needed me to understand what being a vice president had meant to her, the sense of worth and power it had given her, and what it felt like to have all of that ripped away with no warning. She believed she should have seen it coming. She thought maybe she should have refused the package and fought back. "But nobody wins against company lawyers."

As Clare came to realize that there was nothing she could have done, she began to feel the pain of her loss more acutely, and then she could accept the sadness and anger of a grief process. She was surprised to find that on the other side of grief she was less anxious and more able to organize her life productively. It seemed our work was done.

Clare returned four years later. Her consulting firm was now a partnership of two, and they were writing a book. She had also turned her hobby of buying, renovating, and selling houses into a second business. She felt competent and powerful again, but there was something wrong in her marriage. She was on the verge of having an affair. I suggested couple therapy with a colleague, and she saw me concurrently.

Clare had never spoken much about her husband, whom I'll call Geoffrey. They had married in their late thirties and decided not to have children. They had interests in common—travelling, golf, building a cottage. She made him laugh, and he was like a rock for her, "a buttoned-down accountant, but a really good man." In couple therapy they learned that both of them had been feeling lonely and misunderstood for quite a while.

In her own therapy, Clare worked hard to understand what was going on for her. She didn't want to leave Geoff for Larry, she said, but it was so very tempting. Larry was a good time guy, life of the party, "A lot like me," Clare said. He could match her energy in ways her safe husband never could. Clare wanted to break free, "to soar on unclipped wings."

But as it turned out, when Clare pursued Larry a little harder, he played hard to get. To save her self-respect, she wrote him off. Meanwhile in the couple therapy, Clare and Geoff were talking to each other and feeling understood. As energy returned to her primary relationship, Clare's restlessness and anxiety abated. Again it seemed our work was done.

But recently, after another five years away, Clare returned again. She had sold her business interests to younger partners to retire early. It was the pleasant retirement she and Geoff had planned, with time for weekends away and long trips away. However, once again Clare was miserable at home.

"I can't believe I feel this bad," Clare told me in her first session back. "Stuff from years ago is coming back to me. I think about losing the VP position, how that could have been different. If I'd just been smarter, I could have been a CEO. I think about Larry. That maybe I missed my chance for something really 'me.' Who is this 'me' with Geoff? I think about the money I've made—not much, really. Enough for this comfortable life, but nothing spectacular. I'm boring, and fat, and old, and I haven't done what I thought—twenty, thirty years ago—I could do with my talent and energy. In fact, I am consumed, just *consumed*, by self-loathing every day. What's *wrong* with me?"

I decided to take a risk and say what I thought: "My best guess is that chronic shame is what's wrong. It's been under all the other work we've done over the years, but we could never actually see it. Now we can. What do you think?"

Clare was silent. Then she told me a story about golf. She had worked hard with the club pro all summer to take her handicap down. An out-of-town group came to play in September, and the pro contacted four other women—not Clare—to put together the two foursomes.

"I heard about it by accident," she said. "And you know what? I couldn't say to him, 'Why not me?' I couldn't say it because I knew I would just bawl, and yeah, it was shame—that I was such a baby! At my age. But I didn't play again last fall."

Clare hated needing to matter like that. She hated that those things meant far too much—things like being a CEO, being desired by an exciting guy, making a pile of money, having a handicap of nine. Those were her ways to keep shame away. But they were never fail-safe; shame could always break through.

"So if it's there, this chronic shame, where does it come from?" she asked. I sketched the story I know: a child has to have at least one caregiver who is able to respond in an attuned, consistent way to what the child feels. If this is missing in a major way, the child will translate the distress of the mismatch into a feeling like, "I can't make happen what I need . . . so there's something wrong with me." Not necessarily in those words, I said; just a feeling in the bones, and more or less intense, depending on how bad the mismatch is and how long it continues.

Clare was quick to link my explanation to what she knew of her history: Her mom was treated for depression after Clare's birth. Clare was the third of three girls in four years, with a brother, the "beloved," born three years later. Her mother wanted her girls to be pretty and quiet, but Clare was smart and loud. Despite her tough, funny exterior she felt misunderstood throughout childhood and adolescence.

We talked briefly about how a depressed mother can't be available when a child reaches out. We guessed that this miss happened often enough so that little Clare gave up on her mother. But of course, children can't stop needing, so a complicated pattern developed: while shutting down her longing to be really seen and loved, Clare learned to get attention by being funny and smart at school, if "difficult" at home. Feeling good about competence and its rewards took on a life of its own and became Clare's life.

"And I've done my therapy about this!" Clare said, looking me in the eye. I hadn't been her first therapist, so I could only nod. "I know all about that neglected feeling from my childhood, and how I've been trying to get attention ever since. So what are we going to do about this problem?"

Good question, I thought. When in doubt, stay in the moment. So I said, "Tell me more about what it's like to be you right now. There's this self-loathing. I guess there are other feelings too?" She responded by talking about different parts of herself that felt different things.

Suddenly they became a cast of characters—a tough, funny person who can fake anything, a pleaser who cares too much, and a mean bitch who puts the pleaser down. "We'll call her Lillian," she said.

"Lillian?"

"My mother. I know it's not my mother. Well, it is—but it's me, too." Clare began to explore what the pleaser part of her felt when Lillian was mean. With my encouragement, "Pleaser" started to tell Lillian about wanting and being angry and the shame of caring too much.

None of this history was new to Clare. But new energy was sparking and surging in the room. It was connected to a new sense of the problem: we had named the shame and given it narrative context both in the present and the past. Perhaps most importantly, we were going after it not with logic, but with a kind of creative exploration that required each of us to be present to the other and engaged in the moment.

LEADING A DOUBLE LIFE

Not everyone who suffers from chronic shame can rise above it with outstanding performances of a competent self. Shame takes hold in different ways, depending on a child's disposition and on the many possible forms of mismatch between a child's need for connection and a caregiver's ability to respond. Some caregivers respond with a pattern of connection that is more confusing than absence. In some moments with their child, they are intensely present, needing connection themselves, and in many other moments they are oblivious to the child's needs.

The child learns that if connection is going to keep happening, he needs to match the cues coming from his parent. His own spontaneous needs, which would generate his own cues, have to be muted or disappear. A connection like this is more twisted than broken, but it is just as likely to produce a lifetime of chronic shame. Played out across a life-span, it will look more like accommodation to others than like self-sufficiency. Well-being depends entirely on someone else's response. When the response is good, the child feels important and valuable; when not so good, the child feels worthless and low.

Dual or split experience permeates the lives of clients who come into therapy with this kind of history. Some of them, high-functioning pleasers, are able to sequester the dark side of their experience most of the time. Others can't divert their emotions that take them, in a day, from the top of the world to suicidal despair. They work hard to please others, but their relationships are also full of anger about disappointed expectations and dashed hopes.

These split-existence clients don't locate shame in a disowned "baby" part of self. For them, shame lives in recurrent, powerful states of feeling horrible here and now. These states can be forgotten on days when success and good connection sustain them. But when something happens to jolt their self-esteem, shame takes hold as bitter, implacable anger at someone who hurt them, or as a sudden onslaught of feeling so anxious that only "doing something" helps.

My client Gary, a successful, personable professional, manages to keep his chronic shame hidden away on the dark side of his double life. He came to me saying he wanted to get his porn addiction under control. I suggested we understand the problem in the context of the rest of his life. I learned that Gary was in his mid-forties, happily married, proud dad of a seven-year-old daughter. He worked for a bank, doing what he called the people part of solving IT problems. "I'm in over my head," he said with a grin. "I don't have a degree in business or banking. IT is a foreign language to me. But I do trainings really well when I'm on. So they keep promoting me. That imposter thing, you know."

Gary's degrees were in theatre and film studies. When he ran out of time to finish a doctoral thesis, he quit the graduate student life and went to work in a bank. "Finally made my Dad happy," he said. "A real job, real money."

Gary's father was a self-made man. "Four times over," Gary said wryly. "Lots of boom and bust. Boom and he was super-dad. Bust and he was just angry." Boom or bust, Gary's dad drove him to hockey faithfully. "I think he saw me as the star he could have been. But he was never one of those hockey dads, yelling at refs. He'd just take notes during every game and afterwards tell me all the little things he saw that I could have done better."

I asked Gary what that was like. "Good," he said. "He wasn't too busy to talk to me then. I was working at something really important, and I was good and getting better." But Gary's hockey career sputtered as the other guys got bigger than him. "I was scared to get hit. I tried to fake it, but coaches know."

Around that same time, Gary found out that he could act. "I got some big roles in school plays," he told me. "I thought my dad would come. My mom came with my brother, but my dad didn't. I told myself it didn't matter."

I asked about his mom and brother. "He was a special needs kid," he said. "Took a lot of her time. I looked out for him, too, scared off bullies when I could, tried to teach him to fight back."

I asked whether he thought there was anything about his life that would help us understand how the porn addiction fit in. That's when he told me that the problem was more than internet porn sites. It was interactive sites, too. About once a week he'd make a date to pay for sex. "I just get in a zone: it's all I want—to make it happen. Then afterwards I feel horrible about myself. Until the next time when I'm on the hunt again."

Gary had safe sex and got himself tested every six months. "To protect yourself," I said.

"To protect my wife. Gary, the hero." After a long moment of silence, he added, "Gary, the total jerk. I really hate that guy; it's not who I really am. But saying that, I guess I'm lying to myself."

As we continue therapy, sometimes Gary feels intense shame about what that guy does. But he can also easily put it out of his mind. I suspect there's a deeper shame that keeps him split from himself. I wish we could get to know "that guy" better and find out what he feels. I keep hoping to get closer to where the split happens; I wonder if it protects deep shame about a needing, longing self who mattered and then didn't matter, over and over again.

Gary has a wealth of words from previous therapies about needing to be in touch with his feelings, about not numbing out with addictions. Those are sensible thoughts, but they seem repetitive and numbing, too. They don't seem to touch what hurts him. And "that guy" remains terribly elusive.

Gary tells me I do good work. I enjoy being with him—and I still can't quite find him behind his performance of troubled but self-aware, experienced client. I wonder whether I will ever meet "that guy," or even talk with Gary about the "imposter thing" we might be enacting together, my smart therapist-self and his self-reflective, astute client-self.

AN ANGRY KIND OF SPLIT

For some clients who live with this kind of duality, the bitter, hopeless side of self dominates their lives and our work together. They enjoy brief periods of feeling that the success they crave is within reach, but that version of self always collapses like a house of cards. Then all they can feel is that nothing is ever better, nothing helps, and there's no point talking to me about it. I hear their frantic, intense despair, and yet I feel more defensive than empathic. It's as if I am the one making their lives this hell. Then I feel my own angry despair about our work together.

My client Ellen and I share this struggle. Throughout her childhood and adolescence, Ellen dreamed of becoming a concert pianist. At twenty, she gave up the dream and a major scholarship when the stress of competition became more than she could manage. Now, at thirty-five, she has "settled" for a stable career teaching music. Her career may be stable, but her emotions are not. I have come to see in her history and in her emotions a little girl highly attuned to a needy, controlling mom, sometimes the brilliant special child who would prove her mom's value, and sometimes a worthless disappointment. I see how that little girl often felt that she didn't matter, and how she learned to get herself back from an empty place of not mattering by having a messy crisis about feeling horrible. Perhaps then her mother might look at *Ellen,* not at the child prodigy. Ellen's desperate melt-downs also expressed something beyond words about how deeply the relationship with her mother injured her and how awful she felt in it.

In my work with Ellen, my empathy with her despair helps her find some balance by the end of a session, but so far it has not changed the cycle of what happens for her over the course of weeks and months. Hopeless, helpless crisis states keep recurring. Ellen and I continue to explore the sources of her bitter frustration. We examine what happens before she "falls down the rabbit hole." We have revisited her childhood experience of her mother's demands and misattunements until it seems there's nothing more to discover about the double binds of that relationship.

Most of all, Ellen needs me not to fall into splitness with her. I must respond to her crises whole—that is, with calm, containing presence. I must hold in mind what she can't remember: that this hopeless, worthless feeling is not the sum total of her experience. At the same time, I must not encourage the part of her that needs a brilliant performance to feel better. I need to imagine for her the possibility of self-experience not split by shame into either extraordinary or worthless. In a more integrated experience of self, Ellen would be able to move beyond "failed prodigy" and enjoy her success directing well-received music programs. But moderate, solid success doesn't suffice for her. It doesn't stop her from trying to be brilliantly special, nor prevent her from falling into humiliation when she's less than perfect.

I hope that one day Ellen will grasp a whole picture of her dilemma. Maybe then she will be able to feel compassion for the impossible tension she lives with: the specialness she longs for is always out of reach, and the worthlessness she falls into is too painful to bear. But for now she can't seem to stop reliving the terrible moment of falling from "special" to "nothing" in someone's eyes.

FEELING UNBEARABLY ALONE

Some chronically shamed clients don't live out a split existence. Rather, they struggle daily just to survive constant feelings of isolation, despair, and worthlessness. Beneath their current lives of alienation and emotional pain lie histories of physical, sexual and/or emotional abuse at the hands of caregivers they should have been able to trust.

I think of Susie, her father's favorite when he was sober and the one he came to visit at night when he was drunk. Other nights he would beat up her mother. If Susie's mother loved anybody, it was Susie's older brothers, not her. Susie was certain that if she ever told anyone about her father's sexual abuse, everything would blow up, maybe everybody would die.

Susie first tried to kill herself when she was fifteen. When I met her she was twenty-four, living alone and barely surviving on social assistance. Tormented by intense emotions, she desperately needed and often hated the few people in her life. Medication numbed her feelings a bit, but it didn't erase her suicidality.

Susie cycled in and out of hospital emergency rooms and psychiatric wards. Her ongoing treatment was derailed every time she began to trust somebody enough to share her suicidal thoughts. The worker or therapist would take the proper steps to get her safe in hospital. Then Susie would feel like they were getting rid of her, and she would end the relationship.

Susie and I were able to work together for more than a decade, in part because a colleague of mine with hospital privileges agreed to monitor her suicidality. We clarified among the three of us that he and she would chart her suicidal feelings, decide if and when a hospital stay would be wise, and manage her treatment in hospital. I would be her therapist when she was doing well enough to be at home.

Susie and I talked about all sorts of things—about her childhood with its terrors, her relationship with her family now, her struggles with friends, her pets, her dreams of being a writer, and also about what happened when she felt like killing herself. With crisis management in place elsewhere, we were able to talk both when the crises were emerging and when they had passed.

I came to understand that for Susie bleak feelings never went away. But sometimes something worse would happen with her mom or dad, or a brother or a boyfriend. An interaction would leave her feeling especially alone and misunderstood. Then everyday bleakness would turn into wanting to be dead. Following the agreement made with her psychiatrist, she would take herself to a hospital and tell hospital staff she was planning to kill herself, and give his name as her doctor.

Although these hospital visits kept her safe, they were also emotionally devastating for Susie. She wanted hospital staff to feel the intensity of her pain, the agony of her helplessness against it. Instead, nurses or workers would be disgusted with her for using suicide threats to get attention. Although few of them said so, she could tell by the way they treated her, she said, "like get over it already."

It seemed to help Susie to talk to me about her hospital experiences. Our talking seemed to give some shape to the intense feelings of rage, despair, and self-loathing inside her suicidality, emotions that needed to be heard by a real person. Together we "got" what mattered: just not to feel alone with all of those terrible feelings. Even though I was never actually present in her most intense crises, Susie used my understanding to ease her desperate loneliness.

Looking back now, more than a decade after I last saw Susie, I wonder if it might have helped to talk to her about shame, too. I heard her litany of reasons to hate and despise herself. I never agreed with her reasons, but I accepted how awful she felt. I told her that when you're abused, you can't help thinking you deserve it—even though you don't. When your feelings don't matter to anyone, you can't help but feel worthless.

But I didn't talk with her about shame. We didn't speak of the shame-ridden longing for loving care that drove her to crisis. We didn't explore the need itself or the shame that exploded unbearably when the need—to be deeply understood—was denied. Now I see that we might have seen those suicidal times as times when her chronic shame flared up and then others' misunderstanding threw gasoline on the fire.

These days, while working with a client prone to such hopeless despair, I'm alert for moments to introduce the idea of shame. When a client feels overwhelmed with self-loathing, I'll name what's happening as "Shame"—and I'll call it an enemy, a force bigger than she is at the moment, but not the truth about who she is. That gives us more to work with together.

GIVING UP ON LOVE

Sometimes, however, it's wise to hold back on using the word "shame." It was difficult for my client Andrea just to discover her anger about the emotional neglect of her childhood; she needed to discover shame in her own time, too. The household where Andrea grew up would have looked very different from Susie's home, much more "normal," and yet the desolate outcome for Andrea was not so different. She, too, leads a lonely, joyless life. Andrea says she'd never make the mess for other people her suicide would cause, but she often finds herself hoping for an early end to a pointless existence.

On the outside, Andrea's life looks meaningful. She is the well-educated, organized, and articulate executive director of a social service agency that helps marginalized women with housing and employment. She meets friends for dinners or drinks after work and keeps up some online connections. But no one ever comes home to her place, which she shares with two cats and a budgie. She explains her loneliness like this: "I'm not that one special person to anyone on the planet."

Andrea had five brothers, three older and two younger than she. Her father was a family doctor, a quiet, kind man, she says, but very busy with his work. She remembers that her mother was silently but bitterly angry almost all the time. "She should never have had kids, given how she felt about herself. I think 'martyr' was the best she could imagine."

I asked whether Andrea had been pressed into doing housework and taking care of her brothers. But no, her mother hadn't bothered to teach her how to cook or clean. "She didn't care if I wore clean clothes out the door, or if I washed my hair. So I didn't."

When Andrea was bullied at school, she told no one. It made sense to her to be the person nobody liked. She spent hours alone at home in her room, watching a small black and white TV that became like a special friend to her, a friend she took with her to university. "It was better there," she said. "At least I could be smart."

Andrea still takes a great deal of comfort in television. Computer games provide another mind-numbing way for her to spend long weekends alone. She says that her real world is inside her mind. Though she walks around in the world talking to people and doing things, nobody knows what she really thinks and feels.

After some time talking about her life and her history, Andrea began to feel angry about the years of emotional neglect she endured and all the times she clearly needed help and her mother turned a blind eye. At the same time Andrea talked about her fears of becoming a bitter old woman herself. She wondered whether she would ever find the capacity within herself to love another human being.

I wondered about early interactions between Andrea and her mother. Andrea believed she would have felt her mother's absence even as a baby. I told her about the babies in the Still-Face experiments: when the mothers showed nothing on their faces, the babies tried and tried to get a response, but finally their eyes dropped and their bodies slumped. They gave up.[3] "Yes," Andrea said. "I gave up. I couldn't love her, so I can't love anyone."

"I think there's more to it," I said. "In a way, it's even worse than that. Babies can't afford to give up. Maybe for a while, but they'll try again. They have to make emotional connection. If they don't, they'll die."

"Well, I didn't die," Andrea said grimly. "I guess my dad was there for me when he had time."

"And you kept trying with your mom. You made the best of what little came your way. And you were always trying to make sense of it, too. Kids do that. Every time you tried and it didn't work, you had to make some sense of it."

"Like what kind of sense?"

"Like maybe there was something wrong with you for needing."

"I don't let myself need anything from anybody. I hate neediness—I mean in myself, not in other people. I hate needing."

"Maybe you hated needing because it hurt so badly not to get what you needed. You just hated to feel that."

"It is the most painful place," Andrea said very quietly. "You can't be there in that place, you can't survive feeling that. It's just unbearable."

We sat silently for a few moments, and then I told Andrea that feeling wrong and bad for needing to be loved—that unbearable place—is the place where I believe deep, chronic shame starts. "If it doesn't get fixed, it takes over your life," I explained. "There's the unbearable feeling of longing denied, and after a while that pain defines who you are. You feel that helpless and twisted up inside, that despicable and unlovable. Not that a small child thinks those thoughts; the thoughts come later to make sense of the twisted-up feelings."

Andrea nodded. I added, "Not that you think those thoughts all the time now. They're just givens, understood. The wallpaper of your house. The score of your movie."

"But I do feel the shame now if I reach out and it goes badly," Andrea said. "That's always possible. Probable. That's why being in my own head is so much safer than being with people."

It was a relief to Andrea to put a name to shame and to feel the links that made sense of painful parts of her experience. In the weeks following, she found herself less at the mercy of her shame-based habits of thought and more able to reach out. She is now becoming able to talk back to her shame when a small mistake threatens her well-being. She is feeling a bit stronger and more herself, overall. Andrea is still a long way from feeling she is loveable, but I believe she is on her way.

RAGING TO RIGHT WRONGS

Versions of this final story turn up often in work with couples. When couples are locked in a repetitive, vicious fight cycle, shame is frequently what keeps it going. Both shamed partners bring to the relationship the hope that true love will erase their vulnerabilities and undo the deprivation of their childhood attachments. But of course, each partner has moments of failing to understand and appreciate the other. And then, for that other partner, the original trauma of not mattering seems to happen all over again. The vulnerability of wanting to be loved becomes shame and then rage that lashes out in counter-shaming attacks.

Trevor came to me with his girlfriend Megan as a last ditch effort to save their relationship. They had begun as friends. Trevor managed shipping and receiving and Megan managed accounts for a plumbing supply company. Surprised by their mutual attraction and shared interests, they had considered living together, but Megan had backed out when the fights began. Only the fear of losing Megan brought Trevor into a therapist's office. He said he knew it was wrong to lose his temper and call her names, and he didn't want to do it ever again.

Trevor's body was rigid and his voice tense as he and Megan told the story of what kept going wrong between them. Trevor thought he should be given more credit for how hard he tried to be a good boyfriend. "I'm always thinking about you," he said. "Always thinking how I can make you happy. You know that!"

"I know you try really hard," Megan said. "But the least little thing I say that's negative, I get this huge dump of anger about all you do for me. So I tell you to go home and get over it, but instead I get a hundred text messages. It makes me crazy. At least now I can turn off my phone. If we were living together . . ."

"Exactly!" Trevor exploded. "You turn off your phone, you disappear, you cut me off! Is that a way to treat a guy who loves you? I keep texting you because I want to talk about the relationship, get it straight!"

"No, you don't!" Megan shot back. "I know what happens if I see you. Verbal abuse. I grew up with that, and I won't take that from you." She turned to me. "He's got so much going on inside. I was in therapy; I know how it is. But he's got to deal with it. I can't do it for him."

I asked Trevor if he knew what Megan was talking about. "I've got this anxiety," he said. "My doctor gave me pills, but I didn't like the way they made me feel. Dopey."

"And all the stuff about your dad," Megan said.

I asked Trevor about his dad. "He's a cop. He could be a mean bastard. He left when I was ten."

"What was that like for you?"

"Nothing I could do."

"Did you see your dad after?"

"Yeah, weekends. I tried but it didn't go so good. The new woman and all. Then I got older and I got really pissed off with everything, did a lot of drugs and drinking, even my mom kicked me out." I asked Trevor whether he thought some of his past experience was coming back on him when he got frustrated with Megan. He shrugged. "Yeah, I guess."

In our second session, Trevor and Megan reported another break-off and more non-stop texting. We made a deal that Megan wouldn't disappear if Trevor wouldn't send more than one text to say he wanted to talk. She promised she would answer one text and make a time to talk—after work. As long as Megan wouldn't cut him off, Trevor said, he could do it.

But the deal didn't work. Two weeks later it had all happened again, and they were stuck. "I'm only here because I don't know what else to do," Megan said. "I think I'm done."

Now I saw what happened to Trevor when he got desperate. Shaking with emotion, he listed all the things he had done for her and bought for her. *He* was the one who wanted this relationship to work. *He* was the one who was trying, and *she* was the one who was always making it impossible, putting him down, making him out to be the bad guy. "Like you think I'm some kind of a Nazi!" Then Trevor stormed out, saying he had to go to the washroom.

As Megan and I sat in silence, I thought hard about what to do. I know that a shame-based fight cycle always involves both partners' vulnerabilities, and I didn't want to isolate Trevor's behavior as the only problem in the relationship. But Trevor was too upset to do couples work, and Megan was already in therapy. So I said to Megan, "I think that Trevor can't do this couple work with you right now. It's too hard for him. He needs some more help first."

When Trevor came back, we explored the intense anxiety he was feeling right then, the same anxiety that was messing up his relationship. He told me once again that anxiety and depression medication didn't work for him.

"Okay," I said. "There are two ways to treat anxiety and depression. Medication is one way. Psychotherapy is another. Since you're telling me meds don't work, I'm going to suggest that you and I do some sessions of psychotherapy just for you. That means we would talk about your feelings, and not just your feelings now, but when you were growing up, too. We'd talk about your dad and you, for example. I know it seems weird that talking about stuff like that can make you feel better, but I've seen it work for a lot of people."

Since then, Trevor and I have spent a dozen sessions together. He's gotten over feeling like he's in trouble and being punished. We're on the same team now, talking about how he can manage his feelings better so that he can get more happiness and less trouble from his relationship. We've talked about how his dad's angry control always made him anxious—and how he gets angry and controlling, too, when he's afraid he won't get what he needs. Trevor talks to me because he feels safe with me; I won't judge him. I understand that chronic shame is the problem behind his problems with being supersensitive, defensive, argumentative, and prone to rage.

It's not that Trevor needs a new diagnosis. "Depression and anxiety" will suffice. I may never find a good moment to explain shame to him. Trevor doesn't need a diagnosis or an explanation. He doesn't even need advice about making his relationship work, though that's what we often talk about, at his request. As I talk, I try to reflect Trevor's emotional self back to him from my own emotional experience of him. This is what Trevor needs: real interpersonal contact that doesn't get all tangled up in shame. My engaged presence, not my advice, is what helps him feel more aware of himself, more in charge of himself, and better able to make and keep good connection with his girlfriend, too.

WHAT DO THESE STORIES HAVE IN COMMON?

The people I have introduced to you are far from a homogenous group. Some have been able to make their lives work; others hang on by their fingernails. The marks of their suffering are as unique as their life stories are; their symptoms would give each of them a different mental health diagnosis. Yet I'm suggesting that they have something essential in common. I've called that common theme "chronic shame," and now I'd like to trace some other similar themes in their stories, themes that often accompany shame.

Clare's high-octane performance of competence puts miles of distance between her deep shame experience and her usual conscious experience of herself in the world. She's luckier than a lot of shame sufferers in her ability to rise above it. But every one of my cast of characters would tell you that performance is a way of life for them—performance to hide some disgusting or demeaning truth about who they are.

Gary performs the good guy and the jerk in tandem, caught between desires. Ellen, obsessed by the demands of her mother's voice, feels like an utter failure but still desperately hopes to pull off an extraordinary performance of something. She wants to get off the treadmill of performing instead of just being, but mostly, so far, she can't. In their very different ways, both Susie and Andrea perform a facsimile of wellness as best they can, sure that no one could ever know how painfully lonely they are inside. And Trevor performs Great Boyfriend for all he's worth, cut off from the longings and fears that turn him into Boyfriend from Hell.

Gary is more aware than the others of the double life he leads. Most people who manage chronic shame don't know much about their different "selves." Ellen forgets about feeling worthless when the hope of a special performance beckons, and she can't remember competence when she falls to her worthless place. Clare's anxious, unhappy self breaks through only when her performance fails her own expectations. Susie keeps her suicidal self quiet with medication, Trevor disowns the self who flies into rages, and Andrea leaves behind her sad, lonely self for TV, video games, and surfing the internet.

Andrea treasures these addictions. They give her some peaceful pleasure in a world in which she feels no joy or love. Because I want to put addictions where I believe they belong in the story of chronic shame, I have been careful not to highlight them. But they are everywhere in shame stories, so much so that it would be easy to make addictive behaviors the villain of every piece. From Clare's incessant activity (and her wine), to Gary's porn, to Andrea's escapes into fantasy, and to Trevor's adolescent drinking and drugs, addictions block and numb the anxiety that chronic shame spills into a body's system. I haven't mentioned how Ellen's obsession with perfection includes purging after binge-eating. I don't yet know what Trevor does to calm himself on evenings when he can't see Megan and he stops himself from texting. I do know that when a person can't afford to be at home with his or her own anxious self-loathing, a mind-numbing activity or substance can seem like a reliable refuge. Or an only friend.

It's hard to have friends when you're convinced that there's something fundamentally defective about you. You might be able to perform "friend"—Gary is especially good with "buddies," and Andrea is known to be a sympathetic, reliable listener. But you keep crucial parts of yourself hidden. You protect your heart, you hate your own neediness, you pretend not to envy, or you act tough and invulnerable. Nobody knows you, really. And so you are deeply lonely. Perhaps, as for Susie, your aloneness becomes too unbearable to go on living with. Perhaps, as Andrea has done, you decide that you have to give up on loving and being loved in this lifetime. Even though it's what you want more than anything.

People who struggle with chronic shame are deeply lonely, and they have trouble with love. Most of all they have trouble believing that anyone actually loves them. But usually they keep on trying to love and be loved. Something tells them that what they so desperately need is hidden there in "love." They are profoundly right about that, even when they go about it all wrong, hiding their longing behind performance. They are right about what they're missing even when, like Trevor, they rage at the one they love in the doomed hope of getting what they're missing that way.

On the one hand, this is the truth: what they have missed and continue to miss is genuine connection with somebody who understands and accepts who they are and what they feel. On the other hand, it can be a very dangerous enterprise to try to get that connection while feeling so vulnerable to exposure, so sensitive to slight, so damaged and defective, or so extraordinarily misunderstood and angry.

These are all the things I hold in mind when I'm talking with a client and I begin to feel as if there's a lot of shame in the room with us. I wonder whether what's being shared is actually a performance of self. I wonder whether I'm seeing just one version, one "self" today, and who and where another version of self might be. I listen for deep loneliness in the client's story, and I pay attention to the quality of emotional connection between us. If I have a persistent sense of disconnection, I wonder whether the client is able to trust anybody else at all, really. I wonder whether loving and being loved "works" for him or her. As I wonder about all these things, I wonder whether chronic shame is a powerful unknown factor at play.

And if the problem behind the problems is chronic shame—then what? As Clare said to me with challenge in her eyes, "So what are we going to do about it?"

This is the question that matters most to any client: How are you going to help me feel better? As I put it to myself: How can I engage in a relationship with a chronically shamed client in order to be an agent of change? Part II of this book addresses the question of relational treatment. But before we can treat shame, we need to understand it. That's the aim of the rest of Part I. I will propose a relational, neurobiological understanding of what chronic shame is, where it comes from, how it operates, and what it looks like in our clients' lives.

NOTES

1. Patricia DeYoung, *Relational Psychotherapy: A Primer* (New York: Routledge, 2003).

2. Brené Brown, *I Thought It Was Just Me (but it isn't): Making the Journey from "What Will People Think?" to "I Am Enough"* (New York: Gotham, 2007), and *Daring Greatly* (New York: Gotham, 2012); Ronda L. Dearing and June Price Tangney, eds., *Shame in the Therapy Hour* (Washington, DC: American Psychological Association, 2011).

3. Edward Tronick et al., "The Infant's Response to Entrapment between Contradictory Messages in Face-to-Face Interaction," *Journal of Child Psychiatry* 17 (1978): 1–13.

CHAPTER 2

Shame Is Relational

Shame feels like solitary pain, and chronic shame seems like a personal failing caused by one's own negative thinking and low self-esteem. But in fact, shame in all its forms is relational. Shame is the experience of self-in-relation when "in-relation" is ruptured or disconnected. A chronic sense of self-in-disconnection becomes a profound sense of isolation, which in turn leads to feelings of despair and unworthiness. Writing as a Stone Center self-in-relation theorist, Judith Jordan describes the experience of shame succinctly: ". . . shame is most importantly a felt sense of unworthiness to be in connection, a deep sense of unlovability, with the ongoing awareness of how very much one wants to connect with others. . . . There is a loss of the sense of *empathic possibility*, others are not experienced as empathic, and the capacity for self-empathy is lost."[1]

Jordan contrasts this definition of shame with shame seen as the opposite of pride or as the loss of self-respect and self-esteem. Shame strikes not because a person fails to be adored, acknowledged, or admired, she says, but because a person does not have a primary need met, namely, his or her need for connection and emotional joining. When that need is not met, being admired is a poor substitute.

Shame can be healed, therefore, if a person can be brought back into connection where empathy and emotional joining are possible. This is the work of psychotherapy oriented to self-in-relation. Jordan contrasts this relational perspective on healing shame with a therapy oriented to self-development.[2]

A NEW RELATIONAL DEFINITION OF SHAME

I agree with Jordan's relational account of the origin and healing of shame, and I would like to explore it further. I also want to develop shame theory that converses with a broad spectrum of relational theories of psychotherapy and psychoanalysis. To that end, I propose the following definition of shame: *Shame is the experience of one's felt sense of self disintegrating in relation to a dysregulating other.* Chronic shame develops when many repetitions of such shame experience form a person's lifelong patterns of self-awareness and response to others.

As Jordan does, I define shame as the experience of a self-in-relation, not as a person's wounded pride, damaged self-respect, or low self-esteem. But instead of speaking of feeling unlovable in relation, I speak of *disintegrating* in relation, trying to capture the most essential experience of a shamed self, the self's relational experience before it is given meaning. And then, instead of describing a relationship with a disconnected or unempathic other, I speak of a *dysregulating* other, believing the word speaks more precisely to what goes wrong between self and other in the moments when shame strikes.

DISINTEGRATING

Personal well-being depends on a sense of integrated self, and relationships are what hold that self in integrated wholeness. Self psychology speaks to this dual focus; it is a relational theory that stresses the attuned, nurturing relationships a self must have in order to be whole and well, and it specializes in understanding processes of self cohesion and self disintegration. Self psychologists note that from the moment of birth, a drive for coherence turns an infant's patterns of immediate affective/emotional experience into patterns of expectation and response with caregivers. These patterns become unconscious organizers of self-with-other interactions and feelings that persist from childhood through adulthood. When troublesome, they first appear in therapy as a client's experiences of anxiety, depression, depletion, and fragmentation. The self psychologist creates conditions for a relationship of attuned empathy in which, for the client, more coherent self-experience can become possible.[3]

If having a coherent sense of self is psychologically necessary for human beings, then the disintegration of that sense of self threatens psychological annihilation. Clients who struggle with the disintegrating power of chronic shame may not daily or consciously expect to be annihilated by shame. However, the threat is always around somewhere, just out of awareness, kept at bay. What they live with daily is what it costs them to keep from falling into shame. Paradoxically, making sure they don't disintegrate costs them their self-coherence.

Chronically shamed clients can rarely be at home with themselves. A fabricated performance of self covers their need to keep alien, shamed versions of self out of their awareness. For example, my client Clare, despite her power to define her goals and achieve success, found herself time and again being driven by feelings that made no sense to her chosen sense of self. Gary's shamed version of self could find expression only in sexual acts his "hero self" could not bear to think about.

The word *disintegrating* also captures the essence of acute shame experiences. People report that shame makes them feel blank, "vaporized," or incoherent, even to themselves. In moments of feeling humiliated, they can't speak, or even think. They feel shattered, or as if they are falling apart. The threat of psychological annihilation is mirrored by their wish to sink through the floor or to disappear, in some way just to cease to exist. The extreme example of *hara-kiri*, a Japanese form of ritual suicide, comes to mind. Insofar as *hara-kiri* is performed in order to restore honor in place of shame, it also serves as a metaphor for how far a person of any culture may need to go to counteract shame's annihilation of selfhood.

The word *disintegrating* is perhaps most helpful in trying to imagine the shame experiences of young children who are busy trying to put together a coherent sense of self out of their interactions with their parents and other important people in their lives. When a child misbehaves, a parent's displeasure may bring on momentary shame and the danger of the child's shattering or falling apart. In a good-enough parenting scenario, the disciplinary point is made, followed quickly by a return to relational connection, within which the child's self-experience returns to coherence, an internal sense of, "I did a bad thing, but it's over and I'm still a good kid." This sort of small break and repair helps a child integrate emotionally felt senses of "goodness" and "badness" and builds implicit relational knowing about how to be a successful self in social connection and negotiation with others.[4]

By contrast, moments that might eventually coalesce into lasting damage and chronic shame are disintegrating moments that remain unrepaired, with the child left struggling alone to recover a sense of who he is with the other. Without help, the disintegration persists, splitting around "good" and "bad" is reinforced, and the child may just blank out the whole experience in order to move on. Yet a certain kind of implicit knowing about how relationship works—and doesn't work—will have been laid down.

What leads to chronic shame is unrepaired disconnection between parent and child, not a parent's intention to shame the child. A shaming interaction may, in fact, have nothing to do with guidance, discipline, or punishment. Whenever a child can no longer feel connected and recognized by a person who holds him in emotional being, the child's experience of a coherent self disintegrates. Such disintegration happens for infants as well as for young children. For them, the experience remains simply visceral since they don't yet have internal language for "goodness" or "badness."

A DYSREGULATING OTHER

The term *dysregulating other* comes from affect regulation theory, which explores the effects of interpersonal affect regulation and dysregulation on emotional well-being, both in childhood development and in adult psychotherapy. A dysregulating other is a person who fails to provide the emotional connection, responsiveness, and understanding that another person needs in order to be well and whole.

Throughout our lives, having good connections in healthy relationships will help us feel coherent, competent, and lovable. When in distress, we will reach out to someone to listen; compassion and understanding will help us find ourselves again in an adult-to-adult form of regulation. By contrast, painful connections will throw us off balance. If we are in emotional distress, what we get from unhealthy relationships will leave us feeling more shame, doubt, and confusion—the effects of dysregulation. This is adult experience. If others' responses to our adult emotions influence us so strongly, we can imagine the powerful, profound effects emotional regulation and dysregulation have on vulnerable children.

Self psychology and intersubjectivity theory have long held that a caregiver's affective attunement, or lack thereof, profoundly affects a child's chances for emotional well-being. From infant studies, which observe parents and babies in fine-tuned mutual regulation of their interactions, we learn how much of a caregiver's "natural attention" is actually affect regulation. Recent neurobiological studies of attachment and affect regulation, which I will review in more detail in the next chapter, support and expand these ideas.

In brief, and speaking from the perspective of a child's regulated self, a regulating other is a person on whom I rely to respond to my emotions in ways that help me not to be overwhelmed by them, but rather to contain, accept, and integrate them into an emotional "me" I can feel comfortable being. A dysregulating other is also a person I *want* to trust—and should be able to trust—to help me manage my affect or emotion. But this person's response to me, or lack of response to me, does exactly the opposite: it does not help me contain, accept, or integrate.

Then I become a *self disintegrating in relation to a dysregulating other.* This is what happens: as an infant, when I am in an affective state of distress, or as a child, when I am feeling a rush of emotion, the other's response fails to help me manage what I'm feeling. Instead of feeling connected to someone strong and calm, I feel alone. Instead of feeling contained, I feel out of control. Instead of feeling energetically focused, I feel overwhelmed. Instead of feeling that I'll be okay, I feel like I'm falling apart.

This kind of experience is the core experience of shame. All of it has something to do with needing something intensely from somebody important, and something going wrong with the interaction between us. I feel, "I can't make happen what I need from you." If the sequence is repeated often enough in my development to become an expectable experience, I will have a core propensity to feel shame whenever I have strong feelings, need emotional connection, or feel something is wrong in an interpersonal interaction. In all of those situations, I will be likely to conclude, consciously or unconsciously, "There is something wrong with what I need—with my needy self."

As I grow from toddler to young child, I will make that sort of sense of any unintegrated feelings that feel bad to me: I will come to believe that there is badness inherent in my disconnected emotional self who feels those "bad" feelings. This is when felt badness comes to have the meanings we usually associate with shame. As I grow from child to adolescent, I may hang that shame on challenging parts of my expanding self-experience—my body, my sexuality, my emotions, or my competence—that give me some reason for self-loathing. By the time I am an adult, I may have perfected ways to cover and compensate for my propensity to experience shame. However, these very self-protections will alienate me from my own genuine experience and prevent genuine connection with others.

What I have described as the core experience of shame sounds dramatic—feeling affective distress and emotional rush, feeling out of control and falling apart—but it doesn't have to look dramatic. In fact, often this kind of developmental trauma happens quietly. Caregivers don't mean to inflict shame, but for one reason or another, they aren't able to respond to a child in ways that hold, manage, and help integrate the child's affective and emotional experience. A child's response to such misattunement might be dramatic—some kind of enactment of intense neediness or rage. But many children learn quickly to do the best they can with what they're given. They put their "falling apart" or "out of control" feelings away. They block any felt sense of badness as best they can, quietly putting on a good-kid performance or a not-needing face. They show only those parts of themselves that can get along with the range of affective responses that are available to them from important others.

When in my therapy practice I begin to sense the burden of chronic shame a client carries, I have reasons to believe that something like this happened to him in his early relationships. Each story is unique, but these are the kinds of personal meanings that live within the rather terse, technical definition, *shame is an experience of one's felt sense of self disintegrating in relation to a dysregulating other.*

I have come to my definition of shame with reference to relational theory in general and affect regulation theory in particular, but also with reference to a history of psychodynamic theory about shame. Since 1971, when Heinz Kohut re-imagined narcissism for psychoanalysts and Helen Block Lewis began to talk to them about shame, much has been written about shame and the self.[5] Psychodynamic theorists have called shame both affect and emotion. They have defined it as a pattern of thought and as the essence of a flawed self-image. They have described varieties of shame experience, from unpleasant self-consciousness to abject humiliation, and they have disentangled shame from guilt. The rest of this chapter reviews these significant aspects of shame theory in light of my definition of shame.

SHAME AS AFFECT

Affect theorists claimed a spot for shame among the basic affects our human systems produce, even though it is more complex than a direct response to external stimuli. Shame, as Nathanson describes it, is a painful mechanism that limits positive affects, and the degree of pain it causes seems to depend on the contrast between the severity of the felt limit and the degree of "pull" the positive still contains. When a pleasurable pattern of neural firing is suddenly interrupted, the rupture is embodied in downcast eyes, a slump of muscle tone most visible in the head and shoulders, and a sense of confusion and disorientation.[6]

Silvan Tomkins, Nathanson's mentor, argued that for human beings affect is the primary innate biological motivating mechanism, more urgent than drives associated with deprivation or pleasure, more urgent, even, than physical pain.[7] Tomkins' affect theory is a theory of individual experience; shame, for example, happens when one's strong desire meets an unwanted limit. Half a century later, affect theory has become affect *regulation* theory; shame is seen not as an individual's response to a painful stimulus sequence, but as what happens in the interaction between one person's affective relational need and another person's response to the need. In short, shame is essentially a two-person experience.

There's no denying, however, that a fall into dysregulation or shame can be an overwhelming physical experience for one person. Affect is communication, but it is first of all physiological. As Helen Block Lewis pointed out in the early days of psychoanalytic shame theory, the very wordlessness of shame and the concreteness of the autonomic activity it arouses—blushing, sweating, rapid heart-rate, and diffuse rage—make it a powerful and primitive reaction that resists rational solution.[8]

SHAME AS EMOTION

Nathanson explains that affect is only the beginning of the story of shame. When a person becomes aware of having an affect, the affect becomes a feeling, and then feelings, or emotions, become linked to memories and meanings. In his words, "Whereas affect is biology, emotion is biography."[9] Within the narratives we live, shame becomes the complex felt-meanings that accrue over time around all the "neural firing" moments when we feel the slump of a sudden fall from grace, the confusion of a sudden loss of face.

As Tomkins himself said in a passage often quoted by those theorizing in his wake: "While terror and distress hurt, they are wounds inflicted from outside which penetrate the smooth surface of the ego; but shame is felt as an inner torment, a sickness of the soul. It does not matter whether the humiliated one has been shamed by derisive laughter or whether he mocks himself. In either event he feels himself naked, defeated, alienated, lacking in dignity and worth."[10]

This is not the language of biology. This is the language of a self who feels complex emotion in distressing relational contexts, real or imagined. And this is exactly where Donna Orange, a proponent of intersubjective psychoanalytic theory, feels we should begin, if we want to try to define shame.

Orange finds the language of affect reductionistic. As complex processes of subjective experience, emotions cannot ever be reduced to simple entities, she argues. No single emotion can be abstracted from the continuity and layeredness of a person's entire subjective feeling/thought experience. An even more important point is that emotional life is relational. "Emotions are responses to relational events or needs, and emotional expression is an attempt to connect, or to regulate connection, with another."[11] For Orange, the emotion of shame is neither affect nor cognition; when felt, it is a total "world of experience." Furthermore, this shame process is always produced and held in being by an intersubjectively shaming system.[12]

In her pioneering work that charted a relational course for the study of shame, Lewis had also described shame as an interpersonal emotion—an internal emergency response to feeling that one's affectional ties are threatened. The experience of shame begins with a relationship in which one feels dependent and vulnerable to rejection, she said. If one fails to live up to the standards of an important, admired other, one feels a kind of unrequited love—a self crushed by rejection. As a result, one feels humiliated fury, or shame-rage, a feeling that can elicit more scorn from the other, but also more guilt, turned against the self as hateful loathing.[13]

Whether or not we entirely agree with how Lewis parses shame, her description does capture the intensity of interpersonal emotion involved in a "failure of affect attunement"—the phrase self-psychological and inter-subjective theorists use to explain the origins of shame. They speak not of unrequited love, but of chronic misattunement that impairs a child's sense of interpersonal efficacy and forms the foundation for a child's later sense of worthlessness.[14] In Howard Bacal's terms, what the child misses is a sense of communion or affective sharing, an experience of relatedness in which there is *no discrepancy* between infant and caregiver. Thus Bacal calls shame the affect of discrepancy—first, the discrepancy between a child's emotional needs and the capacity of people in his environment to respond to them. Shame also lives in the discrepancy between any person's longing for primary relatedness and his failure to experience it, even while shame is what moti-vates his fear of trusting and reaching out.[15]

Everyday discrepancies between emotional need and emotional response can be powerful events, first of all for infants and children, and then also for our shame-prone clients. Following an unrepaired mismatch of need and response, a disintegration of self may be masked, but it is painfully real in ways that the word "discrepancy" may not quite capture. Lewis's words about the relational pain of unrequited love, with its humiliated fury either unleashed or turned on the self, help us appreciate the emotional cost of misattunement and dysregulation.

Lewis began to write about the excruciating pain of shame when she discovered that failed psychoanalytic treatment can very often be traced to a failure to face shame in treatment. Shame disappears in treatment precisely because it is so very painful to bring to awareness, and espe-cially so when shame becomes part of the treatment relationship. Client and therapist can together bypass shame on a regular basis. Instead of feeling the emotional intensity of shame itself, a client may turn either to obsessive self-hatred or to obsessive thoughts about what went wrong in interactions between self and others, including the therapist. Pursuing these themes may seem like genuine emotional work to both client and therapist. But the real emotion of shame is much more painful. So we all avoid it. That's the point Lewis drives home.[16]

What more can we say to try to capture in words the emotional pain of shame? It's feeling like a failure. It's feeling exposed as inferior or deficient—or as ugly, dirty, and disgusting. Shame includes awkward self-consciousness, blushing embarrassment, and searing humiliation. Shame explodes into rage; it runs quickly to envy and resentment. Because it's so much a part of frag-mented and dissociated states, it also feels like disorganization and panic—or like a profoundly incompetent self. So many words—and yet they can't cap-ture the essence of shame because the experience of shame is fundamentally non-verbal and visceral, a "sickness of the soul," as Tomkins put it.

Nevertheless, as human beings we are wired to bring logic to our experience whenever we can. Though shame is a felt "world" of intersubjective experience irreducible to either affect or cognition, we try to make sense of what hurts us even while it's happening, and in terms we can control. Thus the "thought" aspect of shame experience has become a substantial topic of conversation for shame theorists.

SHAME AS THOUGHT

Lewis, who sees humiliated fury about rejection as the emotional core of shame, believes that shame has a simultaneous cognitive side—ideas of failure.[17] I see the core of shame as self-disintegration, an experience that is not yet as formed as fury, and that by definition does not cohere to "make sense." And so I think that no cognition is *simultaneous* with the core affective experience of shame. In infancy and childhood, meaning forms slowly in response to repeated experiences of self-disintegrating. In adulthood, a certain sense may be made very quickly of disintegration feelings, but only because particular neural pathways have been fired so many times before, not because a particular thought—about a failing or defective self, for example—necessarily belongs to the experience. But if the thought of failure doesn't happen simultaneously with shame, and if it isn't even a necessary component of shame, why is it so commonly associated with shame experience?

According to Francis Broucek, the answer to this riddle lies in the links between shame and objectification.[18] Before we can think about self as a failure, we have to be able to have objective thoughts about "self." We learn how to do this from others who see us from the outside. And it is this objectifying mode of seeing that has the power to instill self-objectifying shame in us, shame that we experience as negative thoughts about ourselves.

Broucek begins with a self psychological definition of self as a relational and contextual entity. In infancy and early childhood, in shared consciousness with caregivers, a sense of self emerges from experiences of efficacy and fulfilled intentionality, and from the joy and excitement that follow. Broucek presents this idea as an alternative to Tomkins' suggestion that a barrier to interest/excitement activates shame. In Broucek's view, felt *inefficacy* in relation to the human environment is what activates shame. Shame happens when the child's experience of sharing intention and consciousness with caregivers is ruptured. The essence of such rupture is being perceived from the outside rather than being joined in the shared "inside" of experience.[19]

This shift from an intersubjective to an objectifying connection can take place in very subtle, non-verbal ways. Broucek suggests that early experiences of failed efficacy or intentionality most likely happen, at least for sighted infants, through mismatches between the infant's cues and the caretaker's gaze and facial responsiveness. (Tronick's Still-Face study comes to mind.[20]) The power of a shame-inducing gaze may explain, Broucek suggests, the lifetime association between shame and the wish to avoid another's gaze or not to be seen at all.[21] In early childhood, a powerful parental gaze will interact with the beginnings of a child's objective self-awareness. Then, when a child fails to elicit a gaze that supports his intentionality, excitement, and indwelling sense of self, he will experience something else: being looked at in a way that objectifies him.

Broucek allows that normal parenting requires reflecting a child as both subject and object, so that a child has a chance to learn both ways of being in the world and in relationships with others. However, in Broucek's view, parents must be firmly committed to first of all seeing the child's subjective experience and feelings. A pattern of noticing things about the child instead of paying attention to what the child feels is a pattern of shame-inducing objectification.[22]

As we might expect, an objectified child—whether objectified in an adoring or a critical way—begins to be preoccupied with a sense of self as an object for others. It doesn't matter whether the child's emotion toward this objectified self is positive or negative; she becomes distanced from her own subjectivity. When this pattern is exaggerated, it becomes pathology. The child loses the possibility of recovering what Broucek calls primary communion with others, communion that would help her dissolve, at an emotional level, the distance and alienation that go with self-objectification.[23]

I would add to Broucek's account my understanding that a shaming moment of objectification is also a relational moment of dysregulation and, for the child, an experience of self disintegrating. Without the communion connection she needs to maintain coherence, the child looks to her own observer self to help regulate her distress, a shift I will describe in the next chapter as a move from right-brain to left-brain functioning. Looking for logic, her observer self borrows her parent's story about her and elaborates from it her own "objective" story. Here is the origin of the disconnection between shame feelings and shame thoughts. Shame thoughts belong to this already objectified self, a self who has exited the intersubjective space where primary communion should be, the space where regulation failed and disintegration rules.

Thus shame thoughts are quintessentially alone thoughts. They are produced by the felt impossibility of communion, and they produce realities that have no primary communion in them. As Wurmser points out, shame becomes a wall of separation that protects fragile selves against intrusive looks and words from others, and guards those selves against the reaching out that might expose their flaws. For shamed selves, their flaws are "objective" givens—varieties of weakness, defectiveness, or ugliness.[24]

In the thought-scapes our shame-ridden clients inhabit, others are always looking, and our clients see themselves through these others' eyes. Lewis proposes that this "other-directed" mindset leads directly to self-loathing kinds of depression.[25] In these isolated worlds, performances of perfection are necessary even if failure is inevitable. Feeling wrong in the presence of others can always be traced to something wrong with self: "I'm too emotional, too boring, too needy, too fat, too dumb." "No matter what I try, I will mess up." Or, "No matter how brilliant my accomplishments, they will never be good enough." As therapists, we learn that trying to argue with any of these thoughts is an effort doomed at the start. They are each the storyline of a lonely narrative that has its own logic for being, a logic buried along with the experiences of broken communion and self disintegration that made the story necessary.

SHAME AS SELF-IMAGE

Nathanson gives the following explanation of how shame affect becomes negative self image: when a child experiences the sudden unrelatedness of shame, he also experiences incompetence, a bad and dangerous state. In a bid for safety, the child links the unbound shame affect with the unbound image of badness and dangerousness. The two experiences "cohere," and coherence is always safer than random chaos. Nathanson describes this safe linkage as an ideo-affective complex of bad-me; "following the establishment of this linkage any experience of shame now brings with it images defining one as defective, weak, or incomplete."[26]

If someone's "bad-me" will be aroused by any shame experience—defined by Nathanson as any sudden drop in positive affect, especially positive interpersonal affect—then bad-me experiences are going to happen whenever that person feels misunderstood or disconnected. This propensity to experience "bad-me" in many relational situations might also be called a disorder of self-image and of self-esteem, or what is often called a narcissistic disorder.

Psychoanalytic literature links shame, flawed narcissism, and faulty self-image. Lewis pointed out that shame and narcissism are related as opposites: Shame is a negative experience of self; narcissism is positive love or admiration for the self. [27] In Wurmser's view, how a person would like to be seen is an "ideal self," how he is seen is his "real self," and any great discrepancy between the two self-images is what he feels as shame.[28] Classic self psychology, which sees shame as the underside of narcissism, believes that shame happens when a person's internal experience of real self falls short of an ideal self-image.

To understand this definition of shame, we need to understand what self psychology tells us about the construction of an ideal self-image, against which a real self fails. And we need to understand how self psychology accounts for the failure of the real self, leading to the discrepancy between the two versions of self. Andrew Morrison, who has written extensively on shame from a self psychological perspective, explains both points.

First of all, a self can feel shame without the immediate influence of an external shamer, Morrison says. When chronic shame is a problem within a person's narcissistic pathology, the trouble is fundamentally internal. This shame is a manifestation not of being shamed by another, but of more general self-deficits. For Kohut the primary deficit is a person's inability to manage his own split-off grandiosity; shame is in the discrepancy between reality and fantasies of greatness that he has never been able to acknowledge and work through. Morrison's picture of shame includes Kohut's account and adds to it experiences of disappointment, failure, and inadequacy when the self fails to live up to its identified ideals.[29]

Morrison focuses on idealizing selfobject experience—what it accomplishes and what happens when it fails. Idealizing emerges after a child's first struggle to get good mirroring and modulation for her striving, exhibitionistic self. Sometimes an idealizing phase can serve as compensation for a less-than-optimum response to a child's healthy grandiosity. To be helped by example to have ideals and to live up to them is a second chance to use another person's presence to create experiences of strength and vitality that cohere as "self."[30]

When this process works well, a child creates a picture of an ideal self that resembles her internal picture of an idealized parent. Her self-image represents her longing for the subjective experience of perfection. And that's why, as the child does her best to live up to ideal self, she needs lots of understanding response from her parent, including calm acceptance about mistakes. When there's a good, mutually responsive fit between the child's experience of her idealized parent and her own picture of ideal self, she has a good chance to grow into a self who can risk both hope and disappointment, and who can accept herself and others with forgiveness and humor. As an adult she will be able to pursue ideals with self-reflective wisdom and to live with imperfection.

On the other hand, if parents fail to provide a child with someone to look up to, including the companionable invitation to "be like" that idealized someone, the child will not have the self-strengthening experience of idealizing. If there's a bad fit between the child's experience of idealized parent and her own ideal self, if the parent fails to respond in an understanding, helpful way to the child's quest for connection with strength and goodness, then the child will carry forward a depleted self who is forever burdened by an unattainable, unrealistic ideal image of self. Repetitive self-critical thoughts will make self esteem tenuous if not impossible.

Morrison's definition of a shamed self seems some distance from my definition, *an experience of one's felt sense of self disintegrating in relation to a dysregulating other.* He has moved well beyond "disintegrating self" to describing a shamed self's enduring, complex formation of shame-based emotion and thought. Yet essential to Morrison's definition of shame is a self who needs a specific kind of interaction with another person in order not to fall into shame. In my paradigm, that interaction is a parent's attuned, affect-regulating relationship with a vulnerable self. In Morrison's, it's a parent's attuned response to a child's vulnerable need to idealize, as well as her need to be mirrored, which are both specific affective needs. In each of our paradigms, shame is produced by a caregiver's failures to match a child's affective need, and that shame is understood first of all as a state of self (disintegrating, fragmented, or depleted, to use self psychology's language) out of which cognitive shame-ideas about the self emerge.

It's remarkable that when shaming thoughts and shamed self-images take over the management of a disintegrating self, shame becomes something of an escape from itself. Such thoughts and self-images are painful, but they are not the direct experience of one's sense of self fragmenting or being annihilated by shame. Broucek and Morrison, along with many shame theorists, chart a trajectory of escape from the core experience of shame even as they describe shame.

Likewise, almost all of what we think of as narcissistic pathology is not an expression of self, but rather, an expression of *escape from self*. More specifically, it is an escape from a self who is prone to feeling a disintegrating, fragmenting state of shame. The self-objectification, the self-aggrandizing or self-loathing obsessions, the unrealistic self images, and the volatile self-esteem that we associate with problems of narcissism and shame—these all belong to the flight-paths vulnerable people take as they flee from the disintegration that's at the core of shame.

VARIETIES OF SHAME EXPERIENCE

So far I have talked about the shame experience as if it were one kind of experience. Our everyday vocabulary suggests, however, that shame comes in different varieties. Susan Miller has attempted a taxonomy of different kinds of shame based on in-depth interviews with subjects.[31] To summarize briefly, she has found that *shame* itself is often connected to feeling inferior, while *embarrassment* is linked to feeling exposed and undone. A person who feels forced into a debased position feels *humiliation*. Seeing oneself in action as if from the outside is *self-consciousness*. Miller sees *guilt* as a form of shame induced by the feeling that one has violated a standard. She calls her study a phenomenological approach to shame, and comes to the conclusion that the crucial elements of shame are as follows: displeasure about the status of self in the context of comparison between self and others.

My definition of shame suggests alternative "crucial elements" of shame, giving perhaps more support to the idea that these various forms of shame are essentially the same experience.

If shame is, indeed, *an experience of one's felt sense of self disintegrating in relation to a dysregulating other,* then in each kind of shame the same three conditions should hold, albeit in different ways and at different intensities: a sense of self is disintegrating, the self is in immediate (real or imagined) ruptured relation to another person, and that person is experienced as "dysregulating," or as a threat to self-cohesion.

For example, the exposed and undone feelings of *embarrassment* are disintegration experiences, though not as intense as full-blown shame. They happen as one feels "looked at" by others, and in that moment their gaze is what threatens a cohesive sense of self. Embarrassed, one is in the spotlight alone—and all the more so when suffering *humiliation*. Humiliation adds elements of intent and psychological violence to the behavior of the "dysregulating other." Humiliation is most powerful when the ruptured relationship in which it happens is an important relationship for the one humiliated. The profoundly dysregulating, anti-relational force of humiliation can produce a profound and lasting disintegration of a person's sense of self.

By contrast, *self-consciousness* is a tame version of shame. In moments of self-consciousness, one is alone, outside the comfort of affect regulation or "communion." Relationship has been quietly ruptured. One is objectifying oneself to stay cohesive—and to stay ahead of any objectifying (dysregulating) others. Acute shame/disintegration hasn't happened yet, but it could at any moment.

What about "shame itself," which Miller defines as feeling inferior, or as feeling displeasure about one's status in relations to others? While her definition captures a sense of a self feeling less than whole in relation to others, it skips over the immediate relational experience of a dysregulated self disintegrating—in just the way a shamed person would. One does whatever one can not to have a direct experience of disintegration. As we have seen, self-critical thoughts help one quickly transform acute shame-experience into something more stable and, though painful, more tolerable.

There are many more words for shame that Miller doesn't explicate—*disgrace*, *indignity*, and *mortification*, for example. They, too, can be understood as a self disintegrating in relation to a powerful other. And then there is *guilt*. Miller believes guilt is the kind of shame one feels about violating a standard. As many shame theorists have done, she blurs the distinction between the experiences of guilt and shame.

One can, indeed, feel guilt and shame at the same time. However, guilt and shame are two distinct emotions, arising from two different worlds of relational experience. The work of June Tangney and Ronda Dearing makes clear for clinicians how important it is to understand each emotion in its own right, and to understand the difference between them.

GUILT IS NOT SHAME

Tangney and Dearing credit Lewis with first noticing what they believe is the critical difference between shame and guilt, a difference they put to the test with the empirical research they discuss in their 2002 study called *Shame and Guilt*. [32] Lewis argued that shame is a negative valuation of the *self*, whereas guilt is a negative valuation of the self's *behavior*. The difference is between feeling, "I am a bad person," and "I am a worthwhile person who did a bad thing." Feelings of guilt, including tension, remorse, and regret, can be painful. But guilt does not affect one's core identity. By contrast, shame is an acutely painful emotion that typically includes the feeling of being exposed as a fundamentally defective or worthless being. One can, of course, feel like a bad person while feeling remorse about bad behavior; guilt can be more or less shame-laced or shame-free. And situation-specific shame, along with guilt, can sometimes be a helpful moral emotion. However, shame and guilt have different origins, meanings, and effects in human experience.

Tangney and Dearing define both shame and guilt as self-conscious emotions because they involve self-evaluation, and as moral emotions because they guide personal choices and behaviors. They point out that shame is always inextricable from the relationship of self with other. [33] However, they do not find the origins of shame in affect misattunement or affect dysregulation; instead, they link its origins to two cognitive milestones: a child's awareness of self as separate from others and his understanding of standards against which behaviors can be evaluated. (Guilt does not emerge until later, they say, not until a child can understand the difference between character— "I'm good"—and behavior—"I did a bad thing.") [34] So although they speak of shame as a painful emotion, their working definition tends toward seeing shame as a thought process.

It's clear that Tangney and Dearing hold a definition of shame that doesn't exactly match mine. Nevertheless, their distinctions between shame and guilt are important to my work with clients. What makes their study so clinically significant? First, clients often speak about guilt feelings when the real issue is not something they have done and for which they feel remorse. Instead, the issue behind their "guilt" is their deep feeling of *being* wrong or inadequate. I don't need to correct their language. I won't press the word *shame* on them. But it's helpful to be able to hear and respond to the shaky, vulnerable self hidden within an admission of "guilt." Sometimes to speak about guilt is as much vulnerability as a shame-ridden person can afford to share. It's almost as if he knows that guilt is a stronger position than shame, and therefore he assumes it's a position more deserving of a therapist's respect.

And in fact, guilt is not only a state of self very different from shame; it's a state of self far stronger than shame. Both of these points have been well supported by the empirical research Tangney and Dearing discuss in their book. Shame emerges from their studies as an emotion and cognition that has destructive implications for interpersonal relationships, whereas the capacity for guilt is a relational strength.

Specifically, their research suggests that shame-prone people are more likely to blame others (as well as themselves) for things gone wrong; they are more prone to bitter resentment or seething hostility, and they are less able to empathize with others in general. By contrast, people who are more likely to feel guilt instead of shame seem to be less self-referential in general, more able to empathize with others and to accept responsibility for things gone wrong. They are less likely to get angry, too, but when angry, they are more likely to express their anger in fairly direct, constructive ways. I see in this contrast a clear difference between people who are constantly warding off the threat of self-disintegration in relation to others and people who can sustain a solid, coherent self in relation to others.

Of course, it's not helpful to point out these contrasts to shame-prone people. They already have plenty of reasons to despise themselves. In fact, I find it very important to remind myself constantly of the vulnerability that drives the emotions and behaviors that make relationships difficult for shame-ridden people. They spend so much energy looking after themselves and defending themselves because they are absolutely sure they have to. Without all this vigilance, avoidance, or aggression, they would find themselves constantly disintegrating in the presence of powerfully dysregulating others—or so they believe. And it's totally beside the point if these "others" are mostly memories from long ago; the threat feels present and real. That's just how it is with people who suffer from chronic shame and who don't quite know it yet.

It's with people who do know and feel their shame that I find the contrast between guilt and shame most useful. When a client has been able to feel his shame and acknowledge its power in his life, he can begin to work through that shame and get to a better place. For the reasons Tangney and Dearing cite, shame and his reactions to shame will have made his interpersonal relationships difficult. As he comes to this better place, he may be surprised that his relationships don't become the perfection that his shamed self once longed for. What's better is that instead of shame about himself, he can feel guilt about his mistakes. He can feel real empathy for others, including those he hurts. He can take responsibility for his actions, his desires, and his anger.

For me as a therapist, it's very helpful to be able to expect this quite unexpected better place on the other side of shame. Guilt *is* better than shame, but it takes some getting used to. I like to be able to help clients make the best of this shift, with all its emotional and behavioral changes; together we can even celebrate their "graduation" from an intersubjective world where shame rules to one where genuine feelings of guilt are possible.

NOTES

1. Judith Jordan, "Relational Development: Therapeutic Implications of Empathy and Shame," in *Women's Growth in Diversity: More Writings from the Stone Center*, ed. Judith Jordan (New York: Guilford, 1997), 147.

2. Jordan, "Relational Development," 152–53.

3. For classic examples of Self Psychology theory, see Heinz Kohut, *How Does Analysis Cure* (Chicago: University of Chicago Press, 1984), and Ernest Wolf, *Treating the Self: Elements of Clinical Self Psychology* (New York: Guilford, 1988).

4. See Louis Cozolino, *The Neuroscience of Psychotherapy: Healing the Social Brain*, 2nd ed. (New York: Norton, 2012), 193: "The return from a state of shame to attunement results in a rebalancing of autonomic functioning, supports affect regulation, and contributes to the gradual development of self-regulation. Repeated and rapid return from shame to attuned states also consolidates into an expectation of positive outcomes during difficult social interactions." *Implicit Relational Knowing* is the term the Boston Change Process Study Group gives to the affective and interactive knowledge we have about how to do things with others, a form of procedural knowledge that is not put into the symbols of language. Boston Change Process Study Group, *Change in Psychotherapy: A Unifying Paradigm* (New York: Norton, 2010), 30–53.

5. Heinz Kohut, *The Analysis of the Self: A Systematic Approach to the Psychoanalytic Treatment of Personality Disorders* (New York: International Universities Press, 1971); Helen Block Lewis, *Shame and Guilt in Neurosis* (New York: International Universities Press, 1971).

6. Donald Nathanson, *Shame and Pride* (New York: Norton, 1992).

7. Silvan Tomkins, "Shame," in *The Many Faces of Shame*, ed. Donald Nathanson (New York: Guilford, 1987), 137.

8. Helen Block Lewis, "Introduction: Shame – the 'Sleeper' in Psychopathology," in *The Role of Shame in Symptom Formation*, ed. Helen Block Lewis (Hillsdale, NJ: Erlbaum, 1987), 19.

9. Nathanson, *Shame and Pride*, 50.

10. Silvan Tomkins, *Affect, Imagery, Consciousness*, vol. 2, *The Negative Affects* (New York: Springer, 1963), 118.

11. Donna Orange, *Emotional Understanding: Studies in Psychoanalytic Epistemology* (New York: Guilford, 1995), 97.

12. Donna Orange, "Whose Shame Is It Anyway? Lifeworlds of Humiliation and Systems of Restoration," *Contemporary Psychoanalysis*, 44 (2008): 83–100.

13. Lewis, "Shame – the 'Sleeper' in Psychopathology," 19.

14. Orange, *Emotional Understanding*, 101–2.

15. Howard Bacal, "Shame – the Affect of Discrepancy," in *The Widening Scope of Shame*, eds. Melvin Lansky and Andrew Morrison (Hillsdale, NJ: Analytic Press, 1997), 97–104.

16. Lewis, "Shame – the 'Sleeper' in Psychopathology," 22–23.

17. Lewis, "Shame – the 'Sleeper' in Psychopathology," 6.

18. Francis Broucek, *Shame and the Self* (New York: Guilford, 1991).

19. Broucek, *Shame and the Self*, 34.

20. Edward Tronick et al., eds., "The Infant's Response to Entrapment between Contradictory Messages in Face-to-Face Interaction," *Journal of Child Psychiatry* 17 (1978): 1–13.

21. Broucek, *Shame and the Self*, 35.

22. Broucek, *Shame and the Self*, 47.

23. Broucek, *Shame and the Self*, 57.

24. Leon Wurmser, "Shame, The Veiled Companion of Narcissism," in *Many Faces*, ed. Nathanson, 78–79.

25. Helen Block Lewis, "The Role of Shame in Depression over the Life Span," in *Role of Shame in Symptom Formation*, ed. Lewis, 29–47.

26. Donald Nathanson, "A Timetable for Shame," in *Many Faces*, ed. Nathanson, 38.

27. Helen Block Lewis, "Shame and the Narcissistic Personality," in *Many Faces*, ed. Nathanson, 95–96.

28. Wurmser, "Shame, the Veiled Companion of Narcissism," 76.

29. Andrew Morrison, "The Eye Turned Inward: Shame and the Self," in *Many Faces*, ed. Nathanson, 271–91.

30. Andrew Morrison, *Shame, the Underside of Narcissism* (Hillsdale, NJ: Analytic Press, 1989), 83–85.

31. Susan Miller, *The Shame Experience* (Hillsdale, NJ: Analytic Press, 1985).

32. June Price Tangney and Ronda L. Dearing, *Shame and Guilt*, (New York: Guilford, 2002).

33. Tangney and Dearing, *Shame and Guilt*, 2.

34. Tangney and Dearing, *Shame and Guilt*, 140–41.

CHAPTER 3

Shame and the Relational Brain

The essence of shame is non-verbal affect. Both in childhood and in adult experience, the emotions, thoughts, and self-images we associate with shame are what accrue to the visceral experience of one's self disintegrating in response to acute or sustained misattunement and misrecognition from a significant other. This account of shame helps me understand some puzzling clinical phenomena.

I have noticed, for example, that many clients who suffer from pervasive, life-long chronic shame are quite sure that their parents and other significant caregivers didn't overtly shame them. They don't have significant stories of childhood shame events. But they do know that, through some combination of caregiver absence and intrusion, they suffered profound misattunement to their young affective/emotional selves. Their chronic shame makes more sense when it's understood to begin with this kind of misrecognition, which could also be called relational trauma.

I have also noticed that most clients who struggle with the after-effects of relational trauma, whether that trauma came by way of blatant abuse, subtle manipulation, or thoughtless neglect, suffer from a very similar kind of pervasive chronic shame. It makes sense to locate the origin of this shame in the profound experience of misattunement they have in common, rather than in specific events of shame or humiliation inflicted in extremely dissimilar ways by their very different kinds of caregivers.

Here's something else I've noticed: When, in the middle of therapy conversations, clients are suddenly thrown into states of wordless, incapacitating shame, it's rarely because I have said or done something they experience as humiliating or belittling. Shame strikes when my presence has failed them and they can no longer feel our connection. These moments of misunderstanding or misattunement between us can quickly become disorienting spirals of shame. Through long force of habit, shame-prone clients make sense of such dysregulation with self-denigrating ideas—*they* are the problem—an action that restores to them a certain kind of equilibrium. If not repaired, these micro-experiences will infuse the therapy relationship with the hidden shame that is the "equilibrium" state for these clients— and all of that will come to pass even when nothing overtly shaming has happened.

Such tenacious tendencies to shame are pervasive and hard to pin down. As I said in the last chapter, trying to talk our chronically shamed clients out of their conviction that they are fundamentally flawed is a project doomed to failure. Our clients may work valiantly at positive self-talk and do their best to think better of themselves, but their sense of shamed self does not go away. This sense, lodged somewhere deeper than words, a "sickness of the soul" with even less form than a feeling, is inaccessible to logic. I can better understand the tenacity of *"I'm despicable"* when I understand its roots in my clients' non-verbal, visceral experience of self-disintegration. This under-standing of their shame gives me a crucial empathic link to their experience.

From this perspective it's also clear why the bad-self feelings of shamed clients will just keep on being produced unless and until their experience of disintegration can be held within the presence of an attuned, regulating other. The idea of preverbal shame meshes well with the emphasis self psychology and intersubjectivity theory place not on interpretation and insight, but on the repair of fragmented selves within a relationship of empathic attunement. The empathy expressed in the non-verbal "music" of attuned response eases the visceral experience of shame, even when shame is neither thought nor spoken. In other words and in summary, my definition of shame has proved to be both relevant and coherent within my clinical practice.

But finding theoretical coherence has been more of a challenge. Self psychological theory left me with some basic questions about shame. Are "fragmentation" and "shame" synonyms for a certain self state? If so, how do we talk about the *emotion* we call shame? How would either the emotion of shame or a fragmented self-state be related both to misattunement and to a failure to attain an ideal self image? I could not sort it out, but I decided to lean away from shame as a self-image problem and toward shame as the result of misattunement to a child's affect. But affect theory did not quite add up for me either. How could I understand the deeply interpersonal pain of shame as a sudden shift in the pace of neural firing? With all these questions, I kept coming back to Tronick's images of infants slumping down and away from still-faced mothers. There was something true about shame there; I felt that truth viscerally, and I let it inform my work.

Meanwhile I was also reading brain theory. I was intrigued by what Daniel Siegel calls the interpersonal development of the human brain,[1] and I noticed Louis Cozolino's recasting of psychotherapy as neuroscience that heals the social brain.[2] I saw how the idea of interpersonal neurobiology dovetails with intersubjective theories of development and psychotherapy. I read Bonnie Badenoch's practical guide to an interpersonal, integrative form of psychotherapy based on Siegel's system of understanding mind, development, and healing.[3] But it was not until I listened to Allan Schore's impassioned argument for "right-brain psychotherapy" that the brain-science penny dropped for me. Perhaps this idea of right brain therapy could provide a paradigm to explain what I intuitively knew about the connections among shame and affect attunement, infant development, attachment, selfobject experience, and relational psychotherapy.

AFFECT REGULATION, DYSREGULATION, AND THE RIGHT BRAIN

Psychoanalysts and psychotherapists of various relational schools feel at home with affect regulation theory, for its description of what the "relational brain" needs for growth and health validates what they have always believed—if mostly on the strength of interpersonal intuition and clinical experience. Since Carl Rogers began writing about client-centered therapy in 1951,[4] many psychotherapists have maintained that the relationship between therapist and client is the essence of therapy and the means to any lasting change. From Rogers to Kohut to intersubjectivity theory, compassionate empathic attunement has been the core of relational practice.[5] Self-in-relation theory takes a similar stand, using feminist language to describe effective therapy as a healing mutual connection.[6] The Boston Change Process Study Group speaks of "now moments" between client and therapist that have the power to change what a client unconsciously knows about how relationships work.[7] A psychoanalyst who works from an interpersonal/relational perspective allows himself to be drawn into his patient's unconscious relational system believing that it is through their shared relational experience that the patient's self-system will become capable of more integration, freedom, vitality, and inner peace.[8]

These relational theories all have a developmental bent. The new relationship between client and therapist matters so much because the client's early relationships are the genesis of his distress. Psychoanalytic and psychodynamic therapists have believed this to be true since Freud. Now, as Allan Schore does with reference to hundreds of brain studies, relational therapists can support their belief with neuroscience.[9]

As a theory of development, Schore's Affect Regulation Theory is twenty-first century attachment theory. Since the early days of attachment theory in the 1960s, Bowlby and Ainsworth have told us that our first primary relationships shape our basic ways of being, and that we carry forward our working models of attachment into all of our emotional and social connections.[10] Schore tells us how the affective interactions of attachment shape our brains for life.[11]

An attachment relationship is a bond of emotional communication between an infant and a primary caregiver. The communication happens through mutual gaze, voice rhythms and inflections, and other bodily responses between the pair. When affect communication is in synchrony, the infant is in a positive state of affect and arousal. When the infant experiences negative arousal, synchrony is lost until the caregiver is able to repair it interactively and in the process help soothe or modulate the infant's distress-affect. Thus the infant's autonomic nervous system remains within an optimal range of arousal, and his relational brain continues to develop well.[12]

A caregiver might also respond in minimal, rejecting, intrusive, or unpredictable ways to the infant's need for emotional communication and modulation, likely because the caregiver is experiencing an internal stressful state of dysregulated arousal. In contact with this dysregulated and dysregulating other, the infant's autonomic nervous system will move first to energy-expending hyperarousal, and then to energy-conserving dissociation.

If these dysregulating interactions happen often, an infant will make a self-protective habit of dissociating from emotional connection. Then the development of his right brain, or relational/emotional brain, suffers.[13]

Emotional communication of any kind, Schore argues, moves between the caregiver's right brain and the infant's right brain. Throughout life, both secure and stressful relational experiences are encoded in unconscious internal working models of attachment that live in the right, not the left, hemisphere of the brain. The fundamental links between attachment experience and its effect on psychic structure throughout life are functions of this right hemisphere emotional/relational brain. The right hemisphere is deeply connected into the body and the nervous system; it processes not only current emotion, but emotion coded as bodily and relational memory. Holding all that we know viscerally and emotionally, the right brain is the well-spring of passion, creativity, imagery, primary process thinking, and unconscious process. It can also be the site of massive dissociation from emotional and attachment stress—from whatever is too painful to know viscerally and emotionally.

In other words, attachment trauma is also a right-brain, emotional phenomenon. And therefore, for any psychoanalysis or psychotherapy to make meaningful, healing contact with that trauma, it must speak right brain-language, which is not linear, rational language. Right-brain language is fundamentally the language of emotion expressed body to body—in quality of eye contact and voice tone, in rhythms of response and modulated intensities, in overt gestures and subtle body-language. The right brain hears the music, not the words, of what passes between people.[14]

PSYCHOTHERAPY AND THE RIGHT BRAIN

It follows, then, that the essential work of intersubjective psychotherapy is not what the therapist interprets or explains to the client—left-brain interactions. Rather, the key technique has to do with how to *be with* the client right brain to right brain, especially in affectively stressful moments when the patient's core self is at risk of disintegrating.[15] Schore and Schore maintain that the core skills of any effective psychotherapy are right-brain implicit capacities such as: empathy, the regulation of one's own affect, the ability to receive and express non-verbal communication, the sensitivity to register very slight changes in another's expression and emotion, and an immediate awareness of one's own subjective and intersubjective experience. All other techniques and skills rest upon this essential substratum.[16]

Schore and Schore propose a theoretical model that makes the most of these therapeutic capacities, and they offer it to psychoanalysts and clinical social workers alike—in fact, to all therapists who work with patients or clients who have suffered relational trauma in their early lives. They describe their model as a blend of classic attachment theory, internal object relations theory, self psychology, and contemporary relational theory, all informed by neuroscience and infant research. Such therapy can be seen as an attachment process through which clients with insecure working models of attachment have a chance to "earn" secure attachment in adulthood. The therapy process depends on accurate attunement and felt being-with, or in other words, on reliable repetitions of right-brain interactions and resonances that help expand right-brain capacities.[17]

The right brain is the home of the capacities damaged by early relational trauma. Not all right-brain trauma develops into a full-blown psychiatric disorder; however, according to Schore, affect dysregulation is a fundamental mechanism of all psychiatric disorders. Even for a highly functional adult, right-brain limitations are likely to become problems in emotional and interpersonal functioning. A person who can't solve personal and social problems in right-brain ways will come to rely on left-brain, explicit analytical reasoning. But left-brain analysis will only contain and manage, not solve, emotional and interpersonal problems.

And so, although right-brain challenged clients will look to psychotherapy for left-brain solutions—conscious, willed changes in thoughts, intentions, and strategies—what they need for lasting change is someone to engage with them right brain to right brain. What does this look like? Right-brain interactions in therapy are insistently and reliably experience-near. As the client talks about whatever is on his mind, the therapist responds with interest, to support and expand the conversation, to explore and to understand better what the client is communicating. The most important part of that understanding is affective resonance that moves moment-to-moment with the smallest shifts in the client's affective state. When there is a moment of affective charge, the therapist holds it with heightened affective resonance. This is also a moment of interactive regulation and an invitation to allow further affect to emerge. The therapist may briefly put words to the moment, but will avoid explaining or interpreting it.

In time and with many safe repetitions of such interpersonally resonant moments, the client will be able to stay with an amplified affective state as it emerges and may even begin to talk about it. This is how unconscious affect becomes sustained, regulated affect, which then can become a subjectively experienced emotional state and a tolerable part of self. Overall, the safely regulated relationship with the therapist begins to be an alternative to the client's habit of self-regulation, which is to disengage automatically from others in order to protect against dysregulating contact. This safe connection with another person also makes it possible for the client to be with himself differently.

Change comes for the right-brain challenged client as he is able to contact, describe, and regulate his own emotional experience. Mentalization theorists call this process mentalizing, which a child learns to do by absorbing how his parents hold his mind in their minds (or as Schore would say, how they regulate his emotions through right brain contact). In adulthood, mentalizing is the experience of *feeling clearly*, which is not the same as thinking clearly, even though it may involve thinking.[18] Right-brain insight follows emotional experience, and it emerges organically and wholistically. With right-brain insight, clients have new capacities to feel connections between their relational history and current patterns of experience. They have a new awareness of self as a thinking/feeling/choosing person, and a new felt sense of meaningful personal narrative.

In terms of neurobiology, an emotionally regulating relationship makes possible more interconnectivity in a client's right brain, both horizontally and vertically, and more brain systems involved in his processing of emotion, with more plasticity. He will experience a broader range of emotion and more complexity in both his emotions and his defenses. This more developed way to self-regulate will prove to be more flexible and useful than pathological dissociation. The client's affective and emotional states, rather than being alien threats to self-cohesion, will now promote the development and unification of his sense of self. He will be in a far better position to solve problems in right-brain ways and to find emotional connection and satisfaction in interpersonal relationships.[19]

THOUGHTS ON SHAME FROM AFFECT REGULATION THEORY

When Schore addresses shame directly, he attempts to synthesize his neurobiological perspective with previous theories about shame and development. He begins by describing shame as a hyperactive physiological state, including sweating, blushing, gaze aversion, and loss of coordination and cognition, all of which reflect a shift of balance from sympathetic (gas pedal) to parasympathetic (brake) components of the autonomic nervous system. He links this shift to Tomkins' understanding of shame affect as a sudden drop from a positive high arousal state to a negative low arousal state.[20]

Schore's narrative about prototypical shame begins with a particular time in a child's development, described by object relations theory as "practicing," a time when a child's grandiose exhilaration about discovery and mastery is at its peak, and is also most vulnerable to misattunement. A toddler in an elated, narcissistically charged state of heightened arousal eagerly anticipates a shared affect state with a caregiver, for example, when reuniting after exploration and separation. Unexpected affective misattunement from the caregiver can then set off a sudden shock of deflation for the excited child.

The shock is due in large part to an attachment relationship that has established an expectable pattern of attunement. The child's expectation of attunement is violated when the smile of contact is missing; for a moment, the caregiver is a stranger to the child. Schore emphasizes that shame does not occur with parent-child separation, but rather when the child experiences a barrier to emotional reconnection. Shame is not about the absence of the other, but about something wrong with presence at a time when a child needs a particular kind of response.

In a good-enough parenting environment, it's both inevitable that things go wrong, and also very likely that they will be repaired. A parent will notice the child's disconnected distress, re-establish attuned presence, and help transform the negative into positive. Shame is modulated and metabolized. Many such sequences of interactive repair build a child's self-regulatory and social skills. Bit by bit the child becomes able to internalize the parent's capacity to recognize, tolerate, and regulate the child's shame and narcissistic stress.[21]

Continuing with object relations theory, Schore carries his shame narrative into the "rapprochement crisis," a time when the child's elation and illusion of omnipotence collapse, and she needs a different kind of parental response. This developmental phase is marked by her resistance and frequent sense of injury, and also by many small, unavoidable doses of shame interwoven with her new sense of being a powerless little person in a world of powerful big people. But in this phase too, when the shame that follows a parent-child difference is regulated as tolerable and repairable, the shame experience can contribute to a life-long ability to reconnect with others after shame-stress, using their presence to recover from narcissistic injury and loss.[22]

From toddlerhood through adulthood, everyone needs a system to regulate shame and self-esteem, Schore maintains, and he borrows psychoanalytic theory about "ego ideal" and "superego" in order to explain the process. He explains both concepts in terms of affect regulation. Schore proposes that optimal (or good-enough) parental regulation is eventually transmuted into a "self-regulatory ego ideal" that regulates shame affect in two ways. It stimulates shame when the self falls short of its ideal. But then it also modulates shame (as parental regulation did), reducing its painful effects and making recovery and reconnection possible. These two components of the ego-ideal continually bring back into balance sympathetic/aroused and parasympathetic/diminished affective functioning, supporting a person's flexible self-identity and self-continuity in the face of life's mistakes and surprises.

And then Schore links this self-regulatory ego ideal with the right brain. Right-brain ego ideal is one part of superego, he says. The other part of superego—conscience—he links with the left brain. This is how he explains the difference between guilt, which requires a verbal, cognitive understanding of moral values and parental standards, and shame, which can be entirely wordless and nameless. More importantly, this move allows him to attribute to the right brain the so-called superego strengths of mood stability and quick recovery from emotional stress. These right-brain functions are clearly in a different class of process than the left-brain functions of cognitive conscience.[23]

In his most recent work, Schore does not return to developmental language about practicing and rapprochement, nor to structural concepts like ego ideal and superego. As his language becomes less psychoanalytic, it also becomes more neurobiologically complex. It seems that as regulation theory advances, a metapsychological context for shame has come to matter less than what is happening in the relational brain/mind/body when shame strikes.

Schore still refers to his early work as valid, and he still speaks of shame as a "sudden shock-induced deflation of positive affect that supports grandiose omnipotence." But he speaks of this shock as an experience common to adults, not just to toddlers. He also links the experience of shame not just to the deflation of positive affect, but to misattuned relational transactions in general, noting especially how shame rapidly enters the intersubjective field "during a stressful misattunement-triggered rupture of right-brain to right-brain therapist-patient attachment communications."[24] This sudden rupture is also a sudden collapse of the patient's implicit sense of self, a sense of self that had been functioning well in right-brain interaction with the therapist just moments before. As the parasympathetic affect of shame takes over, moving the intersubjective field to low arousal, the energies of the patient are withdrawn into a "don't see me" state, and her thoughts run to helplessness and despair.

This is one of Schore's pictures of shame: a parasympathetic low-arousal state that has the behavioural analogue of hiding and the cognitive analogue of seeing oneself as a failure. This affective state of very low arousal can be an ongoing, chronically dysregulated, and very painful experience. In this picture, shame seems to be a steady state that flies well under cognitive radar. The presence and dynamics of this hidden, pervasive shame need to be noticed, tolerated, and regulated in psychotherapy—though that is a daunting task, given how client and therapist alike avoid feeling shame at almost any cost.[25]

But Schore also suggests another picture of shame, or at least another side to the picture: As we noted earlier, the moment of having to apply the parasympathetic brakes of shame on one's own nervous system is an event in itself. It's marked by the momentary hyperactive physiology (blushing, sweating, etc.) characteristic of the shift from up-arousal to down-arousal. In that moment *something happens*, because something complex and relational is happening. We can call the moment dysregulation or misattunement when we focus on the "other" side of this self-with-other relational moment. When we focus on the "self" side of what's happening, we can call the moment implosion or collapse. I have called it a fall into a dysregulated state. The fall itself—that is, the event of implosion and collapse that corresponds to the event of dysregulating misattunement—is the core shame event. When I say that *shame is an experience of one's felt sense of self disintegrating*, I mean to capture that sense of a painful event that happens at a particular time.

And then relational brain processes continue in some way. The other might notice the self's collapse and disintegration and step in to help re-regulate and re-integrate, facilitating the metabolization of the shame experience. Or the other might not notice. Then, in neurobiological terms, what happens next could be called either a continuation of a parasympathetic low-energy shame state or the onset of a withdrawal-of-energy dissociative state. Or perhaps those aren't two names for the same set of phenomena. Perhaps it's helpful to think that two different things are happening at once—that what happens after an unrepaired fall into shame is some combination of continuing shame-affect and dissociation from the acute experience of shame.

Holding both in mind as possibilities would help make sense of the paradox that turns up again and again in psychotherapy: a person feels chronic unhappiness and anxiety, and yet she is profoundly disconnected from her relational history and her emotional self. How can someone feel so bad and yet not feel her own emotional pain, past and present? From a neurobiological perspective, it seems that someone could live in a chronic state of low-arousal shame that is chronically dysregulated because, although she's always somewhat conscious of shame, it is well hidden from others. At the same time this shame-prone person could use various forms of dissociation to keep memories and experiences of acute emotional pain completely out of her conscious awareness, and also to protect herself against any further shame-assaults on her self-cohesion.

FROM DYSREGULATION TO CHRONIC SHAME

Neurobiological affect regulation theory supports my proposal that shame is fundamentally an interpersonal event, an experience of self-disintegration in relation to a dysregulating other. But of course, not every misattuned interpersonal interaction that isn't repaired morphs into debilitating life-long shame. What we recognize as chronic shame has a dynamic and logic of its own that builds on many repetitions of disconnection, in one pattern or another, that are cumulatively traumatic. Shame starts as a simple right-brain to right-brain dysregulating event, but as those events, unrepaired, cluster in memory and wire up consistently with other neural events, shame becomes a chronic relational emotion shaped and colored by the relational contexts in which it came to be. In other words, although a "dysregulation/disintegration" understanding of shame is essential, it isn't the whole story. In the next chapter, I will return to relational theory about shame and the self in order to identify pathways by which repetitive dysregulation becomes chronic, debilitating shame.

NOTES

1. Daniel Siegel, *The Developing Mind: How Relationships and the Brain Interact to Shape Who We Are* (New York: Guilford, 1999).

2. Louis Cozolino, *The Neuroscience of Psychotherapy: Healing the Social Brain*, 2nd edn. (New York: Norton, 2012).

3. Bonnie Badenoch, *Being a Brain-Wise Therapist: A Practical Guide to Interpersonal Neurobiology* (New York: Norton, 2008).

4. Carl Rogers, *Client-Centered Therapy: Its Current Practice, Implications, and Theory* (London: Constable, 1951); Rogers' most widely read work is *On Becoming a Person: A Therapist's View of Psychotherapy* (London: Constable, 1961).

5. For an overview of this theoretical trajectory, see Michael Kahn, *Between Therapist and Client: The New Relationship*, 2nd edn. (New York: Freeman, 1997).

6. See, for example, Jean Baker Miller and Irene Pierce Stiver, *The Healing Connection: How Women Form Relationships in Therapy and in Life* (Boston: Beacon Press, 1997).

7. Boston Change Process Study Group, *Change in Psychotherapy: A Unifying Paradigm* (New York: Norton, 2010).

8. See, for example, Philip Bromberg, *Standing in the Spaces: Essays on Clinical Process, Trauma, and Dissociation* (Hillsdale, NJ: Analytic Press, 1998); *Awakening the Dreamer: Clinical Journeys* (Mahwah, NJ: Analytic Press, 2006); and *The Shadow of the Tsunami and the Growth of the Relational Mind* (New York: Routledge, 2011).

9. Allan Schore, *Affect Regulation and the Origin of the Self* (Mahwah, NJ: Erlbaum, 1994); *Affect Dysregulation and Disorders of the Self* (New York: Norton, 2003a); *Affect Regulation and the Repair of the Self* (New York: Norton, 2003b); and *The Science of the Art of Psychotherapy* (New York: Norton, 2012).

10. Mary Ainsworth, *Patterns of Attachment: A Psychological Study of the Strange Situation* (Hillsdale, NJ: Erlbaum, 1978); *Mary Ainsworth and John Bowlby, Child Care and the Growth of Love* (London: Penguin Books, 1965); *John Bowlby, A Secure Base: Parent-Child Attachment and Healthy Human Development* (New York: Basic Books, 1988).

11. Siegel, *Developing Mind*, 1–4, maintains that "mind" is a more useful concept for therapists to work with than "brain." He notes that the brain is one of several body systems that feed into the patterned flow of energy we call "mind." This flow of energy passes between one's own body systems, and it passes between one's own mind and other minds.

12. Schore, *Science of the Art*, 32–34.

13. Schore, *Science of the Art*, 77–81.

14. Schore, *Science of the Art*, 105–9.

15. Schore, *Science of the Art*, 103.

16. Allan Schore with Judith Schore, "Modern Attachment Theory: The Central Role of Affect Regulation in Development and Treatment," in *The Science of the Art of Psychotherapy*, by Allan Schore (New York: Norton), 42.

17. A. Schore with J. Schore, "Central Role of Affect Regulation," in *Science of the Art*, by A. Schore, 45–46.

18. Jon G. Allen, Peter Fonagy, and Anthony W. Bateman, *Mentalizing in Clinical Practice* (Washington, DC: American Psychiatric Press, 2008), 58–60.

19. Schore, *Science of the Art*, 101–9.

20. Schore, *Origin of the Self*, 203; *Repair of the Self*, 154–55.

21. Schore, *Repair of the Self*, 158–69.

22. Schore, *Repair of the Self*, 169–74.

23. Schore, *Repair of the Self*, 176–86.

24. Schore, *Science of the Art*, 97.

25. Schore, *Science of the Art*, 98–99.

CHAPTER 4

Relational/Neurobiological Narratives of Shame

How do early experiences of dysregulation and self-disintegration turn into the life-long patterns of relationship with others and with self that we call chronic shame? What are the pathways from these early disconnections to the "worlds of shame" that envelop our clients' lives? To track the development of shame as it grows more ingrained and complex in a person's experience, I will return in this chapter to relational theories about the shamed self, this time viewing them through the lens of affect regulation theory.

I find it helpful to understand that the affect dysregulation of early relational trauma is the story behind my clients' chronic shame. But I also know that my clients' shame narratives, their "worlds of shame," have taken shape over many years of complex relationships with others and with self. Together, my clients and I need to find ways to feel into these unique, personal worlds of shame. Here's where a body of relational shame theory is helpful: theories give us storylines for co-creating with clients personal shame narratives that have substance, depth, and emotional clarity.

OBJECTIFICATION

Francis Broucek's account of shame, for example, resonates with any shame-ridden client's sense of being an object to others in her life—and to herself. Where a communion kind of connection should be, there is only the experience of being evaluated or of evaluating oneself. This is what has happened to my client Ellen. She recalls a childhood of being acclaimed as a musical prodigy and her terror of falling from shining specialness to utter worthlessness with a bad performance. In fact, as far back as she can remember, and about "everything," she sees herself cringing at the judgment in her mother's eyes. Objectification happened early and pervasively. She continues to judge herself harshly through my eyes and the eyes of others. She believes we all continually evaluate her. And so she lives in constant fear of not measuring up, her anxiety marked by implosions of shame and explosions of anger.

Affect regulation theory helps us understand how objectification happens in development. As a child's social/emotional right brain develops in tandem with her more linear/logical left brain, she learns to think about affect as well as to feel it. When development goes well, her left and right brain learn to work together. Right-brain relational connection (Broucek's "communion") supports the experience of a coherent self, a self that grows stronger and more expansive as it connects, also with parental help, to left-brain concepts about emotions and relationships.

But when right-brain to right-brain regulation fails—when parents are critical or absent, or when they offer only left-brain "objective" connection— a child's sense of coherent self falters. The right-brain self ceases to "make sense" and is unavailable for left–right integration. Left-brain thoughts have to take over the task of creating coherence. What's available is a rational, from-the-outside-in, judgmental sense of things—including the thing that just happened, the pain of broken right-brain connection. What kind of sense? *I can't make happen what I need . . . I feel bad . . . so there's something bad about what I need, about what I feel . . . so there's something wrong with me.*

Ellen has never been able to feel connection with others that's free of criticism, theirs or hers. By the time she could remember and think about her feelings, she had abandoned her own experience to look at herself from the outside. Again and again, when she felt distress in her relationship with her mother, she made sense of her feelings by seeing herself as wrong and inadequate. To this day, feeling misrecognized or misunderstood sets off shame and a profound sense of failure for Ellen. She then makes the "objective" judgment that there must be something hopelessly, disgustingly wrong about her very being.

DISGUST

Thoughts about being disgusting follow feelings of shame for several reasons. First, it seems that the *affect* of disgust just follows in the wake of disintegrating shame. Schore notes that in theories of development and psychotherapy, the affect of disgust is even more overlooked than shame.[1] He cites a study that shows that persons diagnosed with borderline personality disorder or post-traumatic stress disorder (PTSD)—that is, persons suffering from severe developmental and relational trauma—are especially likely to have a disgust-prone implicit self-concept. Disgust sensitivity is elevated in trauma-related disorders and this self-disgust is also likely to be dissociated.[2]

My client Susie, for example, who survived sexual and emotional abuse in her early years, was barely able to survive the self-loathing that consumed her ever after. When she could no longer numb out her self-hatred, she would hurt herself visibly and then confront the disgusted, quickly averted gaze of others. What she most needed then—and always—was not someone to help her be more rational and responsible, but rather someone to connect viscerally with how unbearably untouchable she felt in her isolation.

It seems that the more traumatic and objectifying a relationship is, the more likely it will be to produce affects of both shame and disgust for someone injured by it. A shame–disgust self-concept will then take up powerful "unthought" residence within the survivor's right-brain self-imagery. This is the case for my client, Trevor, too, who can't tolerate real give-and-take with his girlfriend because even her slightest disapproval sets off his shame/disgust alarm system. He doesn't know that he says ugly things to her to keep from feeling ugly himself. Most of his relationship energy goes into bolstering his inner picture of good boyfriend, so as to wipe out the images of boyfriend from hell.

Both Susie and Trevor had extra help along the path to self-disgust. Not only did Susie's mother fail to protect her from her father's abuse, but her deep dismissive disgust about it also included Susie. Trevor's hard-nosed cop father made him "look stupid" daily. This is a second reason disgust follows shame: disgust is often an integral part of one person's dysregulating response to another. We usually think of disgust as a physical response to offensive sights, tastes, or smells, but an expression of disgust also accompanies interpersonal rejection and avoidance behaviors. If a parent expresses subtle (or not so subtle) disgust in disconnecting, dysregulating moments with a child, the child will register his parent's disgust. Since affect is contagious, his state of shame will resonate with the disgust he has seen in his parent's eyes.

Disgust is easy for a child to translate into a self-concept. This is a third reason that shame dysregulation and disintegration so easily become disgusted thoughts about oneself. As we noted in Ellen's story, when a child becomes an object of others' evaluation, she begins to evaluate herself from the outside too. In early childhood, the options are simply "good" or "bad." When self-evaluation is based on experiences of being enjoyed or rejected, good/bad is easily connected with the basic affect pair, enjoyment/disgust. "I'm bad-disgusting" will make simple, accessible meaning out of the disgust-shame affect she feels.

It's so much easier to understand, "I'm bad and disgusting" than it is to understand, "Something happened outside of my control and I feel like I'm falling apart." It's no wonder that when a child tries to make cognitive sense of the confusion of shame, a simple binary scheme takes over. Feeling like the object of disgust—not of pleasure—creates a simple if painful kind of sense. In later life, disgust infuses the complex emotion of shame with feelings of loathsome ugliness and self-contempt. People carrying chronic shame will be especially prone to judge others as well as themselves harshly and to rely on binary schemes of good/bad or admiration/contempt in their relationships with others.

Knowing this, a relational therapist will be better able to contain and not react to the subliminal but potent contempt that enters the room with a client who is not yet conscious of her own shame. When the client does begin to feel conscious shame, an empathic relational therapist must be able to tolerate feelings and images associated with the client's intense self-disgust. This, too, is a part of self-experience that needs regulation and integration. For all its ugliness, the disgusting side of shame needs to become a known part of the client's shame story if that story is to be transformed in a lasting way.

GOOD SELF/BAD SELF

Any human being prefers enjoyment to disgust. Any child will try to manage her relationships with others so that she can think of herself as good/enjoyable instead of bad/disgusting. And so she pays close attention to what others evaluate as good, not bad, especially as they react to her own behaviors and qualities. Bit by bit, and growing more complex with growth and experience, a picture emerges of a certain self she wants other people to see; a good self that is, by definition, not certain kinds of bad self.

Clients who struggle with shame can usually be quite articulate about the persons they aspire to be. It may seem self-evident that their distress is rooted in the discrepancy between their ideal selves and what they perceive as their defective selves. My client Gary, for example, was committed to the hero version of himself and wanted to banish the guy who kept cheating on his wife. It wasn't him, he said. But the longer we talked, the better I understood that Gary couldn't really inhabit his hero self either. It was above and beyond him, and he knew it. Looking at himself as if through the eyes of others, Gary had concepts and judgments about an ideal self and a failing self, but he couldn't feel from the inside how they came together in his daily lived experience. For many shame-prone clients, bad self is unforgivable while ideal self remains out of reach or at the whims of "what people think." This can also be cause for shame. But these conundrums make sense in terms of affect regulation theory.

Schore links trouble with ego ideal to a right-brain inability to self-regulate shame. Being able to regulate the gap between "ideal self" and "real self" isn't a thought process; it's an internalization of a parenting process that stimulates momentary situational shame and then repairs the break relationally. In repair, parents reflect and accept the child's wholeness, including the best and the worst of him. Likewise, in an internalized process of self-regulation, one's own failure in relation to a sense of good/ideal self stimulates shame. But then shame about failure can be repaired when one reconnects (internally or externally) with a sustaining emotional sense of accepted/acceptable-self-with-other.

Shame persists when self-acceptance remains out of reach. Gary doesn't have access to a relational/emotional process that gives him an accepted, whole sense of self. I wonder whether he learned from his father that striving and failing were incompatible, that one was either a hero or a jerk. I wonder whether his mother's devotion to duty taught him, by example, to dissociate from "selfish desire." In any case, he wasn't able to be a whole emotional self with his parents early on. Now a "bad" part of him has taken on a split-off life of its own.

Resolving the relationships between "good" and "bad" parts of self isn't a cognitive task; it's relational and emotional right-brain work. Self-acceptance is a right-brain accomplishment. This is why it rarely helps to point out to a self-loathing client that her standards are unrealistic and her self-criticisms needlessly harsh. Thinking differently doesn't help her right-brain problem of *feeling* shame and disgust about herself, which she wards off with her rigid standards and righteous judgments. Thinking differently doesn't help Gary make contact with what that "jerk" part of himself might really desire and fear.

Right-brain self-acceptance, grounded in the relational experience of being accepted as an imperfect but lovable whole person, is what makes it possible for a child or an adult to develop the capacity for guilt and remorse. A person with chronically unresolved shame can't be "a good person who did a bad thing." The idea of having done harm may be unthinkable—it just couldn't/didn't happen. Or it may feel like the excruciating exposure of a despicable self. In neither case can good and bad aspects of self coexist in a coherent experience of doing one's best to live up to certain chosen ideals. The left-brain standards and judgments of conscience aren't much use without the right-brain experience of a coherent, acceptable, aspiring-to-ideal self.

ATTACHMENT THEORY, AFFECT REGULATION, AND SHAME

Attachment theory describes the outcomes of different patterns of parent-child affect regulation. For each of us, a certain outcome or "working model of attachment" tends to remain constant across our lifetime. But the first two or three years of life are critical.[3] During those first years, our caregivers responded in certain ways and not others to our needs, wants, and feelings. Their patterns of response elicited our patterns of relating to them, which are still reflected in our adult working model of attachment.

In the working model called *secure attachment*, a calm, emotionally available parent tunes in to his child accurately. Without much anxiety, he fixes the misunderstandings between the two of them as soon as they happen. And so regulation works well on the whole and dysregulation gets repaired. If moments of shame come, they are eased by re-connection, and so they pass. Shame doesn't stick or add up. Able to count on this parent for reliable support and for re-connection if things go wrong, the child can turn toward the world and engage others with confidence.

By contrast, a parent who is emotionally absent—distracted or depressed—won't pick up well on a child's affective cues, and he won't notice a need to repair affective misses. Whatever the parent's intention, the child will experience his consistent dysregulation as neglect or rejection, and she will respond with what attachment theory calls *avoidant* insecure attachment: *If he's not going to be there, best not to need him . . . maybe best pretend he isn't there at all.* If we remember that every moment of dysregulation may also be a disintegration/shame experience, then we can guess that for a child burdened by an avoidant working model of attachment, the shame that builds up will feel especially lonely. As my client Andrea said, "There's not that one special person in the world who cares about me."

Andrea's mother was the parent who gave her no emotional response. For years, Andrea didn't know that she was angry with her mother. She just gave up hope of experiencing love in her lifetime. She didn't know about her own deep, core shame either. She just refused to need emotional closeness with others. Staying cool, contained, and in her head kept her safe from the relationships she "knew" would only hurt her, and it kept her safely disconnected from her own emotions, too.

Clients whose shame is woven into *ambivalent* insecure attachment have an experience very different from Andrea's. The dysregulation they suffer isn't a result of sustained emotional absence. As in my client Ellen's story, the parent is often very engaged—but on her own terms and to meet her own needs. Those same personal reasons also trigger the parent's unpredictable disengagement; it has nothing to do with the child, but the child doesn't know that.

Ellen did all she could to keep her mother engaged, constantly tantalized by the possibility of connection. When connection happened, it happened with stimulating intensity, but it took a lot of effort on Ellen's part to keep it going. Other times she performed just as hard, but she couldn't make the connection work. Then, as now, her obsession kept her anxiously busy, but in a waiting, reactive mode. She was convinced, *If I just knew how to do it better, I'd get what I need!* To this day, she falls apart into humiliated rage whenever she tries hard for a certain kind of recognizing connection and her hopes are dashed.

The shame that builds up from this pattern of dysregulation doesn't feel solitary to Ellen; it feels intensely interpersonal. Her relationships with others are stormy with angry disappointment and unmet needs, while shame keeps whispering, "It's *you*; you're the failure." The best everyday cover for all this anxious, angry shame, the cover that best matches the problem, is Ellen's dogged performance of success, sometimes just patched-together, and sometimes brilliant despite the sucking sink-hole of shame beneath it. There's always the chance, she believes, that her performance will guarantee the kind of connection she longs for.

In the history of attachment theory, these two definitions of insecure attachment patterns—avoidant and ambivalent—sufficed until researchers noticed that sometimes the patterns seemed to break down under stress. To account for this phenomenon, the category of disorganized/disoriented attachment was added.[4] In this pattern, parents who are suffering from unresolved trauma respond in unpredictable and frightening ways to their child's affective needs. Sometimes they are empty and cold. Sometimes they strike out in a rage. Their child will experience them as either frightening or frightened, which is itself frightening.

Susie's father was rageful and needy; her mother was often blank with fear. Both of the people she needed for affective regulation were profoundly dysregulated themselves, and so she had no support for self-cohesion. She was caught between her strong need to approach the only parents she had and her equally strong need to avoid them. A child caught in this dilemma will sometimes go still or frozen, or fall to the floor. Or, as Susie did, she may resort to self-soothing behaviors like rocking or hitting herself. Disorganized attachment offers no reliable comfort. The child is on her own with her distress.

Feeling intense affect and with no regulation from another person, this child will dissociate in order not to feel the pain of a self disintegrating with no hope of repair. Her acute, core shame will be strongly laced with fear, panic, and disorientation. Clients who have suffered severe relational trauma in their early development will carry into adulthood the chance that under stress they will fall into just this kind of frightening, disorienting, self-shattering shame. As Susie did, they may live out enactments of their shame in a desperate search to have it regulated. Many other abuse survivors live severely constricted emotional lives in the unconscious hope that an annihilating fall into such shame will never, ever happen again.

Whatever the nature of my shamed clients' attachment histories, they come to light small story by small story, step by step. I feel my way into the emotional and relational texture of my clients' narratives, the small but telling repetitions of unmet longings and misrecognitions. As I do so, I find ways to share with them my emotional understanding of what attachment feels like to them. I may not speak of shame, but I will be sensitive to their vulnerability, reflecting their needs and fears when it's possible to do so in a non-shaming way. My hope is that they can join me in feeling empathy for the emptiness, anxiety, or confusion that marked their early and formative attachments with others and that remains part of their core experience of life and relationships.

SELF PSYCHOLOGY, AFFECT REGULATION, AND SHAME

Self psychology gives me further templates for understanding shamed clients and for reconstructing their stories with them. For self psychology, as for affect regulation theory, a healthy self is the product of attuned responsiveness to a child's emotional needs. The self-psychological term "selfobject experience" refers to a first-person, subjective experience of being with another person that allows the first person to feel like a cohesive, firm, harmonious self. Many repetitions of various kinds of selfobject experience build self-structure. Selfobject experience is the means by which a child internalizes a caregiver's psychological capacities and thereby grows into cohesive, firm, harmonious selfhood. The self psychology picture of an other who functions as an extension of self corresponds well to the affect regulation picture of an other who through affect attunement makes possible the development of the relational brain.

Self psychology outlines evocative general narratives about the needs children have for selfobject connection and support. It's important to remember that these stories are based on (re)constructed histories coming from the psychoanalytic consulting room, not on controlled experimental studies of infants and young children. But this genesis also gives the stories their resonance for our adult clients trying to make sense of what's missing in their sense of self. Each of the stories is linked to a particular affective need, which is optimally met by a certain kind of selfobject experience a caregiver provides.

In one story, a child needs a "gleam in his mother's eye" that mirrors his displays of power, competence, and specialness. His parent's affective response of "gleaming" confirms his self-esteem, and as he grows and as she becomes more selective in her responses, her accurate recognition and appropriate praise help channel her child's grandiosity into realistic avenues.[5] Such mirroring selfobject experiences help transform childish illusions of power into mature, self-regulating ambition.[6]

In a second story parallel to the first, a child needs to experience a sense of intimate belonging with someone he admires and respects; he needs the selfobject experience of being part of that person's calm, wise, competent power. The experience of being part of this strength brings cohesion and stability to his developing sense of self, and over time the qualities he needs to share can become part of his own self-organization. Thus his mirroring/ ambition trajectory of development is balanced by a second "idealizing" trajectory—toward the development of a cohesive, stable sense of self in the social world, with meaningful connections to values and ideals. Kohut presented these two trajectories or "poles" of development as essential, inter- active components of healthy narcissism.[7]

Later Kohut added the possibility of twinship, a selfobject experience that offers a third chance at developing a cohesive nuclear self. This is the experience of being very much like another person in sensibilities, interests, and talents, a sense brought to life by doing things together in which the essential likeness can be experienced with mutual recognition, understand- ing, and joy.[8]

Kohut's scheme also included an early need for merger selfobject experience—that is, an experience of being one with the mirroring, ideal- ized, or twinned selfobject. To this list of necessary selfobject experiences, Kohut's colleague Ernest Wolf later added efficacy, or the experience that one has impact on the other and can evoke response, and adversarial selfobject experience, which is the need to feel oneself in opposition to another while still secure in the other's support and responsiveness.[9] Robert Stolorow and George Atwood speak of self-delineating selfobject experience—how a self comes to self-conscious awareness within safe, containing affective attunement.[10] Joseph Lichtenberg, who writes about infant development and psychoanalysis in terms of motivational systems that are vitalized by affect, states that "for each of the five basic motiva- tional systems at each period of life, there are specific needs and . . . when these needs are met, the result is a selfobject experience."[11]

In other words, the list of important selfobject experiences could go on. But the list matters only as it illustrates the concept: specific forms of self-experience (such as cohesion and vitality) require specific forms of self- with-other experience (such as being held and being enjoyed). The list helps us think about the different kinds of affective needs and responses that might be included in a process described more simply as "affect regulation," especially as affect patterns become patterns of emotion and of developing self-awareness. The list also helps us think about the different effects on a self when there are different kinds of selfobject failure. Just as attachment theory gave us clues about the different qualities of shame embedded in different styles of insecure attachment, so self psychology might help us understand more about the particular qualities of shame connected with certain deficits in selfobject experience.

SELFOBJECT FAILURE AND PATHWAYS TO SHAME

In general, self psychology thinks of shame as the enemy of well-being, the "underside of narcissism," the state into which one falls when cohesion crumbles.

But different kinds of cohesion crumble, and in different ways. If, for example, a gleam-in-the-eye mirroring sustains a child's cohesive sense of power and specialness, what's the flavor of the child's shame when mirroring fails?

I can imagine that a non-responsive failure of mirroring in toddlerhood will both dampen a child's agency and vitality and produce a flat, empty, shame feeling. Later on, when there's still no resonance for a child's expansive grandiosity, her empty shame will develop into felt meanings of worthlessness, of not being special at all, though she secretly longs to be. Her dreams of greatness and glory will get tucked away in a very private world or will be pushed down to unconsciousness because of the shame they arouse. Showing her power in the world will feel like risking humiliation. With every reaching for success or achievement, she will hear in the background someone saying (or thinking), "Who do you think you are?"

Here we might think of Clare, whose innate energetic talent helped her rise above her shame to exert personal power and achieve substantial success in the world. Yet she has never felt secure in herself. She has always fallen short of the greatness and glory she needs to disprove her deep sense of worthlessness. No matter what she achieves, the threat of humiliation always hangs about. She recognizes her internal denigrating voice as her own, but she knows it also belongs to her mother; the mother who was depressed and unresponsive when Clare was a toddler, and who was never able afterward to repair the connection and get "in tune" with Clare's energy.

In another kind of failure of mirroring, a child will have his specialness noticed in a big way—a taking-over kind of way. A parent whose personal shame has kept her own grandiosity under wraps may merge, psychologically, with a "gifted" child in order to fulfill her own unmet needs. Her affective response to the child's expansive displays of power will feel stimulating to him, but also like too much. He can sense when a pattern of affective response is more about her need for stardom than it is about his own experience of a special self.

Perhaps an over-stimulated gifted child can also sense the warded-off shame behind his parent's need that he be a star. Perhaps the parent's warded-off envy is also implicitly present between them. In any case, this kind of dysregulating "mirroring"—in which the parent's face is actually the face in the mirror—can produce powerful chronic shame. The adult this child becomes is forever caught between his innate desire and capacity to be brilliant at something, and the disorienting shame that strikes at the moment when his brilliance is noticed. The moment of being celebrated echoes many formative moments when his expansive affect was met by an intensely dysregulating affective response. In those moments, he was looked at intensely, yet not seen at all. His expansive self saw brightly mirrored a self whom he could not subjectively recognize—because it was a projection of his parent's need for emotional regulation.

The shame produced within this narrative won't feel flat and empty. It will feel full of anxious, conflicted energy. This gifted child won't stop trying, even as his shame ricochets between hating the thought of failure and cringing about success. His shame feels like an anxious, unmet longing to be seen for himself and also like an anxious conviction that his moment of being seen will once again be a moment of being mis-recognized, and of then becoming alien to himself and others.

Thus two different kinds of failure to mirror a child's grandiosity—under-response or over-response, deflation or inflation—produce two different flavors of shame. Other flavors of shame emerge from the story self psychology tells about the other side of self development, the trajectory called "idealizing." Here a sense of sharing in a caregiver's calm strength is necessary for a child's internal sense of cohesion and stability. Eventually this idealizing selfobject experience becomes an adult sense of a grounded self who can lead a meaningful life guided by chosen values and ideals. What happens to a child who isn't able to connect with an idealizable other in a consistent way? To use Andrew Morrison's self-psychological language, troubles with "ego ideal" emerge.[12]

We can understand such troubles against the background of optimal development: A child constructs an ideal image of her own good self through intimate connection with an idealizable other. When this selfobject connection works well, her sense of best self is well-supported. A powerful, non-verbal kind of modeling helps her know both how to fulfill her ideal and also how to accept herself when she falls short of it. To use affect regulation language, through reliable right-brain contact with her parents, her brain has learned to replicate her parent's way of balancing momentary dysregulation/shame with re-regulation that reconnects. She can move well from self-shaming to self-repairing moments, and this capacity supports resilient self-esteem.

Troubles with ego ideal emerge when a child needs to have idealizing experience with a particular parent, but selfobject connection, or right-brain communion, is not possible with the parent. The child will still want to look up to the parent, and she will still construct a picture of best self related to the parent, but from a distance. Lacking intimate connection with strength and goodness, she will construct a best-self picture that's a cardboard cut-out version, not a complex, three-dimensional way of being in the world. Limited to a child's imagination, her ego ideal will be painted in broad strokes of all good and all bad.

Even Trevor's version of good self/good boyfriend is based on the best picture of a man he could construct when he watched his father from a safe distance. Trevor told himself he wouldn't hurt people as his father did. But he would do his best to become powerful, proud, and decisive, a man in control of situations and the people around him, and especially in control of his own softer feelings. Such a man would never feel vulnerability or shame. This was Trevor's story about himself, a story fashioned after the best he could make of his father.

More often a client has tried hard to idealize a more likeable parent, admired from a distance. The client wanted to participate in the parent's strength and goodness but felt shut out of intimate connection. Andrea, emotionally neglected by her mother, longed for such intimacy with her admirable but distant doctor-father. Because of his unavailability, a kind of "ego ideal" trouble emerged for her, too. She constructed an especially lofty ideal with harsh penalties for failure, as if living up to a rigorous ideal would create the selfobject connection she so wanted to have with him. In affect regulation terms, she wasn't able to connect with him emotionally in a right-brain to right-brain regulation of ego ideal, and so rational left-brain operations took over to fill in for the relational gap.

A child in Andrea's position has to live up to high standards or face harsh self-judgment. Worse, she has to do so without having had the chance to absorb how to be a strong, wise self who can both make good choices and recover from mistakes. Since her self-regulation around mistakes and lapses takes intense effort, it's also prone to breakdown. Again and again, as she finds herself hating her own shortcomings, her shame intensifies, the shame of valiantly striving yet forever failing in the face of relentless judgment.

This is a depleted, exhausted shame burdened by thoughts of faults and failings. When there's no winning and no help, shame feels bitter and full of resentment, too. Sometimes the best "help" is to turn resentment outward, judging others by one's own high standards. Shame feels less like shame, then, and more like righteous expectation and disgusted disappointment with others. It's emotionally stressful, though, to live in a world where "nobody gets it right." The ideal remains as frustratingly out of reach as the idealized other always was and always will be.

It's important to note that a parent's availability to be idealized has little to do with how admirable he or she is in the eyes of the world. We all know self-aware, compassionate, confident people whose parents were unremarkable except for their capacities to love and support them. The idealizing trajectory of development produces ideals and values, but that's not where it begins. In its earliest, most basic form, idealizing is the experience of feeling emotionally safe in the understanding, protective presence of another. The "bigger, stronger, wiser" aspects of the other have to do with his or her capacity to help a vulnerable self manage distress, anxiety, fear, anger, and sadness. Lapses in "idealizability" are gaps in emotional presence, not gaps in worthiness. We are back to the basics of affect regulation and dysregulation.

A self needs to idealize—needs to feel connecting, calming strength from another—when that self is feeling weak and unable to manage. When basic idealization fails, a struggling self feels even weaker, more at the mercy of events and emotions, doomed to passivity.[13] This enervating, impotent form of shame will haunt those who were never able to idealize and whose ideal self is a shaky entity in adulthood. It also taints the experience of those who idealized from a distance and then invented an ego ideal based on a childish understanding of "strong." The strength of the ideal continues to compensate for their internal sense of weakness, and their judgments allow them to be active rather than passive. Yet the shame that haunts them is as much a feeling of being weak as of being wrong.

In addition to shame brought on by failures in being mirrored or in idealizing, there's the kind of shame brought on when twinship or kinship selfobject experience fails. If one's implicit moves to claim likeness with a significant other are rebuffed and if one's desires to have this likeness shared and enjoyed are ignored, a particular kind of shame follows, a feeling of being an outsider, alien, and weird. Often this feeling is layered on other shame feelings. Twinship is a third chance at self-cohesion, but it is also a third chance not to get the connection one needs, and thus a third chance at relational shame.

Ellen's childhood prodigy status alienated her from her peers, and so the twinship she sought was with her mother, an ensemble musician who lived out her hopes for celebrity through her only daughter. More often than not, her mother found fault with her likeness, and so this avenue of connection became charged with ambivalence and volatility, too. Ellen still hasn't found reliable kinship connections in her everyday life; her experience is that people see her as different, weird, and incomprehensible.

Susie has stumbled through life believing that no-one could possibly be as messed up as she is. Andrea, on the other hand, relies on twinship to give her some sense of connection and well-being. Consistent loving attunement, being deeply known and accepted—that's not on the cards for her, she believes. There are some good men, like her father, whom she admires from a distance, but she can't imagine intimacy with that kind of good man. She keeps up with a number of friends, both men and women, however, who share some essential likeness with her. These friends are usually marginalized or wounded in some way, but they are also smart, funny, and kind. None of them is "that one special person," but together they keep Andrea from sinking into unreachable shame and despair.

To sum up: selfobject experiences are myriad, and they often happen simultaneously, creating complex and diverse kinds of self-cohesion. Selfobject failure is complex too, creating many different kinds of problems. What I have described are possible sequences of need and failure that produce different experiences of shame, and my list is far from exhaustive. I have used the categories of self psychology to create narrative contexts for various kinds of affective need, and I have used affect-regulation theory to explain what might happen following failures in selfobject response.

I make similar moves when I join clients in their struggles to make sense of complicated personal narratives. Together we sort out what they needed, what they got, and what implicit relational knowing their experiences laid down. This mode of thinking is also very useful when it gives me clues about how I can best respond affectively to each particular client. We will return to this point in the second half of this book, which deals with treating chronic shame through various forms of affective connection with clients.

Affect regulation theory, a brain science, tells us that our useful conversations with clients won't be scientific discussions. What *will* foster our client's emotional healing and relational development? What can help is the *art* of psychotherapy—the stories, images, metaphors, and feeling words of evocative right-brain language. As we offer right-brain, sensitive presence to our clients who are working through shame, we may never mention attachment theory. But we will probably speak of need, love, hope, and despair. We may never mention selfobjects. But we will share our visceral understanding that a person's need for attunement is also her heartfelt longing to be seen, supported, known, and treasured. We will feel when our "misses" are experienced as personal rejection; our bodies will register the moment when a client's fall into shame is wrapped in interpersonal hurt, fury, and hate, and we will contain what our right brain knows about the shame in the room for as long as our left brain tells us we must.

In the artful creation of narrative, almost any theory can be useful when it helps us resonate more fully with our clients' emotional, embodied experience of shame. Whatever has been written evocatively about shame may become part of what we offer a client who needs precise attunement to her unique shame experience. She doesn't need a scientific explanation of her shame. What she needs is someone—in this moment, a therapist—to be emotionally present to her deep dysregulation and fragmentation in a way that makes her feel deeply, wholly understood and that thus makes reconnection and reintegration possible.

NOTES

1. Allan Schore, *The Science of the Art of Psychotherapy* (New York: Norton, 2012), 99.

2. Schore, *Science of the Art*, 100, cites Nicolas Rusch et al., "Shame and Implicit Self-Concept in Women with Borderline Personality Disorder," *American Journal of Psychiatry* 164 (2007): 500-508, and Nicolas Rusch et al., "Disgust and Implicit Self-Concept in Women with Borderline Personality Disorder and Posttraumatic Stress Disorder," *European Archives of Psychiatry and Clinical Neuroscience* 261 (2011): 369–76.

3. John Bowlby, *A Secure Base: Parent-Child Attachment and Healthy Human Development* (New York: Basic Books, 1988), 119–36.

4. Mary Main and Judith Solomon, "Procedures for Identifying Infants as Disorganized/Disoriented during the Ainsworth Strange Situation," in *Attachment in the Preschool Years: Theory, Research, and Intervention*, eds. Mark T. Greenberg, Dante Cicchetti, and E. Mark Cummings (Chicago: University of Chicago Press, 1990), 121–60.

5. Heinz Kohut, *The Analysis of the Self: A Systematic Approach to the Psychoanalytic Treatment of Personality Disorders* (New York: International Universities Press, 1971), 116.

6. Ronald Lee and J. Colby Martin, *Psychotherapy after Kohut: A Textbook of Self Psychology* (Hillsdale, NJ: Analytic Press, 1991) 128–38.

7. Kohut, *Analysis of the Self*, 37–45; Lee and Martin, *After Kohut*, 139–51.

8. Heinz Kohut, *How Does Analysis Cure?* (Chicago: University of Chicago Press, 1984), 192–210.

9. Ernest Wolf, *Treating the Self: Elements of Clinical Self Psychology* (New York: Guilford, 1988), 54-55.

10. Robert Stolorow and George Atwood, *Contexts of Being: The Intersubjective Foundations of Psychological Life* (Hillsdale, NJ: Analytic Press, 1992), 34–35.

11. Lichtenberg explains that important selfobject experiences happen in the context of the following affectively driven motivational systems: (1) the need for physiological regulation, (2) the need for attachment and affiliation, (3) the need for assertion and exploration, (4) the need to protect self with aversive behavior, either fight or flight, and (5) the need for sensual and sexual pleasure; Joseph Lichtenberg, *Psychoanalysis and Motivation* (Hillsdale, NJ: Analytic Press, 1989), 12. Lichtenberg has expanded on his fifth motivational system, a child's innate seeking of bodily sensual pleasure and its relation to sexuality, in *Sensuality and Sexuality Across the*

Divide of Shame (New York: Routledge, 2007). He proposes that with selfobject experiences of acceptance and approval, a child's sensuality is able to develop shame-free. Responses that inhibit the child's pleasure needlessly and that inappropriately sexualize the child's interest/excitement will infuse his sensuality with shame; lifelong patterns of sexual shame and a disconnection between sensuality and sexuality may ensue.

12. Andrew Morrison, "The Psychodynamics of Shame," in *Shame in the Therapy Hour*, eds. Ronda L. Dearing and June Price Tangney (Washington, DC: American Psychological Association, 2011), 26–27.

13. Morrison, "Psychodynamics of Shame."

CHAPTER 5

Assessing for Shame

Not every cluster of psychological symptoms is a cover for shame. Not all emotional or relational trouble has roots in shame. People struggle to manage stress; they suffer bereavement; they find themselves in personal dilemmas and family conflicts—all without the added burden of chronic shame. Our clients may need to grieve, exercise, meditate, make a decision, or have a difficult conversation. They may not need to pay attention to shame. Furthermore, many of our clients can tolerate carrying around some unexplored shame in their personal baggage. They don't need to unpack it.

On the other hand, when chronic shame is a problem that makes other problems intractable, and when shame itself, however disguised, is making a client miserable, good therapy requires that we recognize it and find a way to address it. How can we recognize it? That's the question of this chapter.

Emotion-Focused Therapy (EFT), which specializes in helping people better use and regulate their affect, offers a handy descriptive definition of the "primary maladaptive shame" we're looking for.[1] We're not looking for "primary adaptive shame", which EFT describes as a direct, rapid response to making a mistake that we can learn from here and now. By definition this here-and-now shame is adaptive, a sign of health.

Maladaptive shame also arises in response to a here-and-now problem, but in contrast to adaptive shame, it mistakes past for present. This shame was once a useful response to interpersonal danger, but now a sense of being worthless or unlovable turns up in response even to minor interpersonal trouble. Maladaptive shame leads to withdrawal and avoidance and to treating self and others badly. Generated by overall self-contempt and self-disgust, it usually carries with it secondary shame about one's primary emotions.[2]

This shame is well-masked in therapy because people who feel contempt toward their own emotions will be especially disgusted by the shame they feel. And yet they can't help but feel it because an interaction with a therapist is an interpersonal risk. Old dangers are called up; old shame is aroused—shame that must be hidden. It's left to us, as therapists, to come to understand what's going on, to "feel out" this pernicious problem hidden behind other problems in a person's life and buried in their responses to us.

In this chapter I will talk about the signs and patterns I see that help me recognize maladaptive core shame, or what I have been calling chronic shame. Recognizing a particular form and "feel" of chronic shame is an essential part of finding out how to be with it effectively. Years ago I was told in social work school that a good assessment is 60 percent of treatment. This may be especially true for shame, kept in dark, closed places by fear of exposure.

WHAT DO I FEEL?

Some of the most important information I receive in a therapy session is the hardest to decipher. But even if I can't make much sense of it, I have learned to pay attention to my own discomfort when first meeting a client. A first meeting is loaded for both of us. Knowing that asking for help with personal problems can be shaming, I make easing a client's situational shame my first priority. I am friendly and welcoming. I ask non-intrusive questions in the spirit of "I'd like to get to know you." I empathize with the client's experience and affirm her choice to get some help and support at a difficult time. In short, I do what I can to let her know that I am on her side.

But with some clients that just doesn't seem to work; I feel shut out of connection. Contempt is one powerful, disconnecting way to counter shame. With a client who defends against contact with contempt, I may feel that my therapeutic approach, my experience, or my credentials are suspect. I may feel reduced to the quality of my website or my office furniture. The client doesn't consciously intend to be contemptuous, but when I start to feel defensive, I know to bookmark this relationship as "Where's the shame?"

With other clients, dysregulation will sneak up on me more subtly. I start to lose touch with my competent self. Internal drop-down menus about "what to do next when . . . " go missing. I find myself stumbling over words; my voice sounds a bit unreal in my ears. I carry on, of course, and if I can pay attention to my anxiety, I wonder, "Did shame come into the room with this client?"

Often, such awareness is all I need to find myself again. Then I can begin to see how this client deflects my bids to make right-brain connection with her. She's looking at me. As I listen, she talks. She nods when I speak. But mostly she's *watching* me. Subliminally I've been feeling, "I'm not in synch with her; I can't make this work!" even while I've been working away at being an attuned therapist. Once I recognize a dysregulated shame situation, I am, in a paradoxical way, back in tune with what's happening to both of us.

Another client might begin therapy thinking the world of me before she even knows me. I accept that good can come from idealizing, but when being put on a pedestal feels weirdly uncomfortable to me, I know it's not a useful, strengthening kind of idealizing for her. Instead, this "special" connection is designed to keep us both safe from the shame of being ordinary—a shame that's now in the room with us. And of course I'm at risk of falling from "special" and into that shame, should I ever prove myself to be just ordinary!

Once I understand this situation, I can predict that therapy will seem to go well as long as we can produce special insights together. I also know that this client doesn't really need special insights. What she needs far more (but can't trust) is to feel someone simply connected to her ordinary emotional self. Her defense against that kind of right-brain emotional/relational connection is what creates the dysregulated feeling between us.

PERFORMANCE, PERFECTION, AND CONTROL

How I feel with a client gives me clues about how he performs self-with-other in the world. I suspect that chronic shame is a problem when our sessions feel like excellent performances of client and I feel like a spectator. You might remember that I feel that way with Gary, my very competent client who leads a double life. A high-performing client may even congratulate me on my performance, as Gary does. Meanwhile I feel little connection between our emotional selves, our right brains. If even Gary's "subjectivity" is a performance, a self-objectification, it's no wonder he has difficulty knowing himself from the inside out.

A client who lives to perform (or performs to live) will track the measures of his successes and failures carefully. He will want to be the best—even if it means cutting corners—but no achievement really satisfies his subjective longing to "feel good in himself." That's the trouble he may bring to therapy. Or he may talk about his struggle with procrastination: He can't get himself going on a project. Why not? Because it won't live up to the perfect success he can imagine . . . and perfection feels so necessary. He has a vision of the self he could be if only he could change a few things, but he can never make those changes. He wants a therapist to tell him how he can overcome his "inner obstacles."

As I listen to all the ways such a client tries to shape and control his relationships with others and his relationship with himself, I see someone who is trying very hard to manage right-brain trouble with left-brain competence. It's a mismatch, of course. His left brain can't "fix" a chronically dysregulated emotional/relational self. His better integration and deeper well-being await right brain to right brain communion. But it will be hard for him to allow himself to be in his non-verbal, subjective, vulnerable self and allow me or anyone to be there with him. Preventing that kind of vulnerability is what his careful control—including his control of therapy—is all about. Having been objectified and judged in that vulnerable place before, he has no idea that being there can feel anything but shaming.

SELF-WITH-OTHER PATTERNS

Since shame is a relational phenomenon, clues to its existence turn up in our clients' patterns of relationship with others, even when they are not aware of the shame they are managing. Shame-ridden relationships can be described in many theoretical languages. We've heard from attachment theory about three different kinds of insecure working models of attachment—ambivalent, avoidant, and disorganized—that are carried forward into intimate yet insecure relationships of adult life. Self psychology talks about the unmet needs adults bring to their way of being with others—enacted "hungers" for mirroring, idealizing, twinship, or merger.[3] Each of these relational styles shores up or protects a shaky, vulnerable self.

Karen Horney speaks of three ways to manage shame anxiety: moving toward people, moving against people, and moving away from people. Each is useful, with a downside. If we move toward people with compliance and self-effacement, we won't lose their love; however, our self-worth comes to depend on being liked, needed, or wanted. Moving against people feels powerful, but we have to keep winning to stay superior and invulnerable. Moving away from people liberates us from needing approval or success. What can shame us then? A small life seems a small price to pay for such freedom.[4]

Donald Nathanson gives us a movement scheme, too: four different directions we may take to escape the direct experience of shame.[5] Facing the threat of shame, we may *withdraw* from others. If the shame persists, *"attack self"* may be our next move. Rather than suffer the internal experience of being humiliated and abandoned by others, we beat them to the punch. Or instead, we *avoid* owning shame, using whatever strategies we need to fool ourselves into believing shame never happened. To completely avoid, we may need to fight harder, using a fourth class of strategy Nathanson calls *"attack other."* The moment we feel that someone might make us out to be weak or insignificant, we turn the tables on them. As we spotlight others' faults and failings, we stop them looking at us. Nathanson goes on to show how taking any one of these four directions on the "compass of shame" can become particular personality styles or "pathologies."

If I'm assessing for shame, I don't need to decide which of these theories gets the picture right. Each of them gives me a different, useful angle on a basic way of understanding my clients' complicated, insecure, and often unhappy relationships with others. They all describe clients who need to protect a vulnerable self while also being in the world with other people as best they can.

Stone Center theorists have described this dilemma as a *central relational paradox*: we use the appearance of being in connection in order to keep ourselves safely out of connection. But this interpersonal "safety" carries a price: a profound sense of disconnection and isolation, a state of self synonymous with shame.[6] So this is perhaps the simplest question I can ask about my client's relationships, as I assess for shame: How does this person's way of being with others (including me) both look like connection and also keep this person fundamentally disconnected and isolated?

From the perspective of affect regulation theory, it's clear that each of these many interpersonal ways to manage shame protects a person from moments of affective connection between self and other. These are moments when an upsurge of emotion could find regulation—that is, attunement, communion, or empathic understanding. However, a chronically shamed person knows in a visceral, right-brain way that what happened before in moments like this—dysregulation, rupture, and misunderstanding—is too painful to repeat. And so he repeats disconnection instead.

SELF-WITH-SELF PATTERNS

Sadly, disconnection and isolation don't shut down chronic shame. Alone, a person prone to shame often continues to treat himself with suspicion and self-contempt. Why would any of us undermine our own well-being so profoundly and painfully? If we want more insight into the mystery of self-inflicted shame, object relations theory may have something to offer.

Object relations theory has its own way of explaining our patterns of relating to others. From birth, it says, our contact with others generates unconscious representations of self and of others ("objects") in particular kinds of relationship, and these relationships between different selves and different objects form the quality of our inner world. Thus our inner object relations—often a mystery to us—are the key to the state of our psychological health.

In an article explaining shame in terms of object relations, Michael Stadter identifies six different kinds of shaming objects, or internal others, each opposite a somewhat different shamed self.[7] In the first internal self-other pairing, shaming is direct. The *direct shaming other* is saying, "You're stupid (ugly/selfish/worthless)." At least the self knows what it's up against, and with some support can fight back. An *indirect shaming other*, an internalized parent who is sad or disappointed on the child's behalf, creates a more confused shamed self. The shame is around, but where exactly is it coming from? Just as confusing is the relationship between shamed self and *neglectful shaming other*, because the shame comes not from things that happen but things that don't happen—loving attention, being seen as special—though they are deeply desired. A *grandiose shaming other* requires a high-performing self for its own self-esteem regulation. In this internal interaction, self falls again and again into the humiliation of being ordinary. A self opposite an internal *abusive shaming other* will be overwhelmed by a shame as intense as her feelings of being violated or manipulated. Something is terribly wrong, and since the internalized abuser is either shameless or completely dissociated from his shame, the victim carries all the shame. And finally, in Stadter's list, there is the *self-shaming other*, someone a shamed self uses as a model for how to treat oneself in a shaming way.

It's important to remember that although these "others" represent the imprint of real people, they are now internal others, according to object relations theory. They are also often unconscious, so the tension a client suffers between different parts of self and these internal others (now parts of self) can be quite inexplicable. Furthermore, an unconscious standoff can be projected into other relationships in the world, with the client playing either the part of shamed self or shaming other—or both, in tandem—in relation to real others in his or her life.

Stadter notes that a shamed self can feel that there's something clearly and palpably bad about self, something that deserves judgment or disgust. Or a shamed self can feel like there's something missing; the list of inadequacies can extend almost infinitely. Or, paradoxically, especially in the presence of a grandiose shaming other, a self will sometimes feel shame in response to success.

However the internal dialectic of shame sets itself up, the shamed self may feel it in one of several ways. The classic shame response is hyperarousal

ASSESSING FOR SHAME 63

and a desperate struggle to contain it: blushing, sweating, trying to "shrink," slumping the shoulders, dropping the head, averting the eyes, covering the face. This state of shame is excruciating. Dissociation is one way to escape the pain; some clients experience shame only in completely dissociated states. Other clients feel the effects of shame only in the aggression they feel towards others. Object relations theory has this explanation for how the experience of shame can move so quickly to aggression: In the split second of feeling shame, a moment so fleeting it doesn't stick in memory, the shamed self vanishes, and the shame-prone person identifies instead with an internal shaming other, turning that bullying energy not against self but against an external target of contempt and disgust.

Thinking about a client's shame as the effect of painful internal relationships gives us a better feel for the unending loops of self-dysregulation shamed clients endure. We can better understand their lament, "I know I do this to myself!" Shame does wreak havoc in self-with-self relationship, sometimes so painfully that a person's core self dissociates permanently in order to escape the constant internal threat of shame. As Stadter explains, following Guntrip, finding this hidden self and coaxing it back to life in relationship can be a long and arduous task.[8]

Understanding the power of internal relationships between shamer and shamed also helps us understand how shaming relationships get replicated again and again in our clients' lives. Shaming and being shamed is just what they know how to do. It's no surprise that the drama gets played out in the world when it's what they are negotiating internally, unconsciously, all the time. This unconscious dialectic between shamed self and shaming object is likely to continue unless it can be interrupted by some empathic understanding of "what's going on."

Getting glimpses of a client's internal shaming objects or shamed selves can be very useful in assessing for shame. An internal shamer can present as someone exceptionally decent—until a contemptuous, judgmental moment gives her away. Sometimes an internal self fights off shame by taking a rebellious stance against a shaming internal other. Often a client will talk more easily about an internal critic than about the internal shamed self beaten down by the constant criticism. It can be very useful to have a sense, however shadowy, of the unmentioned players in the client's internal drama.

If the object relations scheme of psychology and pathology is a helpful way to talk about our clients' self-perpetuated shame, we have to wonder how it fits with my relational definition of shame—*an experience of one's felt sense of self disintegrating in relation to a dysregulating other.* The "dysregulating other" in my definition is a real other in the real external world, and that's where the disintegration happens, too. If the shame-drama has become internal, does the real historical relationship with a real embodied other still matter?

Yes, history matters; it's important never to forget that shame exists because "something happened" in real time in the world. Both can matter, of course—both the historical events and the ways they have been internalized as psychological organizing principles. It's not a problem that object relations theory brings the dysregulating events "inside," as long as we remember the nature of the events. The events were, and are, relational.

Object relations theory suggests that as we populate our inner world, not only do we internalize unconscious representations of self and other, we internalize particular kinds of relationships between those selves and others. In fact, the quality of our inner world reflects the quality of those *relationships*. Internal shamers and internal shamed selves are by definition in a dysregulating relationship; whenever they meet, the event is as profoundly dysregulating as it was when it first happened in the outside world. *And this event is happening internally all the time.* No wonder that people who suffer from chronic shame feel constantly anxious and off-balance!

FAMILY-OF-ORIGIN PATTERNS

Even from the inner-world perspective of object relations, shame is something relational, and it's something that *happens*. It's energy in particular kinds of interactive motion. Since I believe that these patterns started with someone for some reason, I pay careful attention to the stories clients tell me about their families of origin. If I suspect there's shame for this client, I suspect that something happened in his family, is perhaps still happening, to create it.

We have visited several developmental theories, and within each framework I have noted that shame can be seen as the disintegration of self caused by faulty emotional connection with others. So this is the core problem I listen for as I come to understand clients' relational histories. I also recall accounts of shame-bound or shame-prone families in family therapy literature to help me connect empathically with the particular forms of dysregulation a client has suffered.[9]

I listen for the quality of person-to-person connection in the family. Does this client seem to know her parents as people? Does she feel they know her? Do the siblings know each other? By "knowing," I mean understanding how another feels, being in contact with another's subjective world, or in other words, having "right-brain" kinds of connections. Many small moments of attuned responsiveness or affective regulation open up intersubjective space—a shared sense that feelings and thoughts will be met with acceptance and empathy. Many small moments of affect dysregulation shut down intersubjective space.

The family therapist Daniel Hughes believes that the constriction of intersubjective communication is what keeps painfully dysfunctional families locked into their trouble. Therefore the basic goal of family therapy is to expand the possibilities for intersubjectivity—or for what we might call mutually regulated right-brain to right-brain connections. Family therapists make such connections possible by interacting with their clients, both the parents and the children, with playfulness, acceptance, curiosity, and empathy. When families learn how to be "that way" with each other, everything changes.[10] Easy, open, responsive conversation—such everyday stuff! But so much relational/developmental trauma happens when it's missing, and then so much shame.

What does "missing" look like in a client's story? I may hear about a relationship with a mom or a dad in which the kid, my client, knew that the expectations and the stakes were high. There was always a chance to screw up. Or the parent was always worried or angry, or somehow just not present in a relaxed, good-humored way. And so moments of playfulness were few and far between. Acceptance was missing, too; the family system didn't create space where the kid could be confident of an unconditional welcome for his unique being, including his wants, feelings, and failings. My adult client will talk about having experienced constant judgment, criticism, or love that was always conditional.

"Curiosity" may seem like a strange item on this list of essential qualities of being-with. But if there's to be right-brain connection, someone has to have the intention to make the link. Children need to know that their parents want to know them, and that their desire to know their parents is welcome, too. Perhaps "interest" is a better word for clients to work with: "Do you remember your parents being interested in finding out what mattered to you and how you felt about things?" An adult client who struggles with shame may tell me about distracted, emotionally absent parents, or else about parental curiosity or interest that felt intrusive or possessive: "It was about what they wanted and needed, not really about me."

In families where intersubjective connection is unavailable, empathy is unavailable. And so emotions become a problem rather than a form of nonverbal connection and an opportunity for further communication. Clients will very often report, "Nobody talked about feelings at my house!" If a child doesn't know that a parent will try to understand what it's like for him inside when he feels sad or afraid, he will hide his vulnerable feelings. Getting a response that ignores or humiliates his vulnerability is worse for him than deciding to squelch his emotions or deal with them alone.

When talking about "no feelings at my house," clients often add, "Except anger; there was plenty of anger!" But this "anger" had nothing to do with sharing self, we find. The anger they remember didn't ask to be understood, or for constructive change. In fact, the anger at their house was mostly rage— somebody, feeling powerless, was trying to seize or force control. Blowing up (or freezing up) would feel more powerful than falling apart.

I understand that "falling apart" was a constant possibility for all the members of such a family. In the absence of person-to-person (intersubjective, right-brain) connection, there will be affective dysregulation, and selves will feel themselves disintegrating. In everyday language, family members will feel shame when what they need to feel human is withheld and there's absolutely nothing they can do about it. In those "falling apart" moments, rage feels better than shame. In many family systems, chronic rage covers for chronic shame.

Depression is the other side of the coin, another way to feel and express the shut-down of intersubjective space. It's giving up on connection without the show of taking power. In some families, everyone cycles between rage and depression. In other families, some carry the rage full-time while others, for whom expressing rage might be dangerous, carry the depression. However they show their distress, what all these family members are missing is the experience of reliable conversation among themselves in which they feel recognized and understood.

Insisting on recognition and understanding doesn't eliminate conflict in a family. What I listen for in my clients' family stories is whether conflict could be worked out constructively. In healthy families, it's expected that people will get angry if somebody hurts or misunderstands them, and that they will say something, perhaps loudly. Then listening and negotiation will happen. In healthy families, conflict isn't pleasant, but neither is it terrifying or grueling, and that's because people can expect to be heard, no matter what they need to say. The conversation matters more than "winning."

Being able to engage in mutual recognition and understanding not only builds an integrated self, it *takes* an integrated self. You can't be curious or playful if you need all your emotional energy just to keep yourself in balance. Empathy requires you to know who you are and what you feel while you offer someone your genuine presence. Working with conflict constructively means knowing that your point of view matters; this is what gives you space and grace to listen to the other's point of view. My clients who suffer from chronic shame feel shaky on all these counts. What we come to see in their stories is that their families were not *able* to create the intersubjective space that creates sturdy, flexible selves.

It takes self to create self. Regulating or attuning to another's affect requires a self who knows the difference between self and other and can bridge the gap between. An "I" responds to a "you" in a way that communicates, "I am not you but right now I can feel what you're showing me." In this way, affect regulation creates and affirms both self and the boundary between selves. And all of this is why shame is so intergenerationally pernicious. I'm never surprised when, after a while, a shamed client tells me that her mom, or dad, or both, "had a really crappy childhood too." For their own reasons, they just didn't have the selfhood they needed to attune to their children.

By this point it may be clear to my client that many kinds of "crappy" lead to shame. It's always clear to me, and so I make a point of debunking the myth that what causes shame is harsh, shaming parenting. Many clients who suffer from chronic shame can't find evidence of that kind of parenting in their childhoods. They know their parents loved them and wanted the best for them. But at the same time, as their "mostly normal" stories reveal, their parents were too anxious or troubled themselves to create the intersubjective space necessary to nurture cohesion, self-awareness, and confidence in their children. Shame crept in insidiously.

Sometimes, as clients tell their stories, they come to realize that "mostly normal" covered over a lot of "falling apart" in their family of origin. Blame and mistrust ran deep, emotional neglect or emotional intrusion was the norm, and people lived in silos of emotional isolation, harboring secrets and addictions—all while leading a "mostly normal family life" together. Shame was everyone's lonely secret, managed however possible. No one talked about all that pain, or ever tried to make it any better, even though no one wanted it.

There are also some horrible stories, of course. Some caregivers do intentionally mistreat and humiliate the children in their care. They may twist empathy into a sadistic capacity to know the most effective ways to cause pain. A parent's narcissistic self-absorption may demand puppet-like accommodation from a child, if the child is to matter or exist to the parent at all.

A client who has been severely traumatized may have only detached memories of some events, and not much awareness of the relational destruction bound into the trauma. But what I know as I hear the outlines of severe trauma is that the child's right brain will have absorbed "implicit relational knowing" that's deeply terrifying, filled with ugly self-with-other images and the threat of being annihilated. There would have been no attunement with painful, confusing emotions, no regulation for affective storms, because the very people who could have helped were the ones who were causing hurt. The dysregulation experienced by a person severely traumatized as a child is not a unique kind of dysregulation, but it is exceptionally severe and constant. As the dysregulation carries forward unabated, his or her core shame remains intense and debilitating.

TRAUMA AND SHAME

Not long ago, a client told me in a first session, with a determined glint in her eye, "I don't want you listening for the trauma. I don't want to be a 'sexual abuse survivor' like in a book. I want you listening to *me*. I'm going to tell you the mess inside me, and that's what matters, *not the trauma!*" The "mess inside" includes terrible trouble regulating mood and emotion, impulses to kill herself, and intrusive images of violently disgusting scenes that "didn't happen but could happen"—all wrapped in intense self-loathing, because the mess means that *she* is unspeakably disgusting.

So I didn't listen for the trauma behind "the mess." I listened for the shame wrapped around and through it. By naming the shame that possessed her and kept me shut out, we began to be able to speak the unspeakable. With her I hold in mind a crucial point Robert Stolorow and George Atwood make: what persists as pathology isn't the memory of childhood trauma; it's the remembered experience of *nobody there*. "Pain is not pathology. It is the absence of adequate attunement and responsiveness to the child's painful emotional reactions that renders them unendurable and thus a source of traumatic states and psychopathology."[11] The isolating experience that turns painful events into long-term pathology is also the experience that creates acute dysregulation and intense shame.

The trauma survivor's shame may be attached to the story of what happened, or to how she responded to what happened, or to any aspect of her current being. Judith Herman suggests that shame is a core issue for survivors because experiences of abuse that persist over time happen in relationships of dominance and subordination. Victims in such relationships are humiliated, degraded, and shamed, and the shame carries forward. Abused children hate themselves because they are objectified and made helpless in situations where they should be recognized and cared for.[12] I agree that this is the essence of severe trauma and that it creates intense feelings of self-loathing.

And I would add that for many victims, shame runs to an even deeper place than the experience of having been degraded and shamed. It seems Herman would agree, since she also locates the source of the shame suffered by survivors of childhood abuse in severe breaches of their primary attachment relationships, disconnections that leave them with the deep conviction that they are unlovable. Victims of sustained childhood abuse and neglect will have had their bids for emotional connection criticized, rebuffed, or ignored by their primary caretakers. This is what instills in them "a state of chronic humiliation that profoundly distorts their view of self and others."[13]

In other words, even for a survivor of childhood trauma that included domination and degradation, the traumatic state of shame was and is, most fundamentally, a neurobiological state caused by profound interpersonal disconnection. My client knows this when she tells me not to focus on the stories of her terrible confusion and painful humiliation. She may need me to tolerate the stories with her too, but what matters most is that she comes to know that she can share with me her intolerably messy feelings now, her unspeakable self in the room, and that I will *stay*. Above all, I must not repeat the emotional disconnection that is the core of shame. Her shame is addressed and eased as I hear and feel with her *any* feelings about *any* stories, finding what words we can when we can, but with no "outside" agenda for how she should feel or heal.

It's important to listen for shame in a history that includes trauma because, as Herman and others point out, unacknowledged shame about the trauma can prevent any direct therapeutic approach to it.[14] As my client realized, too, once she believed I could see her for herself and not as a "survivor," the essence of what happened to her does need to come into the light, and the shame directly related to the trauma story needs to be understood gently and treated with care. It's also important, however, to assess for the shame that isn't part of the trauma event but belongs to what happens after: feeling utterly alone with memories so disturbing you need not to feel them or think of them; walking through life like an alien, a pariah, like nobody knows you at all; managing an emotional world that lurches between chaos and emptiness; believing that this isolation and despair means that there is something deeply, truly defective and loathsome about who you are.

DISSOCIATION AND SHAME

In her recent article that suggests that posttraumatic stress disorder can be seen as both an anxiety disorder and a shame disorder, Herman cites studies that find significant correlations between PTSD, shame-proneness, and dissociation.[15] Affect regulation theory consistently links shame and dissociation. In Schore's language, dissociation happens as the implicit right-brain self disintegrates in response to affect dysregulation. In this state, the right brain loses synaptic activity; it fails to recognize and process external stimuli and it also fails to integrate external stimuli with internal emotional experience. Thus both subjectivity and intersubjectivity collapse. The self is then protected from feeling emotional pain, which is experienced in "not-me" states. Yet a major marker of this collapse is the amplification of the painful affects of shame and self-disgust.[16]

We will spend more time on what dissociation is and how it works in Chapter 10, when we discuss how best to respond to dissociated enactments of shame in therapy. For now, the question is: As we make sense of our clients' stories and behaviors, wondering about the presence of shame, how do we recognize this companion to shame, a dissociative style of being in the world? It's not hard to recognize when someone at the far end of the continuum of dissociation blanks out in session, or switches between two very different identities. But self-continuity can be ruptured in more subtle ways.

Schore speaks of a dissociative person's inability to sustain an inner sense of aliveness and of her difficulty generating and integrating "present moments"—the continuous small packages of interactions with others that make up the basic fabric of lived, subjective experience.[17] I notice clues to this struggle when I pick up something contrived or forced about my client's conversation. Or I may just notice my own boredom or sleepiness as my body registers her subtle but thorough disconnection from me, even as she seems to be present.

Dissociation may keep a person separated from her own affect, even while some part of her is feeling something deeply. I have seen clients talk right through tears as if they weren't streaming down. I have heard clients tell heart-rending stories from childhood as if the stories happened to somebody else far away who didn't matter. Dissociation may create a barrier between different states of a client's self: one day she experiences a confident, optimistic state, the next day, a state of deep despair, and she has no felt memory of one state when she's in the other.

When dysregulation and then dissociation happen in session, when a client's subjectivity and his access to intersubjectivity collapse, shame and disgust will rush in to fill the vacuum. I may not know about that right away, but I will very likely hear the cognitive sequelae of the collapse. I will hear his thoughts, his utter conviction, that everything is hopeless and that he is helpless in the face of it all. I will also sense an instant evaporation of the safety and trust that had sustained our relationship. The self who trusted is no longer available.

I may have noticed this as an interpersonal style before it happens with us: his capacity suddenly to feel nothing about people, to cut them off without second thoughts. In another less dissociated state, a sense of loss, grief, or a desire to reconnect may emerge. But again, it's difficult for a dissociative person to hold together such complexity of relationship and emotion. When dissociation is a person's default safety setting, his right brain works in rigid, closed ways.[18]

People who function on the less severe end of a spectrum of dissociation don't disintegrate so dramatically when dysregulation strikes, and they are able to recover and reconnect with self and others more easily. But some of them learned early to rely on dissociative splits to manage their emotional and relational worlds, and the splits have taken on a life of their own. Self psychology calls this maneuver and its results "vertical splitting."

Writing from this perspective, Arnold Goldberg proposes that a vertical split in personality begins with a child's experience of negative affect in the presence of a caregiver's emotional unavailability. If the child can't bear the feeling, she can disavow what she feels. She may also find herself doing something that helps her manage her intolerable feeling, but she will need to disavow the behavior as well. The person who disavows is able, on the safe side of the split, to maintain the self-cohesion and competence necessary to get on with life. On the other side of the split there is very different version of self. That self has her moments in the world, but she can't be integrated into a whole sense of self. Perhaps that self is far too grandiose, too needy, or too spiteful to have any place within the "real self." Perhaps she lies or steals compulsively. She may find pleasure in dangerous sex or relief in binge-and-purge eating. But this "she" is "not-me."[19]

Goldberg offers a psychoanalytic explanation for the dynamics of patients who present with two quite different and unintegrated experiences of self, with a retrospective theory about how this psychic split came to be. He doesn't discuss infant affect regulation. But vertical splitting can be seen as a kind of affect regulation: a young child's right-brain response to the dysregulation of only certain specific "negative" affects. The result is less debilitating than an infant's right-brain response to global dysregulation. We could guess that this young child is held fairly well in regulated/repaired emotional connection except when particular affective situations turn up. That's when the caregiver disconnects. The disintegration that happens in that moment is linked with a specific "dangerous" self-state (such as anger, pride, need, or sexual feeling) and the dissociation that happens sequesters just that self-state. The illogical but powerful solution of creating a "not-me" out of that self-state is made possible by right brain primary process.

Goldberg's scheme describes the radical disconnection my client Gary experiences between his sexualized rebellious self and his responsible hero self. We can hypothesize that his overall connection with both parents was relatively secure in infancy and also in childhood—as long as he kept certain feelings a secret from them and thus, eventually, from himself. Ellen's experience of dysregulation was to some extent similar—she too had to accommodate a parent's affect in order to connect. In her case, however, we can hypothesize that her mother's dysregulating responses began in Ellen's infancy and felt like misrecognitions of Ellen's whole being, not just particular affects or states. That's why she cannot sustain the protective barrier of a "vertical split."

The kind of dysregulation Gary experienced was less destructive than massive early misattunement, but it still led to strong dissociation. His capacity to split protects him from feeling the acute distress of disintegration. Nevertheless, any experience of disintegration produces shame and disgust, and for Gary these emotions not only "fit the crime," they are easily recruited into potent reasons not to know the "self" who lives on the other side of the split.

For the purposes of this chapter, which is about assessing for shame, we can say that if a client's way of being in the world just doesn't add up, when he seems quite split and unable to hold the pieces together, invisible shame is bound to be on the scene. In fact, as we'll see in Chapter 10, the client's deep unconscious fear of feeling such shame is what generates the splitting. When there are states of self that can't be known, states that have to be turned into "not-me," what lives in the spaces between "selves" is chronic shame.

ADDICTION AND SHAME

In the decade of the 1980s, addiction and shame became firmly linked in the literature of the "recovery" community.[20] The link remains, for addictions and shame are almost always intertwined. As Ronald Potter-Effron explains,[21] shame generates addiction, since addictive substances can buffer and alleviate the pain of shame temporarily. The relationship with a substance can become a substitute for interpersonal relationships that threaten to stir up far more shame than the reliable isolated activity of addiction does. But then certain addictive events and one's general loss of control to addiction can themselves be deeply humiliating. The addict increases his addictive behavior in order to numb his new, more intense feelings of shame and humiliation, and a shame-addiction spiral is set in motion.[22]

The bulimic binge-and-purge cycle, a powerfully addictive behavior, has been described in much the same way. Binging is an anesthetic against feelings, but then the outcome of binging is shame. Purging is an attempt to undo the damage and also to obliterate the shame of the binge. But however successful it may be in the moment, the purging, as well as the binging, leaves an after-effect of more shame. The shame of the whole cycle and its many repetitions forces the bulimic person into deeper and deeper isolation.

Lisa Silberstein, Ruth Striegel-Moore, and Judith Rodin find the genesis of the bulimic's shame in her internalized sense of failure to live up to a cultural ideal of beauty. The discrepancy between her own body and her internalized ideal body generates further issues around competence and self-esteem; feeling fat leads a woman to feel ashamed of who she *is*. However, they also note that shame is a primitive, irrational, imagistic, and wholistic affect, and/or a global and unarticulated affective state, and that binge eating is very often a way for a bulimic woman to escape anxious non-verbal affective states or intolerable emotions that are themselves shaming.[23] This note allows us to see links between faulty affect regulation (including the objectifying gaze of others), a "right-brain" collapse into primitive, global, wordless shame felt in the body, and the bodily behavior that attempts to manage the affect. In other words, the psychological elements of the binge-purge cycle are quintessentially right brain, though they may seem to be generated by the cultural meanings of "fat/ugly" and "thin/beautiful."

This gives us more to think about when clients talk about a distorted body image and how they hate their shape or their eating behaviors. It's safe to assume that chronic, undifferentiated, dissociated shame is at the core of most eating problems. The shame about failing to be thin is a thought, a cognitive hook, on which to hang something that's diffuse and slippery. That's why counter-thoughts that debunk cultural myths of beauty don't usually have much power to control either the shame or the addictive numbing behaviors.

It's very difficult to change any addictive behavior through insight and force of will, for the addiction has become the fill-in for a deep, desperate lack of something for which it can never really substitute. Gabor Maté maintains that this "something missing" is the experience of attunement—a specific quality of being-with required for the development of the brain's self-regulation circuits. "Attunement is, literally, being 'in tune' with someone else's emotional states. It's not a question of parental love but of the parent's ability to be present emotionally in such a way that the infant or child feels understood, accepted, and mirrored."[24] Poorly attuned relationships leave a child with compromised abilities to regulate his own emotions and with a compromised sense of being a whole, vital, worthy self. Addictions "manage" emotions in ways that further undermine self.[25]

When we understand links like these between the distress of dysregulation and the relief addiction brings, we are not surprised when clients who are burdened by chronic shame eventually tell us about disordered eating, drinking too much, using high doses of over-the-counter drugs every day, or spending hours every night surfing the net or watching porn. Clients often feel intense shame about disclosing their addictions, the same shame they feel about engaging in these often secret behaviors. They then may feel significant relief in owning up to the problem; often they are motivated by a fervent hope that facing the shame of the addiction will give them control over it, and that in beating their addiction, they will also eradicate their shame.

We understand, however, that deep, pervasive shame is the cause, not the result, of the addiction, even though the addiction increases the load of shame. And so we are not tempted by the fantasy that if the behavior ceases, shame will disappear. To have already been speaking about shame will be especially useful when it comes time to address the feelings left when the client is "clean and sober." Then the client's long-term disintegration of self becomes felt reality, along with unremitting feelings of worthlessness and hopelessness. With no capacity to self-regulate and no substitute for regulation, the client will relapse to "fix" this intolerable situation. For clients in these raw, helpless states of shame, interpersonal affect regulation will be the essence of effective therapy. Because they meet some of this desperate need for interpersonal regulation, daily twelve-step groups with personal sponsors are often a lifesaver in the early days of recovery.

Sometimes an addiction isn't secret; it's the problem the client brings into the room. He has to do *something* because it's all "too much"—too much out-of-control behavior, too much strain on crucial relationships, too much lost time, or too much humiliation on having been "outed." Understanding the connections between addiction and shame, we will have some sense of what he, and we with him, will be up against. Believing that addiction is a symptom of shame, we will listen carefully for how his particular symptom masks emotion or numbs affect. We will do what we can to undermine its power. But we will also know that nothing much will change unless we, with our client, can find a way to experience more directly the affective, emotional self that's being shut down by the addiction.

ASSESSING FROM THE RIGHT SIDE OF THE BRAIN

It doesn't take long for a client of mine to understand that my basic question on her behalf is: "How is it working for you—your system of keeping yourself in balance?" We will explore her emotions and self-states in the context of her relationships with others and with herself. I'll be alert to whether shame is a spanner in the works. I become aware of what isn't working for my client by being emotionally close enough to her to feel it. I need to be present in a right-brain way if I am to sense the meanings and the gaps in my client's stories, intuit her unspoken longings and regrets, and bump up against the force-fields of her self-protection.

An assessment from the right side of the brain is always an interpersonal process and a work in progress. It's not a list of symptoms or a diagnostic label. I don't do assessment through structured intake interviews, though such interviews have their uses in some contexts. I have never used a test to measure for a client's shame-proneness, though I appreciate that those measures are essential tools in the ongoing study of shame phenomena. My assessments sound like sketches for a psychological novel based on my client's life, told from my client's perspective. The story is always changing and developing, becoming more complex and nuanced as I keep trying to understand the client from the inside. The only way I know to understand from the inside is to connect as best I can with whatever my client can share of his right-brain self.

Of course, this process of connecting from the inside is the process not only of assessment, but of treatment, too. Theory can give us confidence in what we understand and in what we have to offer, but the bottom line is this: From the beginning to the end of our therapeutic relationships with chronically shamed clients, we have to be there, emotional self to emotional self, right brain to right brain. The rest of this book expands on the various ways we can be present to shamed clients in order to strengthen their emotional/relational selves and ease their shame.

NOTES

1. Leslie Greenberg and Shigeru Iwakabe, "Emotion-Focused Therapy and Shame," in *Shame in the Therapy Hour*, eds. Ronda L. Dearing and June Price Tangney (Washington, DC: American Psychological Association, 2011), 69–90.

2. Greenberg and Iwakabe, "EFT and Shame," 71–73.

3. Ernest Wolf, *Treating the Self: Elements of Clinical Self Psychology* (New York: Guilford, 1988), 72–74.

4. Jack Danielian and Patricia Gianotti, *Listening with Purpose: Entry Points into Shame and Narcissistic Vulnerability* (New York: Jason Aronson, 2012), 29–32.

5. Donald Nathanson, *Shame and Pride* (New York: Norton, 1992), 305–77.

6. Jean Baker Miller and Irene Pierce Stiver, *The Healing Connection: How Women Form Relationships in Therapy and Life* (Boston: Beacon Press, 1997), 81–117.

7. Michael Stadter, "The Inner World of Shaming and Ashamed: An Object Relations Perspective and Therapeutic Approach," in *Shame in the Therapy Hour*, eds. Dearing and Tangney, 45–68.

8. Stadter, "Inner World," 56–58. Stadter's reference is to Harry Guntrip, *Schizoid Phenomena, Object Relations, and the Self* (New York: International Universities Press, 1969).

9. For example, James Harper and Margaret Hoopes, *Uncovering Shame: An Approach Integrating Individuals and Their Family Systems* (New York: Norton, 1990); Stephanie Donald-Pressman and Robert Pressman, *The Narcissistic Family: Diagnosis and Treatment* (New York: Macmillan, 1994); and Merle Fossum and Marilyn Mason, *Facing Shame: Families in Recovery* (New York: Norton, 1986). I will expand on the narratives of shame-prone families in Chapter 9.

10. Daniel Hughes, *Attachment Focused Family Therapy* (New York: Norton, 2007).

11. Robert Stolorow and and George Atwood, *Contexts of Being: The Intersubjective Foundations of Psychological Life*, (Hillsdale, NJ: Analytic Press, 1992), 54.

12. Judith Lewis Herman, "Posttraumatic Stress Disorder as a Shame Disorder," in *Shame in the Therapy Hour*, eds. Dearing and Tangney, 261–75.

13. Judith Lewis Herman, "Shattered Shame States and Their Repair," in *Shattered States: Disorganized Attachment and Its Repair*, John Bowlby Memorial Conference Monograph 2007, eds. Judy Yellin and Kate White (London: Karnac, 2012), 159.

14. Herman, "PTSD as a Shame Disorder," 267.

15. Herman, "PTSD as a Shame Disorder," 266; Herman cites L. Dutra et al., "Core Schemas and Suicidality in a Chronically Traumatized Population," *Journal of Nervous and Mental Disease* 196 (2008): 71–74, and Jean Talbot, Nancy Talbot, and Xin Tu, "Shame-Proneness as a Diathesis for Dissociation in Women with Histories of Childhood Sexual Abuse," *Journal of Traumatic Stress* 17 (2004): 445–48.

16. Allan Schore, *The Science of the Art of Psychotherapy* (New York: Norton, 2012), 160.

17. Schore, *Science of the Art*, 126.

18. Schore, *Science of the Art*, 158–63.

19. Arnold Goldberg, *Being of Two Minds: The Vertical Split in Psychoanalysis and Psychotherapy* (Hillsdale, NJ: Analytic Press, 1999).

20. Gershen Kaufman wrote a seminal work, *Shame, the Power of Caring* (Rochester, VT: Schenkman Books, 1980). John Bradshaw, with *Healing the Shame the Binds You* (Deerfield Beach, FL: Health Communications, 1988), brought Kaufman's shame theory into the self-help world of recovery from addiction. The family therapists Merle Fossum and Marilyn Mason contributed *Facing Shame: Families in Recovery* (New York: Norton, 1986). Kaufman expanded his original book to include a theory of shame-based syndromes, chief among them addictive disorders: Gershen Kaufman, *Shame, the Power of Caring*, 3rd ed. (Rochester, VT: Schenkman Books, 1992).

21. Ronald Potter-Efron, "Therapy with Shame-Prone Alcoholic and Drug-Dependent Clients," in *Shame in the Therapy Hour*, eds. Dearing and Tangney, 219–35.

22. Ronald Potter-Efron, *Shame, Guilt, and Alcoholism*, 2nd edn. (New York: Haworth, 2002), 39.

23. Lisa Silberstein, Ruth Striegel-Moore, and Judith Rodin, "Feeling Fat: A Woman's Shame," in *The Role of Shame in Symptom Formation*, ed. Helen Block Lewis (Hillsdale, NJ: Erlbaum, 1987), 89–108.

24. Gabor Maté, *In the Realm of Hungry Ghosts: Close Encounters with Addiction* (Toronto: Knopf, 2008), 238.

25. Maté, *Hungry Ghosts*, 229–47.

PART II

Treating Chronic Shame

CHAPTER 6

Prerequisites for Working with Shame

Studies show that the efficacy of psychotherapy is strongly related not to particular modalities of practice, but rather to factors common across modalities, such as the client's experience of the therapist's empathy, accessibility, and non-judgmental understanding.[1] These common factors are also markers of the first prerequisite for working with chronically shamed clients: we need to have good right-brain skills for nurturing a therapy relationship—skills such as emotional sensitivity, the ability to communicate affect non-verbally, the ability to express accurate empathy, and the ability to use language in personal and evocative ways. These skills will ground good work with a wide range of clients, but they are absolutely necessary if we are to create trustworthy therapy relationships with shamed clients.

KNOWING OUR OWN SHAME

If we want to do successful relational work with clients whose core problem is chronic shame, there's another prerequisite just as important as the first: we need to have faced and worked through our own chronic shame or shame-proneness. Why? First, because we need to be able to remain connected and gently fearless in the face of a client's intense self-loathing. We will have to tolerate our client's helpless, hopeless thoughts and resist the impulse to talk him out of his negative feelings. Just being present to his world of shame will be very difficult if we have not yet been able to tolerate our own feelings of shame.[2] Second, when our own shame is aroused by our client's shame-defenses of blame or contempt, we need to be able to feel it, name it, and find where it lives in us. A good supervisor is priceless help in this process.[3] But even the finest supervisor will be hard-pressed to help us make direct, useful contact with our shame if we have never before faced it in a sustained way.

The ubiquity of shame provides one of the best arguments for the maxim "therapists have to do their own work." That is, therapists need to have been, or to be, in therapy themselves. This is especially true if we practice longer-term intensive psychotherapy, with all its potential for transference-countertransference entanglements. In Chapter 5 of my first book, written in 2002, I document the time I was blindsided by shame in my transference-fraught relationship with my psychoanalyst.[4] It was a difficult time, but since then I have been far less afraid of shame. In fact, on my own and my clients' behalf, I have been trying to discover what shame is and how to deal with it ever since.

Since shame is such a devious trickster, hiding so well behind masks such as *expert* or *helper*, long-term intensive psychotherapy may be the only way that we will come to know our own shame, and then only if we are working with a shame-wise therapist who won't collude with us to look the other way. We might come to recognize our shame-proneness through self-help videos or books.[5] But even then, we'll need therapy that offers not just insight, but the deep, sustained emotional connection that can make a difference to shame.

There should be no shame in acknowledging our shame (though it seems there always is, at first). Many therapists who write about shame mention a personal connection with the topic.[6] Why might excellent therapists also be shame-prone therapists? First of all, it's a matter of innate emotional sensitivity. Some babies are born needing extra regulation for an emotional response system easily over-stimulated. They become emotionally sensitive children, alert to the interpersonal dynamics that surround them.

Second, it's a matter of family history. If there's emotional trouble in the family, these sensitive children try to manage it as best they can. They feel responsible for the well-being of fragile parents and vulnerable siblings. They spend their childhood offering emotional attunement beyond their years and doing without the emotional understanding they need. It's no wonder that some of them would one day make a career out of their attunement skills and their deep desire to see emotional hurts eased and relational brokenness repaired.

If we were once one of those children, chronic shame remains a liability for us. Knowing about it won't get rid of it. No therapist who writes about shame from personal experience suggests that facing our shame will make it disappear. The process of an attuned right brain therapy will, however, give us a better connection with our own emotional selves and more capacity to relate to others from a grounded, right-brain place.

Even when the threat of shame has been significantly diminished by good therapy and other good relationships in life, lifetime shame management is a strain. But there's another side to the situation. We can use what we know to help others burdened and silenced by shame. We can embrace our unconscious childhood dream of being able to heal wounded people in broken relationships. Now that we understand far better what we're up against, we'll be able to make more of a difference.

READING SHAME THEORY

Reading about shame is a useful exercise in desensitization. Every writer who takes on the topic of shame is proof that shame doesn't have to be an unspeakable secret. Reading shame theory from the inside out is a powerful way to assimilate it. As we make connections between what we read and what we know of ourselves and our history, theory will uncover our own emotionally potent story, and shame will "make sense" in ways we don't forget.

We can also read theory from the inside-out on behalf of our clients. Theory can help us understand the particular ways that clients are self-programmed to protect themselves from feeling their own shame. Theory will give us possible plotlines for the fragmented stories we hear about their childhoods. Theory provides language for educating our clients about shame, words that at just the right moment can make help them make sense out of amorphous ugly feelings.

I'm not suggesting that we read theory in a way that objectifies or pathologizes ourselves or our clients. I'm suggesting that we read in any way that helps us understand more deeply what went wrong for a person whose early attachments left him or her vulnerable to shame-disintegration. I'm recommending that we make compassionate links between puzzling relational behaviors and a person's need to cover or compensate for shame. Reading, pondering, and discussing what we read with colleagues will help us understand the strange things that can happen for our clients and for us when shame comes into the therapy room.

CREATING A SHAME-FREE FRAME FOR THERAPY

All clients need clarity about the parameters of the therapy contract with their therapist. They need to know what they can expect and what is expected of them. This is especially true for clients who are shame-prone, because they are more likely to feel a personal sense of rupture around breaks or misunderstandings. A client who struggles with shame needs to know, for example, exactly what the rules are about payment, including payment for missed sessions. She needs to know what will happen if she leaves a phone message, and whether her therapist will respond to emails or texting. She needs to hear a clear response to any questions she has about how long therapy will take or about what she is supposed to "do" in therapy.

If as therapists we are transparent, clear, and fair about the therapy contract, our clients will have less reason to be fearful about making mistakes or being wrong in relation to us. With shame-prone clients who have a more "attack-other" style that would make us wrong, our clarity will head off their aggressive anxiety about the therapy process. In either case what matters most is subliminal: our clients can relax (somewhat) in the presence of someone who is clearly *not* ashamed, someone who is neither easily made wrong nor interested in making another wrong, someone who is, in fact, just solid and confident in the value of what he or she has to offer.

If we have doubts about our competence, fees, protocols, or boundaries, and especially if our doubts are rooted not in reality but in chronic shame, our chronically shamed clients will sense our doubts and our shame. Since shame stirs up counter-shame, we will have created a shame-loaded interpersonal situation from the very opening moments of therapy. This may provide good grist for the therapy mill, but it's probably better for everyone if we take our doubts, with their roots in shame, to supervision and/or to personal therapy. We need to get ourselves to a relatively shame-free state of inhabiting the role of therapist in order to offer our clients a relatively shame-free space in which to do therapy with us.

CHOOSING A STANCE

Creating shame-free space requires more than a clear, fair frame for therapy. It requires specific "de-shaming" ways of engaging with clients. In their summary of all the contributions to *Shame in the Therapy Hour,* Dearing and Tangney note a unanimous emphasis on developing a supportive, empathic, collaborative therapy relationship. They speak of *relational validation* to capture the essence of this basic "de-shaming" attitude toward clients. It includes commitments to work from the client's values rather than imposing our own, to equalize power and refuse the role of expert wherever possible, and to affirm the client's strengths.[7]

We therapists generally intend to be accessible and empathic. But in fact, a therapeutic stance of relational validation is quite difficult to maintain. It takes hard work. Empathy requires tireless effort to feel into our clients' reality. It would be so much easier just to explain to our clients what their problems are and to give them the good advice they believe they need. Sometimes what we encounter is challenging or uncomfortable to feel. Sometimes the client's emotional experience is opaque or unavailable; then we have to work from what can't be said.

The hard work of empathy also requires clarity about our separateness from our clients. Our separate self is the one who validates the client and who, at a more basic level, is the "other" who tunes into the client's affect in order to regulate and stabilize the client's sense of self. Empathy is a sharing of emotional states in which neither self is taken over by the other; sustaining this clarity in connection requires moment-to-moment attunement to both our own and our client's affective states. In other words, empathy is an energy-intensive activity, not just a state of feeling warm and sympathetic.

Likewise, it takes focused effort to maintain respect for our client's values rather than imposing our own. First of all, we work hard to understand the hopes for change that clients bring to therapy. We validate their hopes even when we might envision different changes for them. We keep quiet our reactions to the cultural or religious commitments that limit our clients' freedom. On a smaller scale we hold back, for example, our "better idea" in the face of a parent's considered decision to cut off a teenage son or daughter who causes nothing but grief. We don't criticize a client's gleeful moment of "perfect revenge" when what we want for her is more capacity for empathy.

Taking a power-sharing, non-expert stance in therapy is also harder than it sounds. We can tell our clients that this is their therapy, governed by their agenda, not ours. But what if they ask us to give some direction to their therapy? We also need to be honest about the power we hold. Even while we refuse to be someone who "knows best," we have to accept the responsibility of having offered clients our educated, professional expertise when we invited them to work with us.

As therapists we are "healthcare providers," but when we take a de-shaming stance of relational validation with our clients, we let them know that we don't see them as ill. They are persons in distress and we will help them, but neither as fixers or healers nor from the outside in. Holding this position requires sturdy self-confidence in the face of our clients' disbelief or misunderstanding. We also have to learn how to communicate what clients *can* expect: help that is based on our clients' strengths and capacities to collaborate with us; help that happens from the inside out through conversation and understanding.

We take a stand for "understanding" because we know that the more shamed our clients are, the less they will be helped by advice or strategies, and the more they will need a sustained experience of being empathically understood. Or to put it another way, with clients who aren't challenged by emotions or relationship, the therapy conversation will be relatively easy. They will be able to use right-brain connection with us to help them manage stress, work through grief, resolve conflicts, or come to decisions that feel subjectively right. For clients whose shame makes emotional/relational connection difficult, just working toward having such conversations is the essence of the "treatment."

A MENTALIZING/MINDFULNESS STANCE

Peter Fonagy and colleagues have been writing for some time about how crucial *mentalizing* is in the emotional and psychological development of children, and then extending those insights to the practice of psychoanalysis and psychotherapy.[8] They maintain that a child learns to know and accept his own inner states, his own mind, by experiencing his mind as it's held in the mind of his parent. The parent uses a combination of empathy and imagination to create in her own mind a moment-to-moment picture of what's going on "inside" the child—his physical and affective body experiences, his emotions, desires, and intentions.

A child comes to know himself subjectively by identifying with his parent's mentalizing responses to him. The process works best, of course, when the parent's mentalizing is a good match for the child's unformed or inarticulate affective experience. Fonagy et al. don't distinguish between right- and left-brain processes, but it seems that the mentalization of emotion that forms a child's sense of "mind" could also be called the right-brain affect regulation that forms a child sense of "coherent self."

The developmental theory of mentalization translates into a psychotherapeutic process in which the therapist's efficacy resides in his ability to communicate what he holds in mind of the client's subjective experience. A commitment to foster mentalizing is another way to describe a therapeutic stance of relational validation. We use our empathy and imagination for a specific purpose: to hold in mind whatever we can contact or intuit about our clients' emotional states, including their motivations and intentions, however unformed, chaotic, or contradictory. We do this so that our responses to them will fit the particular "minds" (emotional/relational selves) we are holding in mind. If, for example, we sense a deep, inarticulate struggle with shame, our responses will be sensitive to this vulnerability, and they will also, bit by bit, help make the shame knowable. Our overall goal is that clients come to know their own minds, their own emotional/relational selves, with a clearer sense of acceptance, ownership, and agency.

David Wallin calls mentalizing and mindfulness the two essential strands of the double-helix DNA of attachment-informed, intersubjective psychotherapy.[9] In the context of choosing a stance for therapy, *mindfulness* means the self-regulated connection a therapist has with his or her own subjective states while he interacts with a client. It just makes sense that in order to connect with our clients' right brains so that we can hold them in mind, we need to be connected in a right-brain way with ourselves. If we are disconnected from our subjective emotional selves, authentic affective attunement with our clients won't be possible.

Our commitment to practice psychotherapy in a mindful way may mean that we enter into specific training in mindfulness. Mindfulness is not an attitude we can easily assume with clients if it's not a comfortable way for us to be with ourselves in our daily lives. But even if being mindful comes easily to us, it's also a way of working that we have to choose hour by hour with every client. When mindfulness is part of our chosen stance for doing psychotherapy and we are able actually to *be* mindful in our work, not only will we have a better chance of staying in tune with our clients' emotional states, we will also be able to notice our own affective responses as they come up. When we can simply notice and be curious about what we feel in response to our clients, our affective responses will give us excellent on-the-spot inside information about underlying issues that a client may not be able to talk about or even to identify consciously—shame issues, for example, hidden behind other layers of self-awareness and self-protection.

THE PLAYFULNESS, ACCEPTANCE, CURIOSITY, AND EMPATHY STANCE

Earlier, when discussing shame-proneness rooted in a client's family of origin, I mentioned Daniel Hughes' emphasis on creating intersubjective space in family therapy and a therapeutic stance that he believes is especially useful in this quest. He calls the stance PACE, an acronym that stands for "playfulness, acceptance, curiosity, and empathy."[10] I find the acronym a useful way to remind me how to be relationally validating with clients.

We've noticed what family interactions look like when these qualities are missing. What would our interactions with individual clients look like if we worked from this stance? The first quality on the list, *playfulness*, might give us pause. We can imagine how playfulness would be helpful to Hughes as he develops connections with the children of stressed families, but how would playfulness make our conversations with adults relationally validating?

Playful, in the context of therapy, doesn't mean silly or meaningless. In fact, the long, rich history of child play therapy teaches us that play reaches into symbolic, primary process realities that the words of linear, secondary process cannot touch. I'm not suggesting here that we do play therapy with our adult clients, but I am keen on the idea that mutual right-brain contact is the name of the psychotherapy game. We know that the right brain is the home not only of subjectivity, emotion, and implicit relational knowing, but also of imagination, metaphor, and play. And so, if we'd like to meet our clients in right-brain space, it's best to begin with a relaxed openness to whatever will happen next in the conversation, that is, with an ability to "play." Our stance of playfulness is our standing invitation that our clients join us in open-ended exploration and discovery.

Playfulness is the opposite of feeling that we have to do therapy a certain way in order to get it right. It's the opposite of believing that any particular diagnosis or treatment plan will be the cure for what ails a client. Playfulness may be difficult to maintain in the face of a client's rigid insistence on answers. It may evaporate under the pressure of the covert shame or blame a client sends our way. Yet it's always worth reclaiming a playful space, since humor is a potent antidote for shame. Playfulness can be reinstated with a self-accepting joke about making a mistake or with a good-humored moment of "I just don't know the answer to that!" Sharing a smile often makes reconnection possible.

For shame-ridden clients, our open, playful stance becomes, over time, deep reassurance that they can't mess up with us. From the very beginning of therapy, playfulness is an invitation for them to open up their thoughts and feelings to new possibilities, to welcome spontaneity and surprise. We can hope that eventually playfulness becomes a mode of being they can claim for their own, having experienced that their own right-brain emotional processes are trustworthy and good to share with others.

In the context of a playful stance, *acceptance* is radical. Nothing is outside the realm of exploration. In a child's play therapy, a mean teacher or a whole school can be blown to smithereens and a bothersome new little sister can be put out with the garbage. Likewise, in a playful mode of adult therapy, resentment, spitefulness, despair, and self-loathing are feelings to be accepted as "just how it is right now." There are no judgments from us that some feelings are better than others, no pressure from us that clients feel or think differently. We say simply, "Yes, I see." Or, "That makes sense." Or, "That sounds painful." Validation is especially powerful when it is experienced in this here-and-now, right-brain way. As clients come to know that we accept whoever they are and whatever they feel in any moment, right-brain rigidities may begin to soften, and right-brain blockages may open up to new connections.

As therapists considering PACE as a way to put relational validation into motion, we will already value *empathy*. We will have worked to develop our empathic capacities. But how does *curiosity* fit? Curiosity motivates useful play—such as explorations of, "What's going on for me?" and, "Why?" Curiosity makes use of the space acceptance creates, spurring a client to roam more freely than before, less afraid of what might turn up, less liable to suffer self-censure. Curiosity tries on different combinations of thoughts and feelings to find what feels true or right to an emergent sense of self. Curiosity doesn't jump to conclusions, and it isn't easily satisfied with what seems to be known. Clients will learn how to be more and more curious about themselves as they take in our relentless curiosity on their behalf—especially if our curiosity is infused with empathy.

In a stance dedicated to relational validation, neither curiosity nor empathy works well alone. The two ways of being-with illuminate and guide each other. Curiosity without empathy can feel intrusive, at worst like a kind of voyeurism. Our clients need to know that we are curious because we care about what's really happening for them. They need to sense that when we keep searching for ways to understand them better, it's because we believe that joining them in making sense of their experience is the best way to help them. If we stay aware of ourselves, we'll know when our curiosity is *not* driven by a commitment to a holistic in-depth understanding of our clients, when it is, instead, driven by our intrigue with the personalities or facts of their stories. Then we can catch ourselves and pull ourselves back to empathically motivated curiosity.

When we work with clients from a validating stance, empathy not only motivates curiosity; empathy also travels along with curiosity to buffer the shock or discomfort of new discoveries. If, for example, we are curious with a client about how terribly anxious she feels at work with a boss who gives her no feedback, and she suddenly remembers her childhood home and a silent, angry father, she may be blindsided by deep sadness or anger. Our curiosity on her behalf will immediately shift into empathy for what she feels now and felt then.

Just as our curiosity needs to be empathic, so our empathy needs to be curious. When a client talks about anxiety in relation to her boss, we do more than feel into her stress and bafflement; we allow our empathy to move into gentle curiosity about what might be going on. In therapy, empathy isn't very useful without curiosity—a quiet, patient, wondering kind of curiosity, which we might also call "interest." Empathy alone can be the end of a conversation; with interested curiosity, empathy opens into new conversations. Together, empathy and curiosity help keep the conversation in the realm of meaningful play, the space of right-brain therapy.

ARE WE SURE WE WANT TO DO THIS?

The therapeutic stance I'm describing may make eminent sense. It may seem like the best way to engage with deeply shamed clients. It may sound like a deeply human, respectful, even noble way to work. And yet it might not be what some of us, on reflection, would choose for a career, not something we'd like to work hard to accomplish every day. Responding warily to the challenges of this work makes eminent sense, too.

Lewis Aron suggests that the measure of expertise for relational psychoanalysts lies in their capacity and willingness to be emotionally vulnerable with their patients.[11] Ronald Potter-Effron, writing about therapy with shame-prone alcoholic and drug-dependent clients, says, "Clients like this need counselors who are willing to become deeply engaged with them, not individuals who use their status to remain emotionally sheltered behind their roles of therapist or counselor."[12] There are easier ways to make a living. There are even less emotionally stressful ways to make a difference in the lives of deeply vulnerable, relationally traumatized people.

Why would we want to do this work? If we undertake in-depth psychotherapy or psychoanalysis to bring our own shame into the light, we may stumble upon a surprising insight; we may discover that this very shame is what has motivated us to be therapists. Just being a helper has helped us feel better about ourselves. We may find that our deep empathy for others in pain has been real (thank goodness), but that it has also been the best we could do to take care of our own shadowy sense of being deeply flawed and unfixable. When we've been through a process of integrating the emotional and relational realities of our own chronic shame, we may find ourselves free to do something else with our lives, something closer to creative dreams repressed or ambitions long denied.

On the other hand, an in-depth therapy process may reveal to us that working closely with vulnerable, relationally traumatized people is indeed our gift and our passion. We may find that the process of facing, feeling, and integrating our own shame sets us free to engage with deeply shamed clients with a profound understanding of their struggle, an exquisite sensitivity to the shame that clouds their relationships, and a rewired right-brain capacity to "play" in what can feel like minefields of potential humiliation and blame. If that's the case, we can take an important first step toward becoming shame-competent therapists by choosing a self-aware, affirmative, de-shaming therapeutic stance. Then comes recognizing and honing the skills and sensitivities we need to do "right-brain therapy," which will be the subject of our discussion for the next few chapters.

NOTES

1. Lester Luborsky, Barton Singer, and Lise Luborsky, "Comparative Studies of Psychotherapies," *Archives of General Psychiatry* 32(1975): 995–1008; Bruce E. Wampold, *The Great Psychotherapy Debate* (Mahwah, NJ: Erlbaum, 2001).

2. For an example of this point that includes session transcripts, see Edward Teyber, Faith McClure, and Robert Weathers, "Shame in Families: Transmission across Generations," in *Shame in the Therapy Hour*, eds. Ronda L. Dearing and June Price Tangney (Washington, DC: American Psychological Association, 2011), 137–66.

3. See Nicholas Ladany, Rebecca Klinger, and Lauren Kulp, "Therapist Shame: Implications for Therapy and Supervision," in *Shame in the Therapy Hour*, eds. Dearing and Tangney, 307–22.

4. Patricia DeYoung, *Relational Psychotherapy: A Primer* (New York: Routledge, 2003), 133–48.

5. For example, Brené Brown, *I Thought It Was Just Me (but it isn't): Making the Journey from "What Will People Think?" to "I Am Enough"* (New York: Gotham, 2007).

6. See, for example, June Price Tangney and Ronda L. Dearing, *Shame and Guilt* (New York: Guilford, 2002); Donald Nathanson, *Shame and Pride* (New York: Norton, 1992); Howard Bacal, "Shame – the Affect of Discrepancy," in *The Widening Scope of Shame*, eds. Melvin Lansky and Andrew Morrison (Hillsdale, NJ: Analytic Press, 1997), 99–104; Donna Orange, "Whose Shame Is It Anyway? Lifeworlds of Humiliation and Systems of Restoration," *Contemporary Psychoanalysis* 44 (2008): 83–100.

7. June Price Tangney and Ronda L. Dearing, "Working with Shame in the Therapy Hour: Summary and Integration," in *Shame in the Therapy Hour*, eds. Dearing and Tangney, 382.

8. Peter Fonagy et al., *Affect Regulation, Mentalization, and the Development of the Self* (New York: Other Press, 2002); Jon G. Allen, Peter Fonagy, and Anthony W. Bateman, *Mentalizing in Clinical Practice* (Washington, DC: American Psychiatric Press, 2008).

9. David Wallin, *Attachment in Psychotherapy* (New York: Guilford, 2007), 307–38.

10. Daniel Hughes, *Attachment Focused Family Therapy* (New York: Norton, 2007), 61–94.

11. Lewis Aron, *A Meeting of Minds: Mutuality in Psychoanalysis* (Hillsdale, NJ: Analytic Press, 1996), 248–49.

12. Ronald Potter-Effron, "Therapy with Shame-Prone Alcoholic and Drug-Dependent Clients," in *Shame in the Therapy Hour*, eds. Dearing and Tangney, 229.

CHAPTER 7

Fostering Right-Brain Connection

Since a relationship of emotional understanding between client and therapist is essential to effective therapy, we try to foster right-brain connection with every client who comes into our practice. Working toward right-brain connectedness is especially important, however, with clients who suffer from chronic shame. These clients have difficulty regulating their own affect and sustaining emotional connections with others because the development of their right-brain connectivity has been stunted by protective dissociation. They struggle with an assortment of emotional and relational problems, they feel inadequate and defective, and whenever they can, they use left-brain rational competence to make up for gaps in their right-brain capacities for emotional/relational connection.

Our shamed clients need changes in how their right brains work for them, but they cannot make these changes on their own. They need to be in sustained connection with at least one other person who is close enough to become someone who can regulate—rather than dysregulate—their right-brain affective experience. We cannot guarantee that this kind of relationship will develop between our clients and ourselves, but we can encourage its development by making ourselves available for right-brain connection.

NON-VERBAL CONNECTION

If our right brains work well for us, we will be able to register our clients' non-verbal clues about the shame they feel even when they are not aware of it. Shame is visible in clients' bodies that are hunched protectively or held rigidly upright. We can hear shame in quick, anxious sentence cadences, in a halting stammer, in nervous laughter or forced jocularity. People struggling to manage shame may avoid making eye contact as well as any contact with emotion. If they are suddenly engulfed by emotion in spite of themselves, it will likely be shame-infused, unintegrated affect that they try to shrug off or put behind them. They may become angry with themselves for showing vulnerability or apologize for their tears.

Clients who struggle with chronic shame receive information from both sides of their brains. However, their left brains and right brains are not well connected, partly because the right hemisphere information is garbled and jerky. Their right brains process interpersonal and emotional stress not as information but as danger, with fight, flight, or freeze responses. These unthought right-brain self-protective measures are not very accessible to left-brain cognition. Our clients certainly can't speak from this right-brain experience. What they present to us verbally makes left-brain sense, not whole-person sense.

But although we can't make direct contact with our shamed clients' emotional experience, we can be sure that their right brains are registering the affective music, if not the words, of the therapy conversation. Right-brain processes turn affect not into verbal cognition but into primary process images, felt storylines, and moments of subjective awareness, including the simple binaries of feeling safe or not-safe and of being enjoyable or disgusting to someone else. We can hope that with better regulation these right-brain processes will come to feel more tolerable and coherent to our clients so that a more harmonious right-brain experience can be integrated with left-brain thought. But at the outset, our most important communication with our clients will be the talking we do to a side of their brains that does not attend to the logic of our words.

Their right brains *do* hear the affect embodied in our tone of voice, our face, and our gestures. These non-verbal affective cues let our clients know about us in relation to them—whether we're anxious or relaxed, assessing or accepting, cold or warm. It helps the process if we're at ease and confident about the therapy process, welcoming in a personal way, and affirming of our clients' choice to come for help.

Our chronically shamed clients won't be able to respond with recipro-cal right brain connection because, at formative times in their development, close contact with dysregulating others shut down their right brain connec-tivity. But even though they can't respond, their right brains are listening, scanning for danger. In this "protect" mode, they have limited ways of being with us, limitations that we see in nonverbal signals of their shame and that we feel viscerally as disconnection.

As we begin with these clients and notice our right-brain emotions and intuitions, our left brains make logical sense of what's going on. And so we are able to tell ourselves to stay the course, resisting impulses to defend ourselves, reassure our clients, explain, argue, or give advice. Our left brains know why it's important to communicate accurate empathic understanding, and they instruct our right brains to keep doing the essential work of being a non-threatening, non-coercive, accepting presence.

Our bodies provide the mix of facial attentiveness, interest, gaze, and gesture that matches our clients' emotional state of being. Human beings with right-brain competency just know how to do this: witness anyone who knows "instinctively" how to connect with an infant or a small child on first meeting. The adult makes connection by matching the child's shifting intensities of affect as well as by mirroring the specific emotions and intentions that the child expresses directly.

Baby-watcher Daniel Stern distinguishes between a child's vitality affect (the rising and falling of affective intensity) and categorical affect (particular emotions such as mad, sad, glad, and afraid),[1] a distinction that's useful in working with right-brain challenged clients. We may find ourselves working with people whose experience of affective connection was so dysregulating that identifying particular emotions is beyond their capacity. Even when they feel safe with us, they can't use our verbal mirroring of an emotion such as sadness or fear. They aren't able to answer the questions, "How did you feel about that?" or "What are you feeling right now?" We have to begin at the beginning with them by matching their vitality affect as we engage them with warmth, acceptance, and empathic curiosity.

Our matching has to be subtle, respectful, and immediately responsive to any clues that what we're doing is causing more anxiety, shame, or disconnection. We have to remember that our best intentions to understand with kind acceptance can be felt as dangerous. Just the prospect of entering right-brain territory, the being-with space where dysregulated affect lurks, may threaten our clients' self-cohesion. We understand that our invitation is perhaps more frightening than it is soothing, but at the same time we persist. We do so because we believe, with Louis Cozolino, that "safe emergency" is part of any form of effective therapy.[2]

Cozolino describes successful therapy as the integration of affect, in all its forms, with conscious awareness and cognition. Useful cognition doesn't come first and it can't be imposed from the outside of affective experience. Change happens not through intellectual understanding (which Cozolino calls the booby prize of psychotherapy), but through emotion coupled with awareness, a right-brain process, which can then be usefully linked with left-brain cognition.

The emotions that make a psychotherapy process work are evoked by safe emergencies within the therapy. Safe emergencies are right-brain emotional experiences that push the client's capacities but are still safe enough to tolerate. A useful emergency can be created by graduated exposure to phobia-inducing stimuli, for example, or by unexpected understanding and acceptance coming from a therapist.

Safe emergencies create mild to moderate affective arousal, and this "optimal stress" leads to optimal integration of dissociated neural networks—which is the neurobiological point of any modality of psychotherapy practice, Cozolino maintains. Furthermore, these moments of optimal stress in which new neural links are sparked have to happen many more times than once; change requires repeated simultaneous activation of the neural networks that need integration.[3] This is why we persist with our right-brain presence, with our playful, accepting, curious empathy, even while our clients, more often than not, need to hold tight to their protective rigidities and keep their distance.

TOLERATING RIGHT-BRAIN DISCONNECTION

We definitely need patience for this work, but even more than patience, we need the ability to keep understanding the big picture of our clients' lives. Any decent human being will feel for another human being in pain, but to work with people who suffer from chronic shame, we need to do something more difficult than this natural form of empathy. We keep inviting our clients to let us know more about how they feel, and they keep refusing to accept the invitation. They just can't share their emotional pain with us. Perhaps they can't even feel it much themselves, at least not directly. And so we have to practice what I call "large empathy." We have to imagine ourselves into emotional and relational worlds where, for example, spreading blame and judgment is the only way to relieve shame, or where being controlling and self-sufficient makes the pain go away. We have to tolerate being there for long stretches of time, sensing but not being able to talk about painful feelings that cannot be recognized.

Large empathy means that while we are being actively denied access to our shamed clients' emotional vulnerabilities, while we are shut out from most ways to show them empathy, we use what we know about them to create narratives that make emotional sense to us, narratives that allow us to feel empathy for the big picture of their struggle. We work with whatever these clients have told us about themselves in order to imagine reasons why they are disconnected from themselves and others. We remind ourselves that their right-brain disconnection is a retreat from intolerable feelings of disintegration and shame. We keep ourselves interested in how each particular form of disconnection works, and what it seems to be protecting.

For example, a client who turns every conversation into an interesting discussion or a lively debate keeps the therapy connection in territory where she can feel like an excellent conversation partner, a person others enjoy. We wonder whether sharing emotion would make her feel incompetent, or maybe even disgusting. A client who tells stories non-stop so that we can't get a word in edgewise is protecting himself from whatever might happen if we entered his space. It seems the kind of dysregulation he fears most is intrusion on his subjectivity. Then we notice that the stories don't give us much of a feel for his subjective experience, either, and we wonder whether he even knows the self he's protecting. Another client gives weekly reports on his symptoms of depression and anxiety, reports that we find hard to connect with because they are so self-objectifying. We wonder whether his habit of watching himself from the outside is part of what makes him depressed and anxious.

When we try to understand what our clients do to avoid being vulnerable and what kind of vulnerability scares them, we're not just tolerating the ways our clients avoid right-brain connection with us. We are working with those disconnections, if mostly on our own without their help. We are making meaning; in fact, we are mentalizing our clients' emotions as best we can, with the information we can glean. Mentalizing, so very useful both in child development and in psychotherapy, can sometimes work its magic without the direct communication of what's mentalized. When we respond to our clients while holding in mind their minds, even if what we hold is mostly fears and defenses, we will indirectly and subliminally communicate our emotional understanding of their minds. If our understanding fits, they will feel somewhat understood and they may even begin to understand themselves better, all without knowing exactly how or why.

When we hold our clients' minds in mind, we also have chances to share directly what we understand about how they protect themselves. What we do with these opportunities is a judgment call; we have to weigh the possibility of their feeling more deeply understood against the risk of their feeling exposed and shamed—even with a comment as simple as, "I wonder sometimes if it's a bit scary for you when I ask you how you're feeling."

We might suspect there's some risk of shame and still decide to speak, thereby creating a "safe emergency" about the therapeutic alliance. Can clients tolerate our seeing something about them that they thought was hidden? Can they allow what we see to inform their own sense of themselves? Will they still be able to feel that we are on their side, offering empathy and understanding, not criticism? If the safe emergency does its integrative work, our right-brain working alliance will have been strengthened by our clients' response to the emergency.

If we decide that our right-brain connection with particular clients is too fragile to risk with an intentional safe emergency, we can just stay with them in the realm of right-brain affective attunement. While responding respectfully to each client's relational style, we can also try to draw conversations into more playful, curious space. We can continue to offer compassionate, empathic understanding. It may be emergency enough—that is, it may cause clients quite enough useful stress and spark new neural connections—if they can just begin to feel understood and then tolerate this disruption to their defenses.

PROVIDING SELFOBJECT EXPERIENCE

Selfobject experience is the name self psychology gives to certain forms of right-brain connection that seem to make special contributions to the development of a cohesive, energetic, and relationally competent self. When selfobject experience is working well for a young child, she simply counts on her caregivers to be emotionally close to her and attuned to her needs. Breaks in connection are tolerable because she is also entitled to protest, and repair is expectable. Because the important others in her life so thoroughly and deeply organize her experience of herself and the world, helping to smooth the rough parts and making life both exciting and safe, a child feels them to be almost a part of herself. From the perspective of adulthood, this intense early form of selfobject experience is called "archaic."

As we mature, we continue to need intimate emotional/relational connections with others to help us feel vital, valued, and fully ourselves. But if our developmental needs were met fairly well in childhood, the selfobject needs we have as adults will no longer be intense and archaic. In brain terms, we might say that when different forms of our right-brain connectivity are established and working well, we don't need to keep creating the capacity for connectivity, even though we do need to have right-brain connections with others for life.

As we know, our chronically shamed clients are not very able to use coherent right-brain connections with others to sustain themselves in emotional well-being. From a self psychological perspective, they carry through their adult lives archaic forms of selfobject needs that have never been met. Those needs were once intensely pressing, and so, even though long denied, they may still survive in muted or altered forms. We hope they do survive, for selfobject needs are our clients' gateway to a second chance at developing a vital, integrated self. If they can allow themselves to need our emotional presence in these more archaic ways, and if we can quietly and consistently fulfill the needs, our clients' longstanding self-deficits may be repaired in the therapy relationship. From a brain perspective, we could say that specific kinds of right-brain interaction will create some important synaptic connections that link interpersonal contact with the safety and energy contact can bring.

A self psychological approach to clients becomes effective right-brain therapy with them. Sustained empathic immersion in their subjective worlds is a right-brain form of gathering information. From this place of emotional understanding, we communicate our empathy about what we understand, and we do so through affectively attuned, experience-near (right-brain) conversation with them. How our clients respond depends on how their archaic selfobject needs are configured. If therapy goes well, some of these emotional needs will emerge and will be met—in right-brain interactions.

As clients start to count on particular needs being met consistently, patterns of relationship will emerge: selfobject transferences, identified by the specific types of need they address. These transferences are potent formations of right-brain connection between therapist and client. To illustrate this point, I'll discuss the three main types of need and transference that self psychology recognizes: mirroring, idealizing, and twinning.

Mirroring

When we mirror our clients, we take in what they say and show that we understand them with simple words, sounds, gestures, and the affect that shows on our faces. At a most basic level, we are mirroring the sequences, intensities, and qualities of their affect. We hope that they see in our eyes that their subjective emotional self exists and that it matters. For clients whose early caregivers were neglectful, distracted by anxiety, or abusive, this may be something they need more than they could ever consciously know. Over time, they may be able to use our mirroring to create a much more firmly delineated sense of *being*, supported by right-brain coherence that synthesizes perceptions, emotions, desires, and intentions.

Useful mirroring responds to all self-experience, no matter how contradictory or unpleasant. Our consistent containing responses support our clients to feel coherent and whole despite the multiplicity and ambivalence of their self-states. A self that feels more whole may also feel more continuity between past, present, and an expectable future. This in-depth, over-time kind of mirroring, when it reflects back to clients a sense of their own "mind" or coherent subjective self, could also be called mentalizing.

Sometimes our right-brain mirroring responses are involved less with our clients' self-coherence and more with their desires to be special. Clients with deficits in the grandiosity/ambition side of self-development may walk through life "mirror-hungry," always looking to the eyes of others for affirmation and admiration. In therapy, this hunger comes our way. We have to remember that for these clients, mirrors are a way to objectify self, and that they are inviting us to join them in this outside-in view of themselves. Their subjectivity has gotten lost in their obsession with their audience. Therefore their original subjective need cannot be met, and their hunger remains insatiable.

The original need was to feel uniquely special while being held in the gaze of another who knew and appreciated them "from the inside." Mirror-hunger tells us that the original need survives, however twisted. What matters in therapy is that we tune in to our clients' need to be special in their *subjective being*. We communicate our appreciation emotional self to emotional self, with "a gleam in our eye," to use Kohut's phrase. The gleam in our eye tells them that we recognize and treasure the special self they are. It tells them that we can feel their passion to be fully, expansively themselves, and that we welcome and enjoy that energy.

It seems that a person's agency, creativity, imagination, and willingness to risk require right-brain connectivity. An organized left brain can make a project or a dream happen, but the idea comes from somewhere less linear. Ambition, too, seems to be more affect than cognition. It makes sense, then, that the bundle of affective energy we call "grandiosity" needs ongoing supportive, right-brain regulation in order to become an important and coherent part of right-brain subjectivity.

Idealizing

The selfobject function of idealizing also takes different forms at different times in a child's development. A child's need to be connected to someone bigger, wiser, and stronger changes over time. In infancy, it's all about calming and soothing—the simplest form of on-the-spot affect regulation. In toddlerhood, affect regulation includes containment of anger and ambivalence in ways that help the toddler learn that moments of shame can be repaired. Within the orbit of a parent's strength and wisdom, a young child can feel confident and strong herself; idealizing allows shared strength to be experienced as subjective strength. An older child absorbs from an idealized parent a sense of the self he might become; idealizing becomes an internal sense of his own values, tested out rigorously during the self-consolidation of adolescence.

If adult clients have missed out on some important idealizing selfobject experience, what sorts of right-brain connections will afford them a belated chance at this aspect of self-development? For some clients, calming and soothing is what they need most from psychotherapy, at least for a while.

And for these clients, since their earliest experience was fraught with dys-regulation, just being able to make safe affective contact with a regulating other is a considerable challenge.

With some of them, we find ourselves patiently eliciting the emotions that they keep tightly boxed in, showing them bit by bit and step by step that not only is it safe to feel, it's safe to share feelings with us. In fact, it feels better to have feelings and to share feelings with us than to keep them locked away. Other clients come into therapy spilling over with emotion but shutting us out of their process. Our empathy seems to be a threat to them instead of a way to connect. They expect that we will try to define, control, or change their feelings to suit our agendas. And so we simply know this, too, and stay near, not giving up on showing empathy but making sure it's not intrusive. Our hope is that they will feel our emotional presence and slowly become conscious that it won't annihilate their affective core self.

And then there are the clients whose affect explodes into the room, a potent mix of rage, helplessness, and despair about all those who keep hurting them instead of giving them the help they need. There's every chance that at any moment we, too, will fail them. The only way for us to prove ourselves safe to stormy clients is by handling whatever affect comes our way with as much calm, empathic presence as we can muster. Right-brain regulation of interpersonal rage requires unflinching interpersonal presence. It's as if the client's self system is yelling, "Regulate this!" and it needs to hear back a firm, clear, "Yes, I am right here!" We have to prove that our powers of regulation are strong enough to hear and contain their feelings, and also that our self-regulation is strong enough to own up, with genuine feeling, to any specific ways we missed them or failed to provide what they needed.

Just as children need to count on their parents to be the guardians and keepers of the parent–child relationship, so clients need to count on us to notice and repair breaks in their relationship with us. In this part of "idealizing," all clients, not just the stormy ones, absorb from us what wisdom we possess about making mistakes and making amends, and about how moments of shame can be resolved with honesty and self-acceptance. They are able to feel and absorb some of the ways our right-brain ego ideal works for us.

Here, too, our own capacity to self-regulate and our mode of self-regulation are very important parts of what our right brains have to offer. Perhaps this is the "brain" definition of idealizing: idealizing is what happens between a self who needs regulation and a self whose capacity for self-regulation makes the mutual regulation process safe and trustworthy. A parent's ability to self-regulate is felt as strength and wisdom, and while a child absorbs self-regulation through ongoing right-brain connection with the parent, her parent's strength and wisdom is felt as her own. And so it is with clients. They feel stronger and wiser while absorbing our capacity to self-regulate.

It's important to note that this developmentally helpful right-brain version of being idealized is not the same as being put on a pedestal. It's not about our clients seeing us as perfect or as someone who offers brilliant insights or deep wisdom. That kind of idealizing is often a way for a client and a therapist both to get some "specialness" from therapy while avoiding more difficult real contact between them.

For right brain idealizing to work well for our clients, they need to feel that our way of being a subjective self is steady, reliable, and safe to be with. It doesn't matter that we're not perfect or even exceptional; what matters is that we know ourselves solidly and act in ways that "add up" with our self-knowledge. In our reliable, fair interactions with them, our clients can experience an attractive, desirable goodness—something worth emulating.

Clients who need to idealize are missing an inner connection to values that feel like part of themselves. They may feel spiritually empty and morally phony. Though they may subscribe to a moral code or a religious belief system in a cognitive way, they have little subjective experience of valuing certain qualities of being, or of aspiring to ideals. A connection with someone they experience as wise and good creates possibilities for them to experience themselves as good, too, and to enjoy the feeling of aspiring to be like someone they feel close to. This is the right-brain creation of right-brain ego-ideal.

We may notice, as particular therapy relationships mature and then move toward closure, that idealizing clients begin to articulate a passionate commitment to ideals that we can see fit especially well with the subjective emotional selves they have come to know in therapy. A trauma survivor takes her law career in the direction of protecting the vulnerable; someone who has struggled to articulate his feelings enrolls in a creative writing course; a community action group becomes the focus of energy of someone who for too long has felt like an alien on the planet.

Sometimes such clients' commitments to particular politics or movements may challenge our own values, whether they know this or not. Even if clients do accentuate their difference from us, we can understand that they are doing something like what adolescents do: having used connection with elders to grow a capacity for subjectively experienced values, they test out values that fit for them as they make new moves toward subjective self-consolidation, or as we might put it, toward mature right-brain connectivity. In the sphere of aspiring to strength and goodness, other-regulation becomes self-regulation.

Twinning

When a twinship transference is in play, clients give us strong hints that they feel we're just like them in essential ways. It could be sharing a certain kind of social location or politics, a certain level of intelligence, or a certain way of looking at the world. Whether or not any of this feels accurate to us, we know that it's an important way for them to make right-brain connection with us, and so we don't discourage them from this emotional "knowing" of us, even when it doesn't quite fit for us.

What deficits might clients be trying to fill as they enjoy this selfobject experience with us? The developmental paradigm is a child-caregiver situation where the two are engaged in an activity that gives the child a sense of subjective likeness with the older adult. There is a special connection based on what they both feel as they do this special something together: On Saturday mornings a little boy and his dad always stir up the pancakes together; summer weekends when a little girl visits her grandpa, they always water the flowers together, remembering flower names out loud. More subtle versions include a child's feeling that when she talks with her dad, they both know they are the same kind of smart, or that when she makes a joke with her mom, they will laugh at the same kind of funny.

Early twinship experiences are a good foundation for finding childhood friends who are "just like me" and a strong adolescent peer group. They undergird an adult's lifelong capacity to find kinship with others in the world. Basic kinship is perhaps the first level of what "twinning clients" are trying to achieve in establishing this kind of connection with us. If we are like them and they are like us, then they are not aliens on the planet. Some clients have deep reasons to fear letting us get close enough for empathic mirroring or letting us be strong enough for them to idealize. But they can tolerate a sense of "being like." It's a safer place to begin making right brain connection, and it lets them come in from the cold just a bit.

SELFOBJECT TRANSFERENCE AS SAFE EMERGENCY

Sometimes the mirroring, idealizing, and twinning links made between our right brains and the right brains of our clients do their regulating and "rewiring" work out of sight and out of mind. The therapy relationship just feels good and our clients feel stronger in it. But sometimes our clients notice how much they look forward to seeing us or how much they count on us for steady support. This awareness is most likely to hit when we are about to take a holiday, but it can bubble up at any time. It may come out as anxiety about counting on someone who could disappear, or as anger that we, not they, control our leaving. Sometimes our clients are ashamed to need us in such intense and basic ways. They have learned from somewhere that "dependency" is a bad thing.

At times like these, we may find ourselves sharing with clients some of our core anti-shame beliefs—for example, that to be human is to need to connect. We might explain that therapy creates a safe place for connection needs to emerge, especially needs that have been shut down for a very long time. Therapy lets us feel those needs again in a natural way, and also lets us get to know the fear, anger, and shame that can be tangled up with needing. If we untangle those feelings, our need to connect can become a helpful part of life again, in therapy and in other relationships. For all these reasons, we say, "dependency"—or needing to connect—is a good thing.

We affirm our clients' courage to let themselves need an emotional bond with us. We recognize their good instincts to use the kind of help we have to offer. We try to calm the anxiety that's swirling around this "emergency," knowing that feeling dependent and needy activates our clients' shame.

We're also aware that different forms of repetitive transference lurk, along with shame, on the dark side of a comfortable therapy relationship. Even though our clients have many moments of trusting selfobject connection with us, in other, more difficult moments, the knowing they hold in right-brain memory undermines that trust. What they know in their bones (their neural wiring) is that bad things that happened before will happen again: their need to connect will only cause them pain; a regulating other will become dysregulating—he or she will turn away or turn mean—and the awfulness of disintegrating shame will happen. It just makes sense that our clients protect themselves from this kind of repetition—even though they also want to trust.

When we intuit that clients are torn between new trust and old expectations, we might share with them what we sense, inviting their left-brain thought processes to step in to make the emergency safer. Sometimes our clients' rational self can help their right brain to stay engaged in spite of fear, and to make space, with conscious awareness, for new relational experiences even while the old feelings are strong.

PROVIDING ATTACHMENT EXPERIENCE

The storylines of self psychology may not resonate in our work with particular clients, or we may feel more general resonance with attachment theory than with self psychology. Attachment categories are also useful ways to think about the kinds of right-brain connections our clients need to have with us.[4] If attachment theory is our idiom, we know, for example, that avoidant clients will dismiss their need to make emotional connection with us or with anyone. Having experienced caregivers as dysregulating in neglectful and rejecting ways, they "decided" very early not to keep going through the pain of needing something they could never have. Their best protection is to limit their conscious awareness to left-brain logic and the rational ordering of experience.

With such clients, it's essential that we ground our "discussions" in right-brain open-ended playfulness—a baffling riddle to them, but useful when offered in a spirit of warmth and acceptance. We can encourage them to be in the moment as we wonder aloud what they happen to be thinking about. The more we can be "right now" with them, the more chances we will have at moments of right-brain connection, even if we often miss. It can also be helpful to explain the value and function of emotions to these clients, enlisting their hyper-functioning left brains to help their right brains approach the "safe emergency" of feeling some emotion.

Clients whose working model of attachment is more ambivalent than avoidant had to cope with hot-and-cold caregiving. They couldn't count on consistent emotional regulation, and now they can't find consistency in themselves. Their feelings and behaviors change drastically as they try to get the regulation they need. With them, we have to be quick on our feet, tuning into whatever emotion is on the upswing in the moment. Our regulating response includes a lot of containment, with perhaps a bit of down-regulating for wound-up, spilling-over affect, and up-regulating for low, despairing moments.

What matters more than anything with ambivalent clients is our calm consistent presence. We monitor the quality of our attunement with them, careful neither to intrude nor be too distant. These clients will give us plenty of affective feedback about how well we are doing, but it may take lots of patience and persistence to discover which disconnected moments between us are causing what kind of distress, and how best to shift dysregulating interactions toward regulation.

Clients with a strong theme of disorganization in their attachment schema have been deeply frightened by a primary attachment figure. As well as learning an avoidant or ambivalent model of attachment, they have learned to cope with intense dysregulation by "disappearing"—suddenly freezing or fleeing into dissociated self-soothing behaviors. With these clients we will hold an overall intention to feel emotion with their highly avoidant self or to contain emotion with their intensely ambivalent self. But first we need to make safe contact with a terrified, non-responsive self. Disorganized, deeply frightened clients need soothing, calming regulation in order, bit by bit, to give up their dissociative self protection. Only then will they be able to be present for more constructive right-brain contact with us.

LINKING EVENTS AND EMOTIONS

Part of regulating a child's affect is helping a child connect particular events with particular emotions. Emotions then become a normal part of life, expectable responses to certain kinds of things that happen. If you lose your favorite stuffed bunny, you will be sad. Turning on the sprinkler on a hot day will make you happy and excited. If your big sister calls you a silly baby, you will be angry. When your mom suddenly loses her temper, you'll be scared. Your feelings make sense because they make sense to the people around you. They are *information* about something that *happened* to you. The information can be useful. When your dad sees that you're sad, he looks for your lost bunny. When your mom sees that she scared you, she says she just got mad for a minute because you weren't listening, but now she's over it, and she's sorry that her angry voice scared you.

Emotional regulation helps develop emotional vocabulary and emotional communication skills. You learn how to feel the difference between sad and angry, and that a hug helps when you're sad, but not when you're angry. When you're angry at your sister for calling you a silly baby, your mom says it's not okay to hit her and that it works better to tell her, "I don't like it when you say mean things!" Then she can say she's sorry. And your mom also tells your sister it's not okay to call names, but it is okay to say, "I don't want to play with you right now." Then she tells you that sometimes you just have to feel sad when something happens that you don't like. But then you can find something else to make you happy.

The foundation for learning how to identify emotions and how to negotiate them with other people is to understand that feelings are normal, expectable responses to events. Children absorb this understanding through their caregivers' responses to them, both through nonverbal emotional attunement and through the verbal mini-narratives caregivers tell them about themselves and their emotions. As we will see in the next chapter, narrative, even in small bits, has exceptionally integrative power.

At first glance, we might see narrative as a link between words and feelings, reason and emotion, left and right brain. However, these linkages reinforce and enhance a more basic integration on the right side of the brain: the ability to feel connection between events and emotions, connections fundamental to a coherent autobiographical sense of self. Our shame-prone clients have trouble making those connections. And that's why, in relational therapy, we have a simple answer to the question, "What do you talk about in therapy?" We talk about *what happened*—and we pay attention to the *feelings* about what happened.

So when clients describe an event to us, we're likely to ask, "How did that make you feel?" or "How was that for you?" Such questions not only keep a therapy conversation going, they also keep it right-brain accessible. For right-brain integration it's equally helpful to ask, "What happened?" when clients tell us about their difficult emotions. In fact, sometimes to ask what happened is more useful than exploring feelings further because it helps link the feelings back into the contextual web of events and relationships that got them started.

SOMETHING HAPPENED . . .

Some connections between events and emotions are easy to make: A client feels terribly sad and angry because her friend died of cancer; another feels anxious because he's unemployed and the job market is tight. Other connections are less obvious—someone can't understand feeling depressed after enjoying her own big wedding, and someone else is baffled by the anxiety he feels on beginning a well-planned retirement.

Perhaps least obvious are the small connections between emotions and events that happen daily, and clients who suffer from chronic shame are especially unlikely to recognize these connections. They are convinced that they feel anxious, depressed, and down on themselves because there is something inherently wrong with them. When they tell us about feeling bad, it's especially important to ask them, "What happened?" Our questions need a helpful frame, for example, "When you started feeling so lousy on Wednesday, can you think of anything that happened earlier in the day, or maybe on Tuesday, that wasn't so great?" And we need to ask in a right-brain way: exploratory, curious, and willing to imagine ourselves into the possibilities with them, perhaps even feeling connections on their behalf.

A shame-prone client will often dismiss the possibility that something happened. As we get to know more about the details of his life, we might be able to ask more useful questions. When he feels depressed and worthless, we might wonder, "You know, that plan to spend some time with your wife this weekend, how did that go?" When he's feeling like a loser, we might say, "Hmm. I'm wondering how things have been going between you and your boss." The last thing we want to do is interrupt his process to browbeat him with questions. But our gentle, consistent wondering about "What happened?" will suggest the possibility, again and again, that maybe his feelings don't just come from weird, wrong places inside him. Maybe his feelings are understandable responses to real events!

For clients who feel a lot of shame, most of "what happens" and leads to bad feelings are things that happen between them and people who are important to their emotional well-being. Once they start to connect events and emotions, what these clients report are many small instances of what we can understand as a sense of self disintegrating in relation to a dysregulating other. Sometimes the dysregulating responses are just remembered or imagined, but even then behind the bad feelings there is an experience of a self out of sorts with others and therefore flawed or diminished.

Maybe the most useful moment to ask "What happened?" is during a therapy session when we sense a sudden disconnection or shift of emotion in a client. We might say that we're aware of something different: "I see you're looking really quiet and thoughtful." We might wonder if the client is aware of feeling something. We might ask, "What do you think happened just now?" We ask in a way that says that we, too, are feeling something; we care what's going on between us. Every time it becomes possible for us to talk with our clients in an emotionally present way about what happened between us in a session, every time we can help them experience here-and-now links between what happened and how they felt, some important new right brain neural networking is instigated.

And every time, at least for a while, being in an affective "here-and-now" with us has the quality of emergency for them. Our clients' implicit relational knowing tells them that things get dangerous when emotions come up between people. They've learned either to shut down or get angry in self-defense. There's no point knowing more about what happened or saying how they feel; nobody will listen to them anyway. In the face of this fear and disbelief, our job is to keep this here-and-now emergency safe. It will take a while, more than a few repetitions, for these clients to believe that things can be different with us, that talking about what happened could be safe, interesting, and helpful to our relationship.

SOMETHING HAPPENED A LONG TIME AGO . . .

As chronically shamed clients notice the events that make them feel bad, they start to see patterns. With our help, they hear their own running commentary on themselves, relentlessly critical, often harsh and shaming. Our clients may notice how frightened and reactive they are with other people, sometimes when they don't need to be. And yet it all seems necessary; the feelings are familiar . . . old. The emotional connection of therapy feels unfamiliar, different from what they expect, and quite different from what they grew up with. They may begin to wonder not only, "What's going on with me?" but also, "What happened to me, really?"

All the past that matters to relational therapy is present in a client's implicit relational knowing. Therapy aims to change how a client is able to be with herself and with others in her world today. Becoming able to speak her subjective mind and emotional self in relation to others in her current life may be all the storytelling a client needs to do. Yet she may also want to understand her historical past—in order to understand her present better. I'm never surprised when a shame-prone client wants to explore "where all this comes from."

Whether the story is limited to here-and-now relational patterns or includes how those patterns came to be a long time ago, the story needs to emerge from what the client's right brain knows and feels. One of the core skills of doing right-brain therapy is being able to help a client develop an emotionally experienced life-narrative that supports a coherent sense of subjective self. Finding out what such storytelling can accomplish in the face of fragmentation and shame is the topic of the next chapter.

NOTES

1. Daniel Stern, *The Interpersonal World of the Infant: A View from Psychoanalysis and Developmental Psychology* (New York: Basic Books, 1985), 53–60.

2. Cozolino notes that Fritz Perls, the founder of Gestalt therapy, coined the term "safe emergency" for the experience psychotherapists create in treatment: Louis Cozolino, *The Neuroscience of Psychotherapy: Healing the Social Brain*, 2nd edn. (New York: Norton, 2012), 44. The classic Gestalt text is Frederick S. Perls, Ralph F. Hefferline, and Paul Goodman, *Gestalt Therapy: Excitement and Growth in the Human Personality* (New York: Julian, 1951, reprint, Goldsboro, ME: Gestalt Journal Press, 1994). Cozolino uses the term to capture a client's experience of tolerating unintegrated and dysregulating thoughts and feelings while being given the support of a collaborative, nurturing relationship.

3. Cozolino, *Neuroscience of Psychotherapy*, 45–47.

4. For further discussion of different ways to connect with clients who present with different attachment styles, see David Wallin, *Attachment in Psychotherapy* (New York: Guilford, 2007), 193–255.

CHAPTER 8

Narrative as Right-Brain Integration

From a neurobiological perspective, the essential work of psychotherapy is to stimulate neural plasticity and neural integration. How do therapists do that? In two basic ways, according to Louis Cozolino: with affect attunement that fosters their clients' affect tolerance and affect regulation, and with narratives that help integrate their clients' neural networks.[1] This chapter is about how to help relationally traumatized, chronically shamed clients create the stories that integrate the neural networks of their right brains in particular and thus diminish their propensity to shame.

RIGHT-LEFT AND UP-DOWN INTEGRATION

Psychotherapists who write about neurobiology agree that narrative seems to foster the horizontal integration of the left and right hemispheres of the brain. As Daniel Siegel describes the process, the left brain provides linear organization, logical interpretation of material, and the drive to understand cause and effect. But the material itself, the "stuff" of autobiographical memory, linked with emotions, relationships, and coherent and contextual meanings, comes from the right brain.[2]

On its own, the left brain's narrator or interpreter will narrate situations in superficially logical ways that are actually confabulations of possible causes and effects. This interpreter ignores contexts and doesn't care to produce a coherent or coordinated view of truth. The right brain, by contrast, seems to be able to make sense of the essential meaning of the input it can perceive and creates context-rich, non-linear, cross-modal *understanding*.[3]

Cozolino describes how clients come in with their left hemisphere interpreter telling its story. But the story doesn't account for what's happening to them. Their narratives aren't making sense of their experiences, feelings, and behaviors. The therapist's task is to help pick up on the right-brain messages that are being transmitted outside of the client's awareness and reflect this right-brain information back to the client in order to make possible a larger, more inclusive narrative. "A primary tool across all models of psychotherapy is editing and expanding the self-narrative of the left hemisphere to include the silent wisdom of the right," he concludes.[4]

But what if the right brain is far from wise? What if it's fragmented, dissociated from parts of itself, and unavailable for interpersonal connection?

This is the situation facing clients who live in chronic shame. At some point in their process of psychological self-integration, the left and right hemispheres of their brains should come to work well together. But that's not likely to happen before their right-brain processes are significantly integrated.

Bonnie Badenoch reserves the term horizontal integration for the linkage between right and left brain that becomes possible once vertical integration in the right hemisphere of the brain is established. [5] Until there's been significant integration of body, limbic system, and cortex on the right side of the brain, a person may be able to tell a *cohesive* story, she explains, but not a *coherent* story. A cohesive narrative makes cause-and-effect sense, but it connects bits of raw right-brain experience in rigid linear ways; for example, "I feel bad because I failed and because that means I'm a failure, a loser." A coherent narrative, by contrast, is an emotionally rich story that makes visceral sense of a person's life in its multiple relational contexts.[6] Perhaps: "I feel bad because I didn't get my part of the project done on time. I'm disappointed, too; I'm always a reliable team-member. But the baby was really sick, Jack was at the end of his rope, and I just couldn't stay late at work again. I was stressed and worried from every direction. My boss is a dad himself—not a gay dad—but still . . . I hope he'll understand.

Our chronically shamed clients don't need left-brain help from us to tell their stories. They have the drive to make cause-and-effect sense of things and the ability to line up an argument. But they do need a lot of help on the right-brain side of creating coherent narrative. They need help arriving at an embodied, emotional/relational sense of self that has coherence enough to be entrusted to their left-brain narrator. How to give that kind of help is what I will explore in this chapter.

RIGHT-BRAIN NARRATIVE PROCESS

The brain theorists I've mentioned think that the left brain instigates narrative. They also agree, however, that on its own the right brain holds an autobiographical sense of self as well as memory and emotions. Allan Schore wants to make sure that we understand the extent and significance of what the right brain holds of "self," especially when the self has been relationally traumatized. He emphasizes that the major debilitating impact of emotional/relational trauma is on the right-brain implicit self system, *not* on the language functions of the left hemisphere. *Self* is much more than a left-brain mental conception, he says; rather, it is a "psychobiological, right-lateralized bodily based process."[7]

Furthermore, this right-hemisphere process *includes* thinking; there is a thinking part of the emotional brain, the right orbitofrontal system, which integrates emotion with ideas and thoughts, and integrates affective information with the selection of actions to take. In states of dissociation due to emotional trauma, this is the structure not well developed and not well integrated with its cortical and subcortical connections.[8]

Schore also explains, with overwhelming supporting evidence from brain studies, that the right hemisphere of the brain is specialized for generating self-awareness and self-recognition and for processing self-related material. Once again, "top" right-brain functions are key. Schore quotes Donald Stuss and Michael Alexander, who say that the right prefrontal cortex plays a central role in "the appreciation, integration, and modulation of affective and cognitive information" and serves as "a specific convergence site for all of the neural processes essential to affectively personalize higher order experience of self and to represent awareness of that experience."[9] Schore calls this right frontal lobe process that connects a person's self schema to underlying emotional experiences and memories the glue that holds together a person's sense of self.

In Schore's view, then, a recognizable self-story does not wait for or depend on a narrative that integrates left and right brain functions. It seems we carry around dual representations of self, one in each hemisphere. The left hemisphere has the advantage of self-description through a verbal, linguistic process. The right hemisphere sense of self is much more dependent on affectively toned non-verbal information received from many body/brain sources. The whole right brain, top to bottom, specializes in cross-modal integration of information received from multiple information channels at once.

When the two sides of the brain aren't synchronized, the "self" a person says he is can be quite different from the self he enacts in his emotions and relationships. His right-brain experience has not yet been integrated into a coherent sense of self. This seems to the case for my client Gary, who knows his intelligent and morally upright side very well, but who has no idea what the "acting out" guy on the other side thinks, feel, or wants, except maybe to flip a defiant finger. He has moments of viscerally sensing "that guy," but they don't hold together as coherent understanding. If we could make better emotional connection with that guy, we could bring more coherence to Gary's right-brain sense of self.

The right brain's capacity for integrating meanings turns up even as it provides material for a left-right integrative narrative organized by a left-brain verbal process. As Siegel points out, inter-hemispheric narratives, those ordinary autobiographical stories we tell, often "tell more than they know" about the implicit aspects of our lives because they touch on emotional themes and meanings that have taken shape in right-brain implicit memory and in right-brain mentalizing activities.[10] In other words, the right brain has its own organization of knowing and "speaks it" even when the left brain hasn't yet put the knowing into words or concepts.

We think, for example, that we're just telling a story of a family outing when our kids were young. But an emotionally sensitive listener may hear not only our nostalgia but also our regret for having been less of a parent than we wish we'd been. He will hear undertones of sadness as we speak of one child and a tinge of pride as we speak of another. He will sense the quality of our connection with our spouse in those days. It's just a story about camping on the beach twenty years ago, yet there's another story there—or more than one—that we don't quite understand.

A sensitive listener, perhaps a therapist, could help us hear the "more than we know" in our own story. He could help us listen to what our right brain knows about that camping trip. We could come to hear in the memories of that family outing emotional meanings that are as yet unformulated, though present in what our story says beyond its words.

PUTTING WORDS TO FEELINGS

Creating and consolidating a coherent sense of self requires different kinds of narrative, "narrative" understood in its broadest sense. The most basic kind of narrative that fosters self-integration is the linking of feeling to words. Studies show that putting emotions into words, or labeling affect, correlates with decreased neural activity in the amygdala, the right-brain subcortical "keeper" of memory and emotion, and an increase in right prefrontal cortex activation. Cozolino notes that even writing about emotions supports the top-down regulation of bodily/emotional affect.[11]

Any new links between subcortical parts of the brain and the prefrontal cortex are important right-brain integrations in themselves. In addition, however, as feelings are brought to words, and thus to the prefrontal cortex, they also become connected with an awareness of self having those feelings. When feelings connect into frontal lobe processes, they become part of what Schore calls the right-brain "glue" function that integrates a sense of self.

This right-brain process of constructing felt autobiography could also be called, more simply, self-reflection. Cozolino distinguishes the language of self-reflection from our socially reflexive language ("How are you?"/"Fine, thanks") and also from internal dialogue we don't stop to think about, the critical or supportive voices our parents have put in our heads. By contrast, self reflection allows us to be in touch with our internal feeling/thought process. When clients move into self-reflective language, they speak more slowly, without clichés or habitual turns of phrase. Emotions rise into awareness.[12] Their left-brain interpreter is temporarily side-lined as they immerse themselves in a right-brain process of finding emotional coherence.

Psychodynamic psychotherapists recognize self reflection as part of a larger process of creating an emotionally coherent life story. But right-brain narratives can also be created in much smaller bits. Cozolino describes a therapist working with symptoms of anxiety. His first step is finding words that help the client identify his anxiety. He then helps the client "feel into it," exploring what scares him and why. Finally the client can "own" the anxiety, understanding its meaning and weaving it into a conscious narrative of his existence. Cozolino notes that here a narrative process has helped integrate cortical and subcortical parts of the brain. [13]

This same kind of integration happens whenever clients are able to link events and emotions in response to questions such as, "How did you feel about that?" or, "What happened, so that you ended up feeling like that?" These questions, though left-brain and verbal, invite our clients to feel into the unspoken gist of what they know, thereby linking up the contexts, relationships, emotions, meanings, and understandings their right brains hold.

ATTACHMENT AND THE CAPACITY FOR RIGHT-BRAIN NARRATIVE

For our chronically shamed clients, feeling into what they know can be as hard as knowing what they feel. It's not just that they block painful emotion; they really don't know their histories. In fact, when it comes to emotions and relationships, it's a challenge for them to tell even a coherent here-and-now story about themselves. It seems that relational trauma severely limits a person's ability to feel and tell a personal narrative. Schore would say: Of course it does, because when that person was a child, no regulating other helped her keep emotions within a tolerable range or helped her integrate emotions into a reliable network of self-awareness. And so her body-affect isn't connected with words. Events aren't connected with emotions. Memories aren't woven into felt autobiography.

Attachment theory describes in more detail how relational trauma affects a person's narrative ability.[14] In optimum child development, everyday parent-child talk provides material for the creation of narratives. These narratives become in time what the child recognizes as inner experience and self-identity. In the context of secure attachment, parent and child are able to talk about all kinds of experiences, feelings, and behaviors. Their co-created narratives provide a medium for the child's brain to integrate all of this multiplicity within autobiographical memory and a coherent sense of self.

If a child is insecurely attached, however (and vulnerable to developing chronic shame), most likely his parent has attachment issues too, which show up as the parent's compromised capacity to tell a coherent self-narrative. A parent who has trouble linking events and emotions in her own coherent, integrative storylines will not be able to model or help her child create a coherent, integrative self-narrative. The child's vulnerability to chronic shame is then exacerbated by a disintegration of self-coherence. He is likely to become an adult with attachment issues, too, who has a hard time telling a coherent story about his life and relationships.

The firm connection between adult attachment issues and adult problems with self-narrative is embodied in a testing tool called the Adult Attachment Interview (AAI), which attachment researchers use to determine adult categories of attachment.[15] Through structured questions and responses, the adults are encouraged to tell the story of their early relationships. Scoring the AAI is a matter of noticing the quality, not the content, of the narratives the adults are able to tell.

Free, autonomous adults with a history of secure attachment tell their stories in a coherent, believable way. They have processed childhood traumas, present a realistic, balanced picture of their parents, and can put their feelings into words. When they co-create narrative with their own children, they are free to understand the children's experience from a child's perspective and have no need to block out any particular kind of emotions or experience.

Adults recognized by the AAI as *dismissing*, an interpersonal style corresponding to an avoidant attachment pattern, tell childhood stories that are factual but thin, full of gaps, and without emotion. As dismissive of their children's emotional needs as they are dismissive of their own connections with others, these parents are far from able to help their children integrate the emotional or relational side of experience into a coherent sense of self.

Adults with an insecure ambivalent attachment history and an interpersonal style called *enmeshed* or *preoccupied* tell their stories with a great deal of verbiage and affect, but the story is disorganized, with blurred boundaries between past and present. The storytellers seem preoccupied and pressured, unable to keep the listener in mind. Those same internal pressures and preoccupations also make it difficult for them to keep their actual children in mind. Their children, likely to develop an anxious-ambivalent attachment pattern, will be hard put to create narratives that truly belong to them. Their parents' needs and anxieties will fill their emotional space, blocking access to their own needs and feelings. What they are able to put together about themselves will probably be as disorganized as their parents' self-narrative, and as unsupportive of grounded, cohesive self-experience.

Emotionally *unresolved/disorganized* adults tell fragmented stories that are shot through with chaotic, intrusive emotion. The stories themselves, as well as the style of narrative, point to chaotic or traumatic childhood experiences that have not yet been resolved. Children of such parents, frightened and disoriented by their parents' emotional disorganization, develop a disorganized attachment pattern themselves. They have no model for making emotional sense of their experience and no one to help them with their fears. Dissociation may be their only recourse, a strategy that will actively discourage a coherent sense of self.

It's striking that in each instance parents with a certain type of attachment style create, *through their narrative style*, the conditions for children to develop the very same type of attachment style. As Cozolino summarizes, "Parental narratives, both coherent and incoherent, become the blueprint not only for the child's narratives, but for the organization and integration of their neural circuitry."[16] These narratives of emotional and relational meanings are right-brain narratives, and the essential circuitry in question is right brain, emotional/relational circuitry.

Cozolino then cites a study by Main and associates that followed six-year-olds who had been assessed for type of attachment at one year old. They found that children in the securely attached group went on to engage in self-talk as toddlers and at six years old offered spontaneous self-reflective remarks. They also tended, more than the insecurely attached children, to be able to talk about their thinking and their memories of themselves when they were younger.[17] These practices of self-narrative and self-reflection can be understood as ways in which these children internalized their parents' right-brain self-regulation and capacities for self-reflection.

Our chronically shamed clients were not so lucky. They internalized their parents' right-brain dysregulation and their parents' difficulty with telling a coherent autobiographical narrative. Therapy gives them a second chance at telling their story. But first they have to learn how to do that, unlearning, as they go, their parents' style of autobiography. As therapists, we become their new partners in co-creating narratives that will integrate a right brain sense of self.

When we understand that our clients need to tell right-brain stories, we know that we are not in the business of co-constructing our clients' factually true histories. The stories in which they recognize themselves viscerally and emotionally are a deeper and more powerful kind of truth than history. We won't get close to that embodied emotional truth by taking a history. Often true self-story exists, untold, in networks of right-brain knowing that clients have never consciously touched in spite of years of "telling their story" in therapy.

RIGHT-BRAIN FAITH IN A RIGHT-BRAIN PROCESS

How can we help our clients discover the emotional storylines that will help them integrate a sense of self? First of all, we need to believe in the process. The test of our faith in narrative process is whether or not we have told our own childhood story well enough to have a free, autonomous relationship with our own internal narrative about our self-in-relationship. If our clients are going to co-construct new narratives that give them "earned autonomy," they need therapists who have either been given that autonomy through secure attachment or have earned that autonomy through an intensive self-reflective process.

We've noted that most therapists have to work through their personal issues of disconnection and shame in order to become effective clinicians. This is that same point from another angle. Therapists need to be in emotional possession of their own story before they can help clients tell integrative narrative. Just as children take on neural circuitry from how their parents are able to tell their own narrative, so clients take on neural circuitry from the ability therapists have to tell an emotional/relational narrative, beginning with their own.

ENGAGING WITH HOW STORIES ARE TOLD

Listening carefully to *how* our clients tell their stories tells us what help they need from us to create narrative that will further integrate a sense of self. With an *avoidant/dismissing* client, for example, it helps to be more interested in her story than she is. I'll tell Martha's story to illustrate. She was a single woman nearing eighty who had been feeling depressed since attending a "homecoming" at a church where she had been the pastor fifty years before. Her keynote speech was well-received; people had remembered her; she was so glad she had made the journey to attend. But now Martha was finding it hard to get out of bed in the morning and go about her daily tasks. A friend suggested that talking to someone might help. Martha didn't believe she was in need of any psychological help, but as a favor to her friend she gave me a call.

Instead of focusing on the symptoms of her depression, I asked Martha to tell me about that parish and her work there fifty years ago. I asked how she had come to be a pastor, and I heard about her magnificent preacher father and her wonderfully capable mother, pillars of every farming community they served, especially through the lean years of the Depression on the prairies. I learned that there was no room for self-pity in the family. There were younger sickly siblings who needed more care than my sturdy, competent client did. Martha worked to send money home for them, and then she worked to put herself through college and seminary.

I didn't question Martha's idealizing picture of her parents. I didn't ask her directly how she felt about any of the events she recalled. But I let my face and tone of voice show my feelings in response to the emotions that moved under the surface of her storytelling. Where her story was thin, I asked for details; where it was flat, I wondered about complexities. In all my wondering, I was letting Martha know that in her stories, *she* mattered to me—the responsible big sister, the lonely working girl, the scared, brave novice pastor driving alone through blizzards between the churches of her three-point charge. I saw her emotional self in her stories. When she told me about a relationship, I tried to grasp how important it was to her—usually more than she said, often more than she knew.

I asked how Martha had come to leave ministry. She told me that it had been just too difficult, and that in the end teaching suited her better. She had loved to see good students light up reading good literature, and she cared about her "bad students" too. Some of them would talk to her about their lives at home, their troubles. It was another kind of ministry, she said. I heard that she had made peace with the change in her life, but I also heard sad resignation in her voice.

I gently but persistently pursued the relational/emotional story her right brain was speaking to me without words. We talked every week for months. I heard many more stories about her northern rural pastoral charge, more about what frightened and exhausted her there, more about what everyday folks expected of their pastor, and more about their kindness, too. I learned that Martha had a drawer full of notes she'd made about her life back then. She was thinking of putting them in order, maybe getting some help writing a memoir.

Finally I heard more about how Martha had come to leave ministry. When the second long winter had ended, her father came to visit. He heard her preach in three places, and stayed with her in the rough cabin that served as "manse." On leaving he looked at her intently, with love and with anger that she didn't understand, and he said, "It's wrong what they're doing!" That was all he said. Later she understood that he was talking about church politics: giving the married men who had graduated with Martha the more prosperous, one-church charges, and sending her, a single woman, to manage an outpost charge alone. Martha did understand, as the days grew dark the next winter, that there would be a place for her at home if she decided to leave her work in the north.

Martha did leave and go home. She and her father never had a conversation about her leaving. No one asked her whether she was upset, sad, or angry. She spent a long time in bed; it seems her family believed she needed a long time to recover from the physical ordeal of the work. She told me that she lost track of time. Then one day she got up and decided to put her failure behind her. It was spring, or maybe summer. She took all of the sermons she had written and burned them on the trash pile in the back garden. No one ever knew that she did that. But then she was ready to go on with her life.

This part of her story made me very sad, and I said so. I said it was an important part of the whole, long story, and I noticed the connection between her staying in bed that winter and staying in bed after the "homecoming" journey. Then Martha saw the connection, too. I wished aloud that she and her father could have talked about what happened to her, about what it meant and how it felt to her to leave ministry. "Yes," she said. "I think he would have understood. But he's been gone now for years. I miss him." Martha allowed that her story was sad, but she didn't cry. That wasn't her way.

Martha and I came to agree that "failure" wasn't the right word for what had happened to her those many years ago. What they had done *was* wrong, as her father had said. She decided to make copies of her notes from her time in the outpost charge and send them to be filed in the archives of the national church offices. A few weeks later, she told me that talking about all that history had seemed to help. Since she was feeling better, it didn't make sense to her to keep coming just to talk—even though she really enjoyed our conversations. I told her I really enjoyed our conversations, too—and that the best part was getting to know *her*, the person who'd lived and felt all those stories.

To be able to connect with the right-brain, emotional essence of her self-narrative, Martha needed to hear her own stories, and to hear them she needed help telling them. Other clients, those with an *ambivalent/preoccupied* style of attachment and of storytelling, don't need any drawing out from us. Stories spill out from them in many directions, with the pressure of disorganized, conflictual emotions behind them. When Ellen tells me stories, for example, either from the past or from the present, they feel more like furious protests and desperate cries for help than coherent narratives. So my first task is not to be overwhelmed by the emotion flying at me. I try to make sense of what's happening for her by listening for the emotional themes that are driving her stories.

I listen, but I don't say much. I know that she expects me to ignore her personal boundaries and impose my needs on her—my need to be heard, perhaps, or my need to be right. Her mother ran roughshod over her like that. I have to be different from her mother; I have to listen to stories (and tell them) differently than her mother did. With Ellen, affect regulation means taking in the intense, ambivalent emotions that drive her stories, holding them, making sense of them, and then, when she's feeling calmer, giving them back to her as *hers*, as a story in which her intentions, her emotions, and her self are seen clearly and compassionately. I can do that only when, unlike her mother, I'm able to be free from preoccupation and enmeshment with my own feelings while I'm with her.

When, in addition to the kind of insecurity that plagues Ellen, a client has frightening, *disorganizing* attachment experience in her background, her stories come to us in fragments, with affect that doesn't match the fragments. Nothing really fits, and we feel disoriented just listening. Here, too, our first mode of listening is just to contain what we hear. But now we're holding in order to "make safe," not yet to "make sense."

For a very long time in my work with Susie, I heard bits of what happened to her when she was young, but we didn't put it together. Mostly she wanted to talk about her daily life: her boyfriend, her part-time job, her many pets. But every time something went wrong in her life and she fell into acute, self-harming shame, a fragment of an abuse story would emerge. Then I needed just to stay present and available to feel Susie's fear and pain; my containing response to her intense emotions made them less overwhelming.

As Susie came to trust me, she spent many therapy hours reading to me from her journals, both past and present. She would read about terrible feelings in a flat monotone voice, but at least the feelings were there in the room and in the pages of her writing. Eventually she found that she could talk about what she had written. Then sometimes she remembered things she hadn't remembered before. Bit by bit her emotions and the story took shapes she could recognize.

Susie began to know what she felt because I was feeling something of what she felt and letting her see my feeling. Her self-narrative began to hold together for her as I was able to hold her terror within myself while remaining present, organized, and stable. With clients like Susie, who suffer from disorganized as well as insecure attachment, non-verbal, sustained right-brain *being-with* creates the essential non-verbal self-coherence that in time can be integrated into a verbal narrative.

Avoidant/dismissing, *ambivalent/preoccupied*, and *disorganized*: these are just three typical styles in which clients tell us an incoherent narrative, signs of an incoherent sense of self. What matters is not the type into which the stories fit; as with attachment itself, mixed types of narrative are common. What matters is that we are listening to our clients in a way that's different from the particular kind of non-listening that created the incoherence in the first place. Our clients find new ways to tell their story just because of our listening, and our listening is grounded, of course, in the right-brain empathic attunement and non-verbal connection we discussed in the last chapter.

MENTALIZING THE TELLER IN THE STORY

The accuracy of the plotlines and details in a client's narrative is beside the point. It's a mistake to become invested in a story for its own sake. Client narratives can be expected to shift and change over time. What matters is the coherence of our client's narrating self; this right-brain connection-making self is what we are attuning to as we engage with the self's story. Developing co-created narrative is an expanded form of mentalizing with our client. Holding a client's mind in our mind also means holding his stories in our mind, and especially his right-brain ways of feeling and telling his stories.

We use a narrative process to mentalize when we let a dismissing client know that we see a lost, lonely child in his stories of growing up and that we hear that child's voice in how he tells his story now. With preoccupied clients, whose stories are bursting with unprocessed conflicting emotions, we contain the emotion and help the client to reflect on (to mentalize) what it feels like, right now, to tell the story. Disorganized clients desperately need us to hold their trauma narrative—not the details, but the affective reality of it—in our emotional mind. As we let them know that we can feel their fearful chaos in how they tell their story, they can absorb the possibility of mentalizing from us and eventually find their way to a more coherent sense of self through a more coherent narrative.

Holding our clients' minds in mind is right-brain work, even though our imaginations are fed by the theoretical (left-brain) stories we believe about trauma and self-development, psychotherapy and healing. As we notice particular attachment styles in how our clients are able to tell their stories, we imagine ourselves into a probable attachment history. Then, when we respond from that understanding, we are mentalizing the storyteller in a very particular way. Our mentalization is a story we have constructed out of knowing them, a reflection of the workings of their minds as we hold their minds in mind.

We never tell our clients what actually happened to them or what their stories "really mean." Likewise, we hold lightly our mentalization of how their minds work. If co-created narrative is to be an expansive form of mentalizing, whatever we suggest from our side must seek to match what our clients already "know," even if that knowing hasn't yet taken shape. Our mentalizing involvement with their stories must enact our empathic curiosity, not our knowing. Instead of closing down options, our reflective narrative bent must encourage our clients' self-reflection, opening space for them to play with what they know, space where new self-coherence may coalesce on its own.

PROCESS, NOT CONTENT

Narrative fosters integration, not because the stories told are accurate histories, but because they enact the teller's agency and capacity to tell. When the telling is freely chosen, it can integrate pain and joy, pride and regret, relief and resignation. Our clients may need our help to find the links that feel emotionally true to them, but they have to feel their own visceral "*yes*" for any part of any new story to be *theirs*. When they make the link themselves, they feel their capacity to tell and to possess emotional truth. The best in-depth narratives in the world won't help them feel like more whole, true selves if they are our stories *for* them, if the telling is our doing, not theirs.

And so we practice the art of eliciting and co-creating narrative as naturally as possible. The therapy conversation follows our clients' agendas and our clients' flow of thought and feeling while we remain alert for chances to expand the process. A client might be talking about being afraid he made a mistake at work, for example, and we might find a quiet moment to be curious about what happened when he was a kid and made a mistake. We wait to see if the narrative line we throw gets picked up, and if not, that's okay.

It's his story, not ours. We'll at least have dropped the subliminal clue that we think it's always worth pursuing more story than meets the eye.

Chronically shamed clients know things, but they can't put them together in ways that make emotional sense. In fact, the bits and pieces of their stories are disconnected precisely because "emotional sense" isn't available to them. Right-brain regulation, creating connectivity between emotion, memory, and sense of self, makes the process of coherent storytelling possible. Right-brain dysregulation, by contrast, actively blocks connectivity, and also the process of emotional/relational storytelling. It's not just that our shamed clients lack the linking skills to tell a coherent story; it's also that something tells them it would be dangerous to know it. This warning comes from a visceral right-brain place, likely from fear they absorbed from a parent's visceral aversion to emotional/relational knowing and being known.

That's why, until we've developed a secure foundation of attunement with our clients, their storytelling won't become a more authentic, integrating process for them. Our clients need to feel that our co-creation of narrative is part of our deep, responsive attunement to them. As we earn their trust, we tread carefully in this narrative process, not intruding, not imposing, and always aware that the process of telling true stories is risky. Emergency is inherent in the telling; the ground shifts as strange new feelings and exciting, scary possibilities emerge. Our job is to make this risky process of storytelling a *safe* emergency.

ON SHARING WHAT WE KNOW

We intend to help our clients integrate affect and become stronger selves from the inside out. At the same time, we "co-create," sharing what we know, see, wonder, and imagine. This can feel like a tricky business. For example, how do we question or even highlight the negative things our clients say to themselves without breaking empathy with their self-experience? Is it wise to speak about patterns we see in our clients' present behaviors, or to suggest that a current pattern may be connected to past experience? Isn't it best to wait until they see patterns and connections for themselves so that they can have the "aha" moments, the self-consolidation of discovering and telling their own story?

Questions like these have no easy answers. As therapists we always hold a delicate balance between the wise use of our expertise on the one hand, and our responsibility to foster our clients' development in their own terms, on the other. This balance can be maintained in a practice that first invites clients to tell whatever events, feelings, troubles, or stories they want to tell, and then engages with this narrative in ways that understand, expand, and integrate it. The model for this way of "helping" is in how parents co-create a child's narrative, sharing what they know non-intrusively and non-coercively in order to foster the child's own integration.

As we've seen, securely attached children are good at developing their own coherent stories. There is also a strong correlation between parents' coherent self-narrative and their ability to support secure attachment in their children. Summarizing a study of the relationship between infant security and reflective self-functioning in parents, the researchers comment:

"The caregiver who manifests this capacity [self-reflexivity] at its maximum will be the most likely to be able to respect the child's vulnerable emerging psychological world and reduce to a minimum the occasions on which the child needs to make recourse to primitive defensive behaviour characteristic of insecure attachment."[18]

In other words, a parent who has an integrated self-narrative, a parent who knows from the inside how self-story "works," will be, of all parents, best able to help his child tell her own story. He will also be the least likely to intrude on that story—on his child's sense of self—with his own needs and emotions, or his own story *for* the child.

We are not the parents of our adult clients, and they are not children. However, if we have done the work on our own narrative that undergirds a practice of relational psychotherapy, we bring to our clients our capacity for reflective self-functioning, along with the implicit claim, "I am a well-enough grounded and coherent self to help you with this." As a relationship develops between us, our clients come to know what we embody of how to regulate emotion and negotiate relationship. When they can feel the trustworthiness of this implicit story, they will also trust our attempts to help shape their narrative in more explicit ways—as long as our attempts fit. And as self-aware "parents," we are always looking for the fit. This is especially true when we are looking for ways to help our clients face and work through their chronic shame, born of profound mis-fit.

NOTES

1. Louis Cozolino, *The Neuroscience of Psychotherapy: Healing the Social Brain*, 2nd edn. (New York: Norton, 2012), 26.

2. Daniel Siegel, *The Mindful Brain: Reflection and Attunement in the Cultivation of Well-Being* (New York: Norton, 2007), 46.

3. Daniel Siegel, *The Developing Mind: How Relationships and the Brain Interact to Shape Who We Are* (New York: Guilford, 1999), 32–327.

4. Cozolino, *Neuroscience of Psychotherapy*, 110.

5. Bonnie Badenoch, *Being a Brain-Wise Therapist: A Practical Guide to Interpersonal Neurobiology*, (New York: Norton, 2008), 33–35.

6. Badenoch, *Brain-Wise Therapist*, 195; Siegel, *Mindful Brain*, 309.

7. Schore, *The Science of the Art of Psychotherapy*, (New York: Norton, 2012), 296.

8. Schore, *Science of the Art*, 294.

9. Donald Stuss and Michael Alexander, "Affectively Burnt-In: One Role of the Right Frontal Lobe?" in *Memory, Consciousness, and the Brain: The Talin Conference*, ed. Endel Tulving (Philadelphia, PA: Psychology Press, 1999), 223, cited in Schore, *Science of the Art*, 296.

10. Siegel, *Developing Mind*, 331–33.

11. Cozolino, *Neuroscience of Psychotherapy*, 168–69.

12. Cozolino, *Neuroscience of Psychotherapy*, 170–73.

13. Cozolino, *Neuroscience of Psychotherapy*, 22.

14. For discussions of how attachment theory and neurobiological theory inform each other see the following: Siegel, *Developing Mind*, 67–120; Badenoch, *Brain-Wise Therapist*, 52–75; Cozolino, "Building the Social Brain: Shaping Attachment Schemas," and "The Neurobiology of Attachment," in *Neuroscience of Psychotherapy*, 197–236.

15. Carol George, Nancy Kaplan, and Mary Main, The Adult Attachment Interview (Berkeley, CA: University of California at Berkeley, unpublished manuscript, 1985); Mary

Main and Ruth Goldwyn, Adult Attachment Scoring and Classification System (Berkeley, CA: University of California at Berkeley, unpublished manuscript, 1998). *The Adult Attachment Interview* can be reviewed online: Mary B. Main, "Adult Attachment Interview Protocol," available from http://www.psychology.sunysb.edu/attachment/measures/content/aai_interview. pdf; accessed January 18, 2014.

16. Cozolino, *Neuroscience of Psychotherapy*, 208.

17. Mary Main, Nancy Kaplan, and Jude Cassidy, "Security in Infancy, Childhood, and Adulthood: A Move to the Level of Representation," in *Growing Points of Attachment Theory and Research, Monographs of the Society for Research in Child Development* 50 (Chicago: University of Chicago Press, 1985), eds. Inge Bretherton and Everett Waters: 66–104.

18. Peter Fonagy et al., "The Capacity to Understand Mental States: The Reflective Self in Parent and Child and Its Significance for Security of Attachment," *Infant Mental Health Journal* 12 (1991): 208, cited in Cozolino, *Neuroscience of Psychotherapy*, 208.

CHAPTER 9

Giving Shame Light and Air

We have come to a third chapter about treating chronic shame, and we still have not discussed how to address shame explicitly in therapy. We have talked about creating an emotionally attuned, non-shaming therapeutic relationship with chronically shamed clients. We have discussed helping clients tell stories that integrate emotional and relational selfhood. In both of these ways we hope to bring connectivity to their dysfunctional right-brain neural networks. Awareness of right-brain disconnection and shame shapes our entire conversation—but we are approaching work with shame obliquely, not directly . . . not yet.

So it goes in therapy. It may take a long time of building trust, working through relational misses and repairs, and co-creating narrative before clients are able to identify and speak about the ugly secret they keep under deep cover, the shame feelings that erupt from time to time when they feel wrong and disgusting to someone. When that someone is us, they'll be especially reticent about what shame does to them.

When clients finally speak of the pain and destruction that shame wreaks in their lives, they often ask, "Can anything make this better?" I often respond, "Shame needs light and air." This answer seems to make intuitive sense to them. I'm not the only therapist to find this a useful metaphor. As Shapiro and Powers discuss how group therapy can help resolve participants' shame, they write: "The most natural response to the experience of shame (i.e., to hide) is the most toxic, whereas the least automatic or natural (i.e., to expose the source of the shame) is the most healing. As the old adage goes, one needs to 'let the air get at it.' It is only when shame reaches the light of day that the healing process can begin. The presence of others allows in that light of day."[1]

The presence of others helps only if clients know those others won't further shame or blame them for their suffering. Our clients need to be able to trust that we will understand them from inside their story, not judge or criticize them from the outside. Only then does it become useful for us to speak of light and air for shame.

When we speak this metaphor, we tell our clients we are comfortable being in company with what they feel is loathsome. We communicate implicitly that we are not afraid of shame in general or of our own shame; we can help regulate this. Recommending light and air also signals our belief in a narrative of healing, not of doing, and our commitment to a healing process that takes place naturally when wounds are attended to properly. This settles anxiety too; the last thing chronically shamed clients need is something else to do (that they can't do) to make themselves feel better.

Of course, by the time a client asks, "Can anything make this better?" shame is already in the open. The first question of this chapter is: How do we bring shame into the light? How can we make safe space in therapy for shame to be identified and spoken?

BRINGING SHAME INTO THE LIGHT

When we discussed assessing for shame, we noted the clues of shame clients give us, from their posture and manner of speech to their need to control the therapy situation. It is one thing to notice the clues, however, and quite another to let clients know that we can hear their unspoken shame, and to do so in ways that cause no further shame.

Clinicians who write about treating shame disagree about whether using the term "shame" is necessary for treating it effectively.[2] I think it's a matter of sensitivity and timing, and that pushing the word "shame" early is probably a bad idea. That's because shame, most essentially, is our clients' experience that their needs to be understood by a connected, caring other cannot and will not be met. They have no idea it could be any different with us. This relational deprivation has become personal pain that is just a given, something to live around. When we speak of shame, we expose something they try not to know or feel, something they believe cannot be helped, and our "help" may cause the very fragmentation of which we speak.

So we don't expose our clients' shame; we protect them from fragmentation. We create right-brain connection with them, using affect attunement, empathic curiosity, and our best story-making skills. We create a relationship where emotional understanding becomes possible. But what then? Does relational psychotherapy tell us how we might make it more tolerable for our clients finally to speak their shame and work through it directly?

With its specialty in issues of narcissism, self psychology would seem to be a modality of choice for treating chronic shame. Self psychologists offer support, understanding, and insight to clients who suffer from profound forms of self-fragmentation and depletion. But in its classic form, self psychology may still fall short of what shamed clients need from their therapists. Shamed clients need their therapists to take a stance that involves more than empathic immersion and empathic interpretation.[3] They need to feel the person of the therapist within and behind her empathy. After a lifetime of profound disconnection (often with others who *seem* to be in connection while staying out), they can't simply trust the authenticity of their therapist's presence. Chronically shamed clients need interaction and engagement with their therapist so that they can feel her as an embodied, emotional human being.

Self-in-relation therapists and interpersonal/relational psychoanalysts call this contactful quality of therapy "mutuality." They also call it the essence of a meaningful, useful therapeutic relationship.[4] Diana Fosha, a relationalist and proponent of interpersonal neurobiology, suggests that there are two important strands in the parent/child and the client/therapist connection: the *attachment* strand, providing empathy and affect regulation, and the *intersubjective* strand, in which "the therapist's delight *in* and *with* the patient is a powerful antidote to his or her shame."[5] This important intersubjective strand of connection is expressed through "mutuality."

The most powerful therapy for shame is one that provides both attachment connection and intersubjective connection, both attuned affect regulation and the lively contact of mutuality.

Self psychology teaches a powerful practice of empathic attunement and it offers a profound, complex understanding of how affect can be regulated through selfobject experience, both in childhood and in transference. Can self psychology also be practiced with lively engagement and deep interpersonal contact?

Connectedness

The answer is *Yes*, if we listen to Richard Geist, a self psychologist who brings empathic immersion and mutual contact together in what he calls *connectedness*. According to Geist, the heart of every self psychological treatment is the client's need for connectedness. This is more than a need for the therapist to provide "one way" empathic attunement. Connectedness is mutual empathic understanding between the interpenetrating selves of client and therapist, so that each is a strongly felt presence in the other's life. In connectedness, mutual empathy creates mutual implicit knowing of each other's being, a powerful, mutually affective bond between two people.[6]

As he describes our essential need for connectedness, Geist touches on what shamed clients missed in childhood: the dance of *mutual emotional engagement* between child and parent that creates a lively, whole, and secure self. Shamed clients never had a chance at this sustained connectedness. The absence of mutual connection was where their chronic shame started, and that absence continues. They bring this absence and longing when they bring shame to therapy.

In self psychological therapy according to Geist, we invite these clients not only into our empathic understanding but also into mutual emotional connection with us. When this connectedness is the heart of treatment, the therapy will naturally create mutually experienced selfobject transferences that lead the client toward health.[7] I have noted that having selfobject experiences with us is one of the ways our chronically shamed clients get a second chance at the right-brain regulation they missed when they were younger. Merging Geist's perspective with mine, we can see that this form of affective regulation happens within connectedness. The selfobject transferences of mutual connectedness regulate a self who becomes better able to self-regulate and less fragmented and diminished by shame.

Geist suggests that three kinds of engagement are important for developing connectedness: mutual empathy, nurturing the tendrils of selfobject transferences as they emerge, and interpreting from inside the client's world.[8] The first two belong to the implicit treatment of shame. As we know, mutual empathy is a form of resonance that creates right-brain connectivity. Providing selfobject experience is also an enacted, mostly subliminal response to unmet emotional need that comes our way. But "interpreting from inside the client's world" gives us, finally, some direction about speaking directly to shame and inviting shame itself to come into the light.

Interpreting from inside the Shamed Client's World

Self psychology has always understood a client's symptoms and defenses as efforts to maintain his self-cohesion. When a client enters therapy guardedly, a self psychologist understands this resistance as necessary; the client needs to protect his self-organization from being re-traumatized in this new relationship. Even as trust slowly takes on substance in the form of selfobject transference, selfobject failure will cause him to fragment. When this happens, the self psychologist interprets from within the client's experience of having been misunderstood and let down, believing that repairing the empathic connection will bring the client back into cohesion.

Geist shifts the focus of this picture in a simple but profound way. At the dynamic center of every client's world, he maintains, is a hidden but powerful drive toward health—health understood not as cohesion but as connectedness. And so interpretation must always be in the service of restoring connectedness. Geist might say that if we take care of connectedness, cohesion will take care of itself. I would say that if we take care of the client's experience of connectedness, we take care of the client's experience of shame—the fragmentation caused by disconnectedness.

With his eye for connectedness, Geist adds another dimension to the self psychological understanding of resistance, too. Clients resist trusting the therapy process when they experience it as disconnecting. This kind of resistance happens far more often than we expect because despite our best efforts at empathy, therapy often feels to clients (especially to chronically shamed clients) like a place where they are evaluated and objectified "in treatment." That's how they often experience our empathic listening—as shame-inducing disconnection.

Yet, with their unconscious drive for connectedness, our clients also clutch at any chance to make of us something that matches their need. So in spite of their anxious mistrust, they come back. More stories are told; mutual engagement and interpenetrating connections happen; selfobject transferences germinate. *Connectedness* begins to happen!

And we begin to "interpret." We begin to reflect back to our clients our tentative understanding of their emotional experience. If we follow Geist's lead, we will understand that the distress our chronically shamed clients feel is not just about feeling misunderstood or undervalued. It's more than their struggle to carry on with a self that has far too many missing pieces. It runs deeper than their compulsion to perform, the rigid ways they ward off failure, or the destructive things they do to keep themselves from falling apart.

These are all aspects of their distress, but most fundamentally, their pain is about wanting connectedness and having no reliable way to make that happen. This sense of our shamed clients' core dilemma is what we hold in mind for them. Our interpretive responses implicitly and explicitly build this shared understanding of the connectedness they long for and just "know" they can't have.

With my client Ellen, for example, whose obsession with perfect performance is all that protects her from falling into utter worthlessness, it's essential for me to remember that her moments of shining in her mother's eyes were her best moments of connection. These days it may seem that a need to be special is behind her compulsion to compare herself to others and then to spiral down into abject shame. But really, what's behind her constant striving is her longing for connectedness. When she shares yet another failure to prove herself worthy with peers and colleagues, I can respond, "I wonder if what you want most of all is connection with them, like you belong with them in a way you can feel."

If, when I speak, Ellen can feel my compassionate connectedness with her, she may be able to sit still for a moment and feel the truth and pain of her longing for connection. If she touches that truth and cringes away, I may tell her that there's no shame in needing connectedness; it's what makes us human, what makes us whole and well. And then the "shame" word would be out—exactly where it belongs, where connectedness should be and never could be.

If Ellen can feel how her need to be special is driven by her heart's desire for connection, she may become able to grieve her real losses. Failure isn't the core of her shame; at the core of her shame is an absence—the absence of connectedness. She doesn't know what it feels like to be known and loved for herself, to "matter" in her being and in her being-with. This absence is what she needs to feel and to grieve. In this grieving process, which integrates split-off emotional pain, she might find some relief from her compulsion to perform. From a more integrated place, she might find herself able to trust connectedness—with others and with me—in ways that aren't yet possible for her.

For Ellen, it's also essential that I understand the turbulent times in our relationship as times when our tentative mutual connectedness is failing her and she's doing whatever she can to get it back. Geist describes such turbulence like this: "Resistance tends to occur when an analyst, though attuned to the patient's experience, does not allow himself to be included in the patient's self-structure, molded and shaped according to what the patient metaphorically needs him to be."[9]

From this perspective, we can understand even angry demands as a client's healthy attempt to maintain the particular kind of connectedness she needs. And we can certainly interpret from this perspective. For example, when Ellen tells me that nothing I do helps her, I can say, "I'm wondering whether I've done or said something to make you feel disconnected from me right now." Whatever her answer is and wherever we go with it, this interpretative lead isn't likely to be felt as evaluative, blaming, or shaming, especially since it rests on my unspoken belief that her desire for connectedness is her movement toward health. Instead, it communicates my understanding that she's in distress because something has happened between us that prevents her from getting a legitimate, valuable need met.

Making Our Emotional Selves Available

Yet none of this may reach Ellen when she's in an active state of shame. Repair may not be possible until I can find a way to continue in a self-disclosing direction, beginning with something like, "I'm thinking about my part in it—when I might have disconnected." I may share a moment when I was distracted or my defensiveness flared up. Or I might not know what happened for me, and I can ask what she noticed.

Geist strongly recommends this final step: that in moments of repairing connection, we disclose our here-and-now experience of the relationship and our thoughts about how we might have come to disconnect from the relationship momentarily. This is the natural outcome of Geist's belief that empathy is most therapeutically useful when it expands into mutual connectedness, permeable boundaries, and an interpenetration of selves.[10] These moments following rupture are perhaps the most important moments to put a "connectedness" principle into practice, especially when working with chronically shamed clients.

Self psychology has always taught us to understand a client's experience of empathic failure from inside his world. When there's a break between us, we say genuinely, "What you feel about what I did makes sense, and I can understand how it hurts you. There's nothing wrong with you or with your experience." It seems this should be exactly what it takes to resolve a client's shame about a rupture. But in such an exchange, we remain invisible behind the function of our understanding. And behind each rupture a client experiences, there's shame that exists as a client's unmet, intense need to *feel* us in a personal way. Chronically shamed clients need for their therapists to take a further step—from, "There's nothing wrong with you," to, "I'm feeling the rupture, too, and I'm wondering who I am in it," or as Geist would put it, "You are a felt presence in my being, as I am in yours."

Furthermore, when relational rupture is met by, "I wonder what was going on with me when that happened," chronically shamed clients can no longer assume that when a relationship doesn't work it's because there's something wrong with them. Clearly, "wrong" can be elsewhere, and if it's with a therapist who thinks about it with calm, connecting curiosity, "wrong" loses its devastating knock-out punch. Over time and with many repetitions, our clients' general experience of relational rupture can become less of a cliff edge of "something's terribly wrong" and more of a chance to repair a misunderstanding.

As we repair rupture by honoring our clients' need for mutual connectedness, there's opportunity to notice with them how their feelings of shame subside. There's time to talk with them about what they feared and expected would happen. We can explore what it feels like when their need for connectedness feels wrong, and they feel deeply wrong for having it. We can notice the force that demands punishment for need and vulnerability, and we can call it shame.

When we finally get to these conversations, we're no longer dealing with a wave of self-disgust that has just obliterated our clients' sense of coherence and value. Shame is not what's happening here and now; it's what happened earlier, or almost happened, or what would have happened had relational events gone as the clients expected. From a here-and-now, non-shamed place of connectedness, clients can look into the shadows, put the name of shame to the dark force lurking there, and call it into the light. What happens next may be unpleasant and take further work, but it won't be annihilating.

HONESTY AND DIPLOMACY

We help clients call their shame into the light because we believe that when they can know and feel what's hurting them, they can heal. The "light and air" metaphor is especially apt for the concealed emotion of shame, but it holds true for all painful emotions. Disconnecting from anger, grief, or fear isn't good for our clients' emotional health either. Being able to integrate a range of difficult emotions into a conscious, balanced, resilient sense of self is a key component of emotional and psychological well-being.

But shame is particularly difficult to own. And so we bring our diplomacy skills to the therapy room. As long as clients can feel the emotion and talk about it in some way, they don't need to put the label of *shame* on what they feel. What matters is the essence of the feeling. We can empathize with the pain of longing and not receiving. We can recognize the bleak and utter conviction that "something is just so wrong with me!" We can notice how terribly hard it is for clients to need something from someone. In short, even as we're honest in our responses to our chronically shamed clients, helping them bring their pained vulnerability into the light, we can also steer clear of the word *shame* for as long as necessary.

Sometimes there are strong reasons to be extremely careful with the word *shame*. Some abused and tortured clients have suffered humiliation that is more than a person can bear to describe. Judith Herman quotes Cloitre, Cohen, and Koenen on helping clients deal with such narratives of shame:

> In the same way that narratives of fear must be titrated so that the client experiences mastery over fear rather than a reinstatement of it, so too narratives of shame should be titrated so that the client experiences dignity rather than humiliation in the telling.[11]

Even when humiliation does not appear to be the storyline of a traumatized client's history, the profound relational violations of physical, emotional, or sexual abuse will have thrown the client, as a child, into extreme and catastrophic states of shame, felt as intense self-disgust and self-hatred. Those states of shame live on, and when they are aroused in adult life, they can feel extreme and catastrophic once again. We don't want our clients to be re-traumatized by catastrophic shame experiences, and yet we know that completely dissociating their shame will block integration. Since we want to help them integrate their experiences of shame as well as of trauma, we introduce shame delicately and with substitute words that aren't as strong—for example, feeling *silly, dumb, weak, small, worthless, uncomfortable,* or *embarrassed*. In this way feelings of shame can become part of the clients' stories, material that can be explored again as the feelings become more tolerable and speakable within a deepening therapy relationship.[12]

With some clients it's not so clear why *shame* is a dangerous word. But the danger is signaled by the intensity of what masks or disguises their shame, whether the alternative state is one of judgment, envy, hostility, or grandiosity. If such states come and go, we may still have chances to help our clients speak what they feel about their own needs and vulnerabilities. But if one of those states has become their personality style, we will have to accept that theirs is a story of shame that can't be told for now. Here diplomacy means not speaking something that can't be heard and that will only put the therapeutic relationship at risk.

By "diplomacy" I mean what we do to be genuinely present with our clients while making constant small decisions about what will help them the most. With some of our clients it feels right not to insist on too much reality. However, if our diplomacy slips into dishonesty, the therapy relationship will suffer, and we will fail to be helpful. We do our clients harm if we protect them from the reality of shame when they could face and integrate it.

When our clients are able to feel their shame, letting the light and air get at it, we must stay honestly present with them. We have to encourage them to feel this most difficult emotion when what we want to say is: *No, you are not ugly or worthless. No, I have never experienced you as selfish or stupid.* Of course we would like to convince them that they are worthy, lovable persons. Instead, we must help them push through the language of *ugly, stupid,* and *worthless* to the even more painful feelings of deep shame, feelings of not mattering at all to anyone, feelings of needing someone and finding no one, and feelings of disintegration and annihilation.

Within safe connectedness, our chronically shamed clients can touch that reality again. We need to trust that this is their best way, perhaps their only way, out of *ugly, stupid,* and *worthless*. When a client sobs, "I . . . don't . . . matter!" we need to reply, with quiet, steady presence, "Yes, that's how it is for you inside. That's truly what you feel. It's just awful. It just hurts."

There will come a time for us to say, "You matter now!" But first the shame must be experienced for what it is. And in fact there's no better way to let our shamed clients know that they matter now—to us—than to take their shame seriously enough to feel it with them. We invalidate their need to be fully understood if we try to "make it better" to protect them or to protect ourselves. But we can help them feel that their wounded self matters deeply if they can feel our deep intention to stay a difficult course with them, this process of owning and integrating their lonely, disintegrating experience of shame.

TEACHING ABOUT SHAME

Giving clients some basic information about shame can make it easier for them to bring their shame into the light where they can see it and feel it. It often helps them to hear that shame is probably the most painful emotion human beings can feel, and that not only does it feel excruciating, it's so disconnecting and isolating that it can go on for a very long time without anyone noticing—except the person who feels the shame.

Hearing that shame is an experience common to humanity helps relieve the loneliness of our shamed clients and ease the shame they feel about feeling shame. Hearing shame defined as an emotion helps normalize it for them. We might add that like other emotions, shame is a response to something that happened, and it needs the same kind of attention that sadness, for example, needs so that it doesn't become a chronic, draining feeling. We might say, "To get over shame, we have to feel back in connection with people who love us."

I always welcome a chance to talk with clients about the difference between shame and guilt. When clients tell me that they feel a lot of guilt in their lives, I'll ask if they feel they've done something wrong. If they're puzzled, I explain where I'm coming from: "I think guilt is about something we've *done*; if we feel bad about who we *are*, I think that's *shame*. With guilt we can say we're sorry and make amends, but shame is a lot more complicated to fix." Most clients understand this difference quickly and intuitively. And I have let them know that I'm as comfortable talking about shame as about guilt. I have spoken the unspeakable word, with an invitation to join me in discussing shame whenever they can.

If shame becomes speakable, we can link the emotion of shame to events in our clients' stories of daily life, noting, for instance, the difference between experiences of shame that are repaired in relationship and those that are not repaired, and the difference between shame that's a learning experience and shame that's an annihilating experience. Bit by bit, we can also share with these clients what we believe about the origins of chronic shame. As they tell their stories, they will notice patterns in their personal feelings and their responses to other people. They may wonder how shame just "took over." That's when we might make available to our clients some of what we know about the generation of shame in family systems.[13]

ELICITING FAMILY SHAME NARRATIVES

Family systems theory outlines major topics related to shame, but in the spirit of open-minded curiosity and playful co-creation, I don't teach clients about these topics. Instead, I wait for a moment to ask a "topical" question. To keep things open-ended and to create space where events and emotions can be linked, I usually ask my questions in the form of "*What happened when . . .?*"

Stories about Conversations

If my clients are finding it difficult to talk in therapy, I may ask, "What happened when people in your family had conversations?" Some clients answer that question with a laugh: "*What* conversations!" They don't remember anything that could be called conversation.

So I might be more specific: "What was it like around the dinner table when you were eight or ten?" Whether we begin there or on a family vacation, a client and I discover a story about communication in his family. I ask some basic questions: Were his family members open about what they felt and wanted? Were they good at listening? I might say that communication can fail in two ways: when people don't say what they mean and when people don't listen.

Clients may mention family members who always said what they meant—"and made other people feel like dirt!" I will answer: "I don't think that counts as being honest. Making somebody *be* bad because you *feel* bad is hiding how you feel. Blaming is a tricky, dishonest move, and it causes huge shame in families."

There are other ways family members avoid saying what they feel. People hide behind silence or behind a lot of pleasant chatter. Maybe nobody wants to talk because nobody will listen. Maybe people are afraid to get hurt. It's hard to speak up if you think the others will ignore you or attack you. And you can't listen while you're preparing your defense or counter-attack.

As my clients and I wonder what was going on in their family to make conversation so dangerous and impossible, they come to see what *did* get communicated: (1) who I am and what I feel doesn't matter, and (2) communicating doesn't work. We can see how these conclusions lead to isolation and despair—the core experience of chronic shame.

Stories about Emotions

When I ask, "What happened when people in your family had emotions?" I'm asking about affect regulation. People who struggle with chronic shame usually report that emotions were either shut down or out of control in their family. Often clamp-downs led to explosions, followed by more silence. Or somebody in the family was always in danger of going "out of control," and everybody else tried to keep it from happening. In short, when people had emotions, what happened was some kind of emergency or emergency shut-down.

Against this background, I ask clients questions that offer clues about what might have been. I ask whether anybody in their family could say "I feel . . ." to somebody else. I wonder whether their parents helped them learn to name sad or angry feelings when they were little. Can they remember a time when a parent was there in a calming way, even though he or she couldn't fix a problem? Were there times when their parents were upset themselves and talked about what they were feeling?

When I ask about "feeling-talk," I am also asking about how my clients' families handled emotional vulnerability. I might say: Most families don't have trouble explaining facts or giving directions to each other. But many families have trouble talking about feelings like sadness, fear, or shame. Sharing so-called "negative emotions" makes people feel vulnerable. It feels like weakness to say, "I feel sad," or "I feel scared." Even to say, "I feel angry with you," (instead of yelling and blaming) is being vulnerable.

I tell my clients that emotions make us feel vulnerable because they come from our core self. In our emotions, we feel alive and real, even when what we feel is painful or disturbing. If we have no help learning to care for our own emotions—if we feel abandoned or annihilated in that vulnerable place—we will feel that there's something wrong with us in our core being. After a while, just having emotions will make us feel like *"there must be something wrong with me."*

As I tell my clients this, I am aware that I am suggesting an alternative story that I believe can become possible between us, a story where emotions can be safely expressed because they can't be "wrong," a story of emotional connectedness instead of disconnection.

Stories about Needs

People who live in a chronic state of shame are very likely to believe, whether they know it or not, that their deepest emotional needs are what make them despicable. At times when those feelings seem not far away from a client, I look for a way to ask, "What happened in your family when you needed something?" As we explore how needs were met in their families, clients may begin to reflect on the meanings they attribute to neediness in general.

I wonder whether it was okay for my clients to ask for what they wanted, and whether their parents would respond in fair, reasonable ways. As clients think about needing, they may become aware of some intangibles: a sense that they'd be wrong to ask for more than was given them, for example, or a sense of emptiness from parents who gave lots of stuff but little time and attention. I might ask, "Was it totally fine to want and need something and hope to get it? Or was it important not to need too much?" And also, "Are people in your family stingy or generous with their understanding and affection?"

People who suffer from chronic shame are likely to carry around a sense of emotional impoverishment, of somehow never getting enough. Some of them spend their adult lives acquiring material goods and satisfactions to make up for what's missing. Our conversations about needing may help them link unmet emotional needs with other kinds of insatiability they experience. The most important narrative link we make, however, is between emotional need and shame (the shame they may feel about their insatiability, too). How is it that emotional needs turn into chronic shame? Sometimes, when we are deep into the story of having emotional needs, a client asks me that very question.

I'm happy for this chance to "teach" the core story of shame as I understand it: When you're little and you need to be seen and understood, when you need to matter to someone and it seems you don't, that hurts. Even the hurt is invisible. That's how it feels—you feel bad, and nobody cares how you feel. So you decide that these needy feelings are useless and having them makes you stupid. You tell yourself, "What's wrong with you anyway, to feel this? Get over it!" That's how shame takes over when emotional needs are ignored or denied. The needs themselves become something wrong with you. And then your hurt feelings about not having your needs met cause you even more shame.

I have never had a client tell me that this answer doesn't make sense.

Stories about Mistakes

Instead of asking, "What happened when somebody in your family made a mistake?" I usually ask, "In your family, what happened when somebody spilled the milk?" I find a way to ask this question when I sense that a client worries a lot about making mistakes with the people in her life, including me.

What I usually hear is, "Somebody got yelled at." My client and I find that even if she wasn't the one who got yelled at, the yelling made her anxious. Somebody was made to feel bad; next time it could be her. And the message was clear: mistakes are dangerous. Why are they so dangerous? Because they prove you are careless or stupid. You are always just one mistake away from proving yourself to be a worthless idiot.

"Wow!" I say. "That's a lot of anxiety to live with all the time!" I go on to wonder what happened in her family when "real mistakes" were made. We may figure out that in her family, there was no sense of proportion about mistakes; all mistakes were just the same kind of *bad* in the moment when they happened. We may find that there wasn't even a sense that someone could mean well and by accident make a mistake. And nobody in the family seemed to understand that doing a bad thing was different from being a bad person.

Here's an opportunity to do another bit of teaching about the difference between shame and guilt. You can make a mistake and still be good person who did a bad thing—or just a "mistaken" thing. You can find a way to say you're sorry for mistakes and make amends. That's completely different from being annihilated by "bad self" shame.

My client may realize that she never saw her parents able to be "good people who sometimes made mistakes." In a family system poisoned by "bad-self" shame, saying "sorry" meant being the bad person in the wrong. So everybody threw blame back and forth, desperate to be the right one who'd been wronged by the other.

Often there's a spin-off story here about taking responsibility in general. My client may tell me about power being abused in her family. I suggest that responsible power has in it a sense of being in control of oneself, and that it's personal and respectful. It says, *"I am here; I see you; I am accountable for what I do in relationship with you. I respect you as I respect myself."* Implicitly I'm saying to my client, *"This is the kind of mutual relationship you and I could have."*

Stories about Difference

It's not a big narrative leap from mistakes, shame, and blame to the question, "What happened in your family when there were differences between family members?" In shame-prone families even different opinions lead to conflict, and again people can only be good or bad, right or wrong. Clients say: "In my family it wasn't okay just to be yourself. People wouldn't be *interested*; they'd have judgments or criticism. It was like you'd always fall short of some standard, even if you didn't know what it was."

Clients tell stories about two different kinds of families who can't deal with difference. One kind of family is in constant turmoil over disagreements; fights are loud and emotionally bruising. People shout each other down and stomp out. There's no "working things out," there's just trying to win, and you win by being the angriest. The other kind of family is quiet and tense. People don't know what other people feel because nobody feels safe enough to say. Nobody talks about the things that matter most to them. Conflict may erupt briefly, but there's no talking it out to come to some kind of understanding. You can't even agree to disagree. The fight will go underground, with people giving each other the silent treatment for days . . . or years.

Neither family's story has in it a way to accept difference as a normal part of life, something that's good to talk about. In each story, conflict means that somebody will get hurt and there will be no repair. Nothing gets resolved; even if people "get over it," resentments smolder. Clients are quick to notice when they are still living this story—they still expect judgment just for being themselves, for example, or they fear conflict because they "know" they'll just get hurt. They may even come to notice that their fears of conflict shut them down in their therapy relationship.

Stories about Achievement

So far all of these "what happened?" approaches to shame storylines are closely related to the everyday regulation of affect in family relationships. Sometimes I will ask a question that seems to come from a somewhat different place: "How did your family help you learn skills and achieve goals?" or, "What got you noticed or praised in your family?" The skill or goal won't fall into the category of affective regulation. And yet there will have been potent affect in my clients' trying to achieve their goals and in how they saw their strivings recognized.

Some clients who struggle with chronic shame as adults remember having been shamed by their parents for failing at school or in sports. But for most of them the shame storyline is more subtle. Some of them remember having to figure things out for themselves and doing them badly without the help they needed. Others take pride in having "made it with no help." Some remember working hard to meet their parents' expectations while feeling unclear what their own goals were. Others remember constant praise about being smart and talented no matter what they did—but they could never settle on something to be good at.

These are memories that invite snippets of teaching. I explain that missing out on the experience of being guided by somebody who cares about us can leave us with an empty feeling—even when we reach our goals in life. I note that the unrealized dreams of parents can turn into powerful expectations that take over their kids' lives. I mention studies that show that praise for being smart or talented doesn't help kids feel good about themselves; instead, praise can just make them more anxious about living up to the mark the next time.[14]

I explain how I make sense of this: parents who suffer shame themselves feel afraid of failing as parents. They give lots of praise so that they can feel like the good parents of competent, happy children. But this kind of praise doesn't help the kids. It doesn't really *see* them; it's about the successful, well-adjusted child their parents need them to be. The kids try to keep up the image but without being really connected to their parents or to themselves, which is where genuine self-esteem comes from.

What these shamed clients needed growing up was close contact with parents who were happy to share skills and knowledge with their kids, and who also saw their kids clearly for who they were. That's what these clients missed. Praise or "positive feedback" doesn't help them much now either, unless it comes from someone who can see them as a whole self—a self who can be known, not just praised. In my understanding of their dilemma, I invite them to let me see and know them whole.

WHEN HISTORY DOESN'T MATTER

Opening up family stories may make more explicit the power of shame in our clients' lives. But sometimes chronically shamed clients aren't interested in talking about family history. Then we need to accept that a revised autobiography is not what they need to gain a more coherent, less shame-prone sense of self. For some clients the new relationship with us provides a secure base for developing a new story not about the past, but about who they are now and hope to be tomorrow, and that's not only good enough, it can be a deeply strengthening process.[15]

With these clients we can address shame explicitly by paying careful attention to shame that they feel in relation to us, especially when shame feelings enter a therapy session. There are no more transformative moments in therapy than when shame has created profound disconnection between a client and ourselves, and then, with a "moment of meeting" that's a moment of compassionate mutual understanding, shame dissolves and we can feel our connectedness again.[16] This becomes a powerful new story of what's possible beyond shame.

Whether clients' shame stories are about the past or the present, change happens because in the interpersonal place where new stories are taking shape, a new kind of implicit knowing about relationship is also coming to be. Here our clients' memories, thoughts, and feelings matter to someone, and so a self who matters can come to conscious coherence. This experience runs exactly counter to the experience of a self disintegrating in relation to a dysregulating other.

WORKING WITH PARTS OF SELF

For some shamed clients, their first conscious experience of a right-brain process at work is a troubling awareness of feeling in pieces and at odds with themselves. Until now, they have lived mostly in one part of self with occasional out-of-character breaks for low moments or "cutting loose." Their troubled parts have been sealed away from their conscious thoughts and emotions. They've never before felt their internal disconnectedness. But now they can feel "self" as having disconnected "parts," and this self-awareness, however incomprehensible and incomplete, is also a self-experience that is larger than any one part. The experience begs for comprehension and completion, and so it may bring them to therapy.

Why Working with Parts Helps

Feeling like a self in parts makes clients aware of their dis-integration. Working with these parts calls forward an integrative part of them who can pay attention to internal disconnections, often related to shame. Paying attention in the presence of an interested, engaged "regulating other," such as a therapist, helps that integrative self grow beyond shame to new experiences of agency, confidence, and competence.

There are other reasons, too, why working with parts of self is a useful way to bring more light and air to chronic shame. Talking about a part of self who is terribly wounded or bitterly angry is not as risky as saying, "I hurt," or, "I hate." With parts language, clients can speak about vulnerability without having to be entirely vulnerable. As one part feels humiliated or worthless, another part has enough distance to see what's happening. In this way, the pain of shame can be titrated and integrated a bit at a time.

Talking about parts explores clients' internal worlds, and it also brings the tensions of clients' family histories to life. Even clients who don't want to revisit the past are able to visit formative relational dynamics as they animate their inner cast of characters. For example, a Judge may stand in for internalized parental criticism, a Blamer for clients' early learning about how to manage conflict, a Sneak for how they managed to survive criticism and blame, and a Whiny Baby for the vulnerable sense of self they despise.

The noticing, exploring "main self" part of a client will have relationships with various other parts of self. The parts will also have relationships with one another. Working with the parts often involves exploring how they relate to each other. A Blamer and a Sneak, for example, can be at odds forever in an internal system that's never had an adult model for taking responsibility for one's own behavior. In Richard Schwartz's model, called Internal Family Systems Therapy, parts of self may have many names but they all fall into three groups—*exiles, managers,* and *firefighters*—all of whom are defined by their relationships with one another.

Exiles are the hurt parts of self, often child parts, that are sent away—disowned, repressed, or dissociated—because they can't be tolerated, much less understood. *Managers* can't tolerate the exiles' vulnerabilities and hurt feelings. Whether they are controlling, distancing, or perfectionistic, whether they act as pleasers, worriers, or caretakers, managers live to keep the exiles out, both for the exiles' safety and the safety of the whole system. They may seem like adults, but in fact managers operate more like parentified children who had to take over adult roles too quickly and with too little support. *Firefighters* turn up when a system contains badly wounded exiles and, despite the managers' best efforts, an exile's feelings are activated and break through. Firefighters douse vulnerable feelings in ways that are less "adult," using drugs, alcohol, binge eating, self-harm, or outbursts of rage, for example.[17]

Schwartz believes that if clients can get to know these internal parts, honoring each one's intentions and working through their impasses, they will come to enjoy a more balanced, harmonious "internal family system" in much the same way that an external family system can reorganize relationships in order to work together and help one another.[18]

In Bonnie Badenoch's somewhat different model of "internal community," parts of self spring from actual experience and resemble real others whom clients have known and internalized. She also recognizes parts she calls watchers and protectors, who help clients negotiate the environment to get nurturance and to avoid injury. And then there are the very important internal parent/child dyads, for example: caring-parent/nurtured-child, unempathic-parent/hurt-child, and abandoning-parent/abandoned-child.[19]

Badenoch speaks of parts of self in a case example of working directly with shame. At the core of her client's experience of shame she imagines "a small child relentlessly pursued by an angry and condescending parent, an internalized pair implanted early and unchanged since then."[20] But before approaching such a dyad directly, she says, we must take time and care to be calm, attentive, and consistent, soothing a client's interpersonal terror, disarming internal protectors, and making a place for trust. In words I have been using, fostering right-brain connection comes first. Then, Badenoch says, we use left-brain access to suggest a new narrative that includes awareness of those parent/child shaming interactions, a narrative that can then be slowly but deeply embraced in emotional/relational (right-brain) ways.

Badenoch describes moving from soothing what hurts the child to understanding what drives the parent "until they both settle," while constantly attending to here-and-now affect. As a client's "watcher" is able to feel compassion for his own shamed inner child and eventually for his parent's inner child as well, previously isolated neural networks become connected. Prefrontal cortex becomes wired into limbic regions; vertical integration happens; self-regulation becomes more possible.[21] As parts of self make peace, the brain heals itself; so says contemporary interpersonal neurobiology.

What's old is new: some of the earliest psychotherapy theory in North America spoke both "parts-of-self" language and what we now could call "right-brain" language. To this day, Gestalt therapists do not offer to diagnose or treat clients; instead, they invite them into bodily, emotional awareness of here-and-now experiences of self with other. Holistic processes of sensing, feeling, and expressing are the "stuff" of Gestalt therapy; the left-brain skills of interpreting, explaining, and conceptualizing just get in the way of change. Change happens not through insight, strategies, or efforts to be different, but rather through radical emotional acceptance of what is. And of course the trademark Gestalt technique for discovering and integrating "what is" is active, emotionally engaged dialogue with and among parts of self.[22]

If shame is fundamentally the felt experience of self disintegrating in the presence of a dysregulating other, using any of these models of working with parts of self can be profoundly counter-shaming. Each creates a safe, emotionally potent reality where vulnerability and shame can be given symbolic substance and voice—light and air. But perhaps even more important, the identified, personified shame is integrated through a relational process. What once could not be known by another is brought into interpersonal connection.

Now, in the presence of a regulating (therapeutic) other, a nascent regulating self makes contact with disintegrated parts of self in affectively charged moments of meeting. In interaction with and among these parts of self, and with a therapist as guide and model, a client can learn the integrative relational/emotional skills of empathy, compassion, accountability, forgiveness, courage, and respect. All of this expanded sense of self and connection "comes home" not as lessons, but as a series of holistic, embodied, emotional experiences—a lived, right-brain narrative of self in active relationship with self.

How to Work with Parts of Self

Schwartz and Badenoch have both written handbooks on how to work with parts of self, and they teach others how to work within their respective models. There are Gestalt institutes across North America that offer valuable training, too. But we don't need specialized training in "parts-of-self" work in order to do such work from a relational, psychodynamic perspective. If we understand in our own terms *why* working with parts of self helps integrate a self disintegrated by shame, we can be flexible and creative with the *how*. We can also expand our imagination and prime our creativity by listening to what others have to say about how to do parts-of-self work.

From Schwartz we learn that integration comes by way of resolving polarization and fostering communication. So, for example, bringing shame to light often illuminates a needy part of self who is despised by a tough, independent part of self. Listening respectfully to both parts and helping each to find compassion for what drives the other brings better balance and harmony to the whole self system. Schwartz helps us see how important it is that clients feel their agency and leadership as they do this work. Badenoch chooses, instead, to emphasize the client's attachment relationship with the therapist. Within this attuned emotional holding, parts of self slowly become known, cared for, and integrated. The brain heals itself within a "we-ness" of compassion.

Each of these perspectives gives us good clues about what to try to accomplish when we work with parts. Agency and compassion both matter. Gestalt reminders are also helpful: working with parts of self can instigate organic integration when it's all about here-and-now, I-and-thou, spontaneous, emotional relationship among parts, and when it's not about interpreting, explaining, controlling, or prescribing anything.

Working with parts of self can be surprisingly effective—and yet I don't propose that we make it a required project for our shamed clients. In my practice, I don't suggest that chronically shamed clients use parts language; the language just turns up. I have something to do with it when I say something like, "So there's a part of you that's excited about your party, but another part that's feeling quite anxious." This may be "therapy-speak," but it's also a fairly common way for people outside of therapy to talk about internal conflict or indecision, similar to: "On the one hand. . . . On the other hand," or, "I'm of two minds on the issue."

Yet when I casually introduce the language of parts, I often find that shamed clients jump at the chance to talk about themselves in this protected yet immediately engaging way.[23] As my client Clare did, many of them enjoy the energy of the game. I like to meet their parts and help them speak because I, too, enjoy this edgy, engaging, creative kind of play. And play-spaces are, of course, exactly where right-brain connectivity happens, both within and between minds.

Exploring parts of self can slide in and out of larger ongoing co-created narratives. Narratives that are *experienced* are especially integrative. When a form of therapy, like Badenoch's, expands into the arts, parts of self can be brought to life explicitly in psychodrama, dance, sandplay, or visual art. In talk therapy, parts of self emerge as metaphors and images, most often just within the client's mind, but sometimes speaking out as the client moves between different voices or even different chairs. Some clients identify parts of self that aren't personified, that feel, for example, like a wall, or a tiny light, or the roots of a tree. It can still be quite useful to ask, "What does the wall know?" or, "What do those tree roots want?"

In short, for certain clients (they will let us know who they are), working with parts of self is a powerful, useful way to give voice to their divided, fragmented self-experience, and thus to let light and air get at their shame. Parts of self can find space to speak the unspeakable about need, longing, and humiliation, and in their speaking and being heard, integration happens. Often a time of working with "parts" comes and goes in therapy, and later clients look back with fond nostalgia on parts they once encountered as "other" but that are now just everyday aspects of the self they know.

Working with parts is not for everyone. Some clients do intense integrative work without the help of metaphors. And then there are other clients who can't give any voice at all to vulnerability; they can't face their shame even obliquely. They have no access to parts of self that are hidden away for safety, and in fact, they have no felt sense of their own splitness or fragmentation. Their shame is dissociated—and yet it is generating all kinds of distress. How can therapy help them? That's the subject of the next chapter.

NOTES

1. Elizabeth Shapiro and Theodore Powers, "Shame and the Paradox of Group Therapy," in *Shame in the Therapy Hour*, eds. Ronda L. Dearing and June Price Tangney (Washington, DC: American Psychological Association, 2011), 124.

2. A wide diversity of opinion on this score is summarized in June Price Tangney and Ronda L. Dearing, "Working with Shame in the Therapy Hour: Summary and Integration," in *Shame in the Therapy Hour*, eds. Dearing and Tangney, 384–85.

3. Philip Bromberg describes the limits of a pure self psychological empathic/interpretive stance in "Interpersonal Psychoanalysis and Self Psychology: A Clinical Comparison," in *Standing in the Spaces: Essays on Clinical Process, Trauma, and Dissociation* (Hillsdale, NJ: Analytic Press, 1998), 147–62.

4. See, for example, Judith Jordan et al., *Women's Growth in Connnection: Writings from the Stone Center* (New York: Guilford, 1991), and Lewis Aron, *A Meeting of Minds: Mutuality in Psychoanalysis* (Hillsdale, NJ: Analytic Press), 1996.

5. Diana Fosha, "Emotion and Recognition at Work: Energy, Vitality, Pleasure, Truth, Desire, and the Emergent Phenomenology of Transformational Experience," in *The Healing Power of Emotion: Affective Neuroscience, Development and Clinical Practice,* eds. Diana Fosha, Daniel Siegel, and Marion Solomon (New York: Norton, 2009), 181.

6. Richard Geist, "Connectedness, Permeable Boundaries, and the Development of the Self: Therapeutic Implications," *International Journal of Psychoanalytic Self Psychology* 3 (2008): 130–36.

7. Richard Geist, "The Forward Edge, Connectedness, and the Therapeutic Process," *International Journal of Psychoanalytic Self Psychology* 6 (2011): 246.

8. Geist, "The Forward Edge," 236.

9. Geist, "Connectedness," 140.

10. Geist, "Connectedness," 133–36.

11. Marylene Cloitre, Lisa R. Cohen, and Karestan C. Koenen, *Treating Survivors of Childhood Sexual Abuse: Psychotherapy for the Interrupted Life* (New York: Guilford, 2006), 290, quoted in Judith Herman, "Posttraumatic Stress Disorder as a Shame Disorder," in *Shame in the Therapy Hour,* eds. Dearing and Tangney, 270.

12. Herman, "PTSD as a Shame Disorder," 267–68.

13. For example, James Harper and Margaret Hoopes, *Uncovering Shame: An Approach Integrating Individuals and Their Family Systems* (New York: Norton, 1990); Stephanie Donald-Pressman and Robert Pressman, *The Narcissistic Family: Diagnosis and Treatment* (New York: Macmillan, 1994); Merle Fossum and Marilyn Mason, *Facing Shame: Families in Recovery* (New York: Norton, 1986); John Bradshaw, *Healing the Shame that Binds You* (Deerfield Beach, FL: Health Communications, 1988); Gershen Kaufman, *Shame, the Power of Caring,* 3rd edn. (Rochester, VT: Schenkman Books, 1992).

14. Polly Young-Eisendrath, *The Self-Esteem Trap: Raising Confident and Compassionate Kids in an Age of Self-Importance* (New York: Little, Brown, 2008).

15. See Morton Shane, Estelle Shane, and Mary Gales, *Intimate Attachments: Toward a New Self Psychology* (New York: Guilford, 1997). They believe that effective transformative therapy can be carried out in various combinations of a client experiencing an old or a new self in relationship with a therapist experienced by the client as an old or a new other. Thus it is quite possible, they say, for a client to experience the therapist as a completely new, non-threatening other, and to be able, then, to have a fundamentally new experience of self in response.

16. The Boston Change Process Study Group defines significant change in psychotherapy as significant change in a client's "implicit relational knowing," that is, in his/her unconscious structures for feeling and knowing self-with-other, which I understand as right brain patterns of relational knowing/feeling. Shifts in a person's implicit relational knowing come by way of the repetition of direct, potent, and novel relational experiences between client and therapist. Opportunities for this kind of experience are "now moments" in therapy, and when their potential is realized, they are, in BCPSG language, "moments of meeting." Boston Change Process Study Group, "Non-Interpretive Mechanisms in Psychoanalytic Therapy: The 'Something More' Than Interpretation," in *Change in Psychotherapy: A Unifying Paradigm* (New York: Norton, 2010), 1–29.

17. Richard Schwartz, *Internal Family Systems Therapy* (New York: Guilford, 1995), 46–53.

18. Schwartz, *Internal Family Systems Therapy,* 122.

19. Bonnie Badenoch, *Being a Brain-Wise Therapist: A Practical Guide to Interpersonal Neurobiology* (New York: Norton, 2008), 76–89.

20. Badenoch, *Brain-Wise Therapist,* 105.

21. Badenoch, *Brain-Wise Therapist,* 109.

22. Frederick S. Perls, Ralph F. Hefferline, and Paul Goodman, *Gestalt Therapy: Excitement and Growth in the Human Personality* (New York: Julian, 1951; reprint, Goldsboro, ME: Gestalt Journal Press, 1994).

23. Philip Bromberg, an interpersonal/relational psychoanalyst who invites his patients' multiple selves to speak with him if they will, comments, "Used judiciously, I have found that an approach which addresses the multiplicity of self is so experience-near to most patients' subjective reality that only rarely does someone even comment on why I am talking about them in 'that way.' It leads to a greater feeling of wholeness (not *dis*-integration) because each self-state comes to attain a clarity and personal significance that gradually alleviates the patient's previously held sense of confusion about who he 'really' is and how he came, historically, to be this person." Bromberg, "Standing in the Spaces: The Multiplicity of Self and the Psychoanalytic Relationship," in *Standing in the Spaces*, 290.

CHAPTER 10

The Challenge of Dissociated Shame

We all know clients who are unhappy in their lives but who seem determined never to make contact with what they feel most deeply. They avoid vulnerable connectedness with everyone, including us, because feeling vulnerable means feeling shame. For them, shame is simply intolerable; the last thing they want is to give it light or air. Their therapy conversation allows no teachable moments about shame, no links to childhood vulnerability felt here and now, no curious playfulness about alien parts of self. For these clients, defenses against feeling shame have become their way of being in the world. Their self-with-other operating systems are what Karen Horney would have called "character solutions" to the problem of shamed vulnerability, solutions that make shame disappear but do not really solve it.[1]

When these clients come to us for treatment, they want to feel better, but at the same time, since just being in therapy carries the threat of shame, their defenses intensify. Our therapeutic diplomacy immediately tells us to keep quiet with them about shame, to live within the constraints of their operating system, and to offer them the consistent empathic attunement that over time will calm their fears about being shamed by us in therapy.

These clients often try very hard to be good clients. They may be able to share a personal history that includes painful memories, but the self who felt or feels the pain is not in the room with us. These clients may be able to identify different aspects of themselves, but those parts don't come to life. In sessions it's hard to *feel* these clients with emotional immediacy; something is missing. Someone is missing. An absence is present because a vulnerable, shamed self is dissociated.

It might seem that the best we can offer these clients is sympathy for their mysterious, debilitating symptoms of anxiety and depression. But if we understand how relational trauma and dissociation affect them, we can do more. They can't tell us directly about either the trauma or the dissociation. With "large empathy" based on unspoken clues, however, we can imagine for them an internal reality that they can't yet afford to know. This leap of imaginative mentalizing gives us a chance of real contact with them, first with how their protective splits work for them, and maybe one day with the "self of shame" who is so thoroughly dissociated from their awareness.

To set the stage for understanding dissociated shame, I'll summarize how the term *dissociation* is used in understanding and treating trauma. The meaning of *dissociation* shifts slightly to fit each user's frame of reference. I'll begin with a neurobiological frame.

DISSOCIATION AND THE RIGHT BRAIN

In Allan Schore's understanding of relational trauma and its effects on the brain, dissociation is essentially a right-brain relational event. A vulnerable, affectively flooded self fails to receive attuned, integrating affect regulation, and so in reflexive self-protection, the self freezes. This primitive coping strategy is best understood, Schore maintains, as a loss of vertical connectivity between cortical and subcortical areas of the right hemisphere of the brain.[2]

Locating dissociation in the right brain helps us understand that it's not primarily disconnection from a reflective, verbal thought process. Dissociation is disconnection within primary consciousness, which relates visceral and emotional information to a felt sense of self. "Dissociatively detached individuals are not only detached from the environment, but also from the *self* – their *body,* their own actions, and their sense of *identity.*"[3] At the same time, dissociation interrupts a right-brain kind of cognition about the external world, the kind of knowledge acquired through processing faces and social cues and held within implicit knowing about "what always happens" in relational interactions.[4]

With repetition, such dissociation can become a highly rigid, closed right-brain system and a matching personality style. In Schore's words, "The endpoint of chronically experiencing catastrophic states of relational trauma in early life is . . . a progressive impairment of the ability to adjust, take defensive action, or act on one's own behalf, and a blocking of the capacity to register affect and pain, all critical to survival."[5]

When a person's felt sense of self is impaired, she has difficulty sustaining an inner sense of aliveness. It's also very hard for her to generate and integrate "present moments"—those small packages of interactions with others that are woven into the basic fabric of lived experience.[6] It's no wonder then, if we are in a therapy relationship with her, that she often feels more emotionally absent than present, even when she is doing her best to connect with us.

DISSOCIATION AND TRAUMA THEORY

Before the days of interpersonal neuroscience, dissociation was most often discussed in the context of trauma understood as an intense, overwhelming assault on a person's psychic integrity. Combat veterans, survivors of kidnapping, torture, and sexual assault, and adult survivors of sustained, severe childhood abuse were all seen to share a cluster of symptoms, identified as PTSD. Chief among the symptoms of PTSD is dissociation.

This trauma literature describes dissociation not in interpersonal but in intrapsychic terms. It explains that when traumatic experience is too shocking and painful for individuals' emotional and psychological systems to process, they dissociate from the experience, perhaps even "leaving the body" as the trauma happens. The trauma experience is imprinted as sensations or feeling states that are protectively blocked from becoming verbal narrative. If no one intervenes to help trauma survivors process what happened, the experience is never integrated into narrative memory. Their self-systems continue to believe that experiencing the emotional pain of the trauma will be psychologically annihilating; therefore, the trauma experience continues to be dissociated from explicit narrative memory and from coherent selfhood. This failure of symbolic information processing is what generates the symptoms of PTSD.[7]

Though dissociated, the traumatic experience doesn't disappear. It is stored as isolated sensory fragments, affective states, or behavioral reenactments, and it may intrude on consciousness as flashbacks, nightmares, and inchoate feelings that threaten to overwhelm a trauma survivor's sanity. And so a trauma survivor's ongoing life in the world demands ongoing dissociation from these disturbing intrusions. Such dissociation, as Judith Herman points out, is but one of the many forms of constriction that deaden and diminish the lives of traumatized persons.

Herman, along with many others who specialize in psychotherapy with trauma survivors, believes that a central task of this therapy is to allow implicit memory to become explicit narrative, working slowly from what is known to what is not yet known. Within the respect and care of a witnessing, supportive therapeutic relationship, a client becomes able not only to remember the trauma, but also to mourn the losses that the traumatic experiences inflicted. In Herman's view of the trajectory of recovery from trauma, integration—a comprehensive undoing of dissociation—is central: the integration of memory and narrative, the integration of self through a profound grief process, and the integration of self-with-other relationships as the trauma survivor reconnects with the world.[8]

In concurrent writing on trauma and recovery, Jody Davies and Mary Frawley referenced the research literature on trauma and sexual abuse that was available when they wrote (the early 1990s), and at the same time they brought a psychoanalytic perspective to the challenge of treating adult survivors of childhood sexual abuse. From this perspective they took the meaning of dissociation and integration in a somewhat different direction.

It's true, they say, that a trauma survivor needs to remember and feel events that have been dissociated from awareness; however, this is just one aspect of the intrapsychic work that must be done. Theorizing from an object-relations point of view, they understand the trauma experience to exist as a dissociated but powerful segment of the survivor's world of internal selves and internal others. The overriding goal of the survivor's therapy should be "the emergence, containment, encoding, and integration of this entire split-off aspect of experience."[9]

What begins as dissociated memory becomes a walled-off internal self-with-other system that contains the effects of the trauma. The system is a terrified child's speechless world of abusers and victims, longed-for saviors, and those who look the other way. Dissociating this inner world makes it possible for the rest of the child to develop into an often remarkably competent adult, though plagued by inexplicable anxiety, depression, and self-loathing. Effective therapy requires that the dissociated system be integrated into consciousness.

Dissociated states may emerge as a child who remembers trauma in the fragmented voice of flashback. They may take the form of battles between a punishing adult part of the client's self and a subversive, angry child.[10] They may be enacted as co-transference dramas, in which parts of the child's dissociated world are assigned to client and therapist: the non-abusing parent and the neglected child; the sadistic abuser and the helpless, enraged victim; the idealized rescuer and the child who demands to be rescued; and the seducer and the seduced.[11]

Davies and Frawley do not identify these personified self-states as "alter" parts of a multiple personality. They do recognize that a small proportion of abuse survivors live with dissociated states of self that have become distinct personalities, some of whom have no awareness of the other personalities within the self system. Dissociation is, indeed, the central dynamic that governs the operation of the complex mechanisms of what has been called multiple personality disorder, now identified as dissociative identity disorder.[12]

The literature on treating these so-called disorders explains how dissociation exists on a continuum from, at one end, our everyday doing of tasks absently, through a middle ground of deliberately induced hypnotic trance states, and on to the far end where spontaneous self-hypnosis produces amnesiac fugue states of consciousness and completely separate personalities within one human being.[13] Here dissociation does more than just manage traumatic memory, though it is often the case that certain "alters" or identities hold specific memories that others know nothing about.

In this powerful form, dissociation is also a highly creative way for a trauma survivor to escape the constriction of the after-effects of trauma. Many different parts of self can find ways to engage with life, expressing talents, skills, and energies that might otherwise never see the light of day. As will become clear in a case example later in this chapter, it's also possible for these different identities who share one body to cohere in an unusual but genuine form of integration, one which these dissociative clients often call not "I," but "we."

DISSOCIATION AND "THE UNCONSCIOUS"

A psychoanalytic understanding of trauma and dissociation belongs within a long tradition of "making the unconscious conscious." Contemporary relational psychoanalysts think more about the return of the dissociated than the return of the repressed when they think about achieving more integrated consciousness.[14] And they include in the unconscious (that is, in *unconsciousness*, not defined as a thing or a place) not just what a person has known and then repressed, but also a person's implicit relational knowing,[15] the psychological organizing principles that operate outside a person's conscious awareness,[16] and whatever a person has experienced but never known in symbolized form.[17]

In this larger sense of the unconscious, not just trauma is dissociated from a trauma-survivor's awareness. Trauma creates implicit knowledge and psychological organizing principles that are also dissociated from consciousness—even while they operate to keep certain thoughts, emotions, desires, and insights out of awareness and in what might be called "the dynamic unconscious." Furthermore, any of these unconscious structuring aspects of the mind may be the result of relational trauma that no one would call abusive—and yet they may seriously undermine a person's psychological integrity and emotional well-being.

DISSOCIATION AND SHAME

Here shame theory intersects with trauma and dissociation theory. Physical, sexual, and emotional abuse wreaks relational trauma and intense chronic shame on its victims. But intense chronic shame can also emerge from caregiver–child relationships that are not overtly abusive. Whether the relational trauma of affect dysregulation happens to a child in horrific or subtle ways, shame will follow. Left unrepaired, the disintegrating experience of shame will become a chronic state of self. That has been my argument, and I have also noted that this unspeakable shame at the affective core of the self soon becomes untouchable and unknowable. As a person finds ways to hide, protect, and compensate for shamed vulnerability, chronic shame itself becomes dissociated.

Making contact with dissociated trauma is not the same as making contact with dissociated shame. It's possible to help clients integrate trauma into authentic narrative memory and not notice a shamed self slipping out of sight. And it's not only the shamed abused child who disappears; so does the shamed adult. As a client explained to me, "It's not just what you felt when it happened. It's how you've felt about yourself ever after. You don't want *any* of that feeling!"

And so with survivors of acute, sustained abusive trauma, it's essential to remember that the return of dissociated memories of traumatic experience, including bodily and emotional feelings, is only part of the integration that needs to happen. They also need to make contact with the shame, past and present, that they can't bear to feel. This truth became unmistakable in my work with a client who lives her life through several identities.

DISSOCIATION AND SHAME: A CASE EXAMPLE

Cynthia came to me with what she understood to be intrusive flashbacks of sexual abuse that she had "sort of" known about before in a previous therapy. "That therapy was ten years ago," she said. "Things have been quiet for a long time." I listened with no agenda but to understand, and one day her eyelids fluttered and she was no longer Cynthia but Sid, clearly somebody else, a person as masculine in mannerisms and speech patterns as Cynthia had been feminine. Yet Sid was still a "she," a stellar woman sales rep in a man's world of high-end sports equipment, and also the star of a woman's rugby team. "I've got this bumper sticker," she told me, dead-pan. "Rugby players eat their dead."

Sid also told me that she'd had no intention of participating in therapy. She was just putting up with me, checking me out, making sure I didn't do wrong by the others. But things were bad. Lots of nights she thought about taking them all off a bridge together, and the night before she'd walked to the bridge. "So I've been thinking you're not a fucking freak therapist like the fucking last one. You've got some sense. Also, Hilary says we got to talk to you."

It was clear to me that I needed to join Sid in a tough guy place, match the cadences of her vitality affect, give no-nonsense, pithy responses, and ask direct, fearless questions. I learned that she had warned "the rest" off the last therapist, but they hadn't listened, and the kids had ended up being abused. I found out that Hilary was the group's therapist-alter who had then quit being a therapist. Sid respected Hilary, but she thought Cynthia was a pussy and a wimp—"Too chicken-shit even to be multiple." Sid made a deal with me that she wouldn't jump and kill herself (and all the others) until after we next met.

The deal was extended until, after some months, it became superfluous. I met the kids. Some days they brought me books to read to them and stuffed toys to "charge up" as protection against the dangerous world outside. Other days, Sid and various kids remembered a complicated history of sexual abuse including basements and cameras when they were young, and a gang-rape later. The kids lived through flashbacks in session and with outside-session help from Hilary. Everybody started to feel a bit better. Even Cynthia was beginning to remember dimly some of the things that happened when she lost time. And then Sid fell in love.

Sid, the invulnerable, had never fallen in love before. It was a whirlwind affair that ended badly, no matter how hard Sid, the one who could build, fix, and manage anything, tried to make it work. Sid fell apart, and then the whole group fell into a psychotic break—but with enough lucidity to spend two weeks in hospital and not give away the dissociative identity disorder (DID) secret. After the breakdown, our work was very hard and painful. Cynthia wished she could just be dead, and the others had vanished. "I think it's over," Cynthia said. "I'm not multiple any more. That must be a good thing. The breakdown was like a blender—dump everybody in, push the button, chop and whir and they're all gone."

I felt sad to hear that because it was so unlike what Sid had told me early on: "If you'd come on like a fucking DID expert who was going to *integrate* me, I would have been out of here in one second." And I also missed Sid. She'd been the life of the party, a source of energy and vitality for the whole group. I wondered whether vitality would become available for Cynthia in some other way now.

Cynthia struggled on in deep depression for many long weeks. And then one day Sid came back, though not the Sid I had known. She was silent, but I knew that she knew that I recognized her. I said, "Hi," but she wouldn't speak or look at me. Shame was thick in the room. I decided to say that I could feel it.

"I didn't do my job," Sid said quietly, bitterly. "I look after everybody; I take care. Instead, I cracked up and put them all through hell. If I can't be strong and take care, there's no reason for me to be here. I tried not to *be*, but that didn't work either."

This was what Sid needed to talk about, and so week after week she came back into some part of a session to work through her shame, despising every tear she cried. I affirmed her strength and courage to do such terribly painful work. She would say, "I hate you, too, for making me do this." Then she would crack a very small grin at me. I watched her develop emotional depth, become a much more three-dimensional person.

Meanwhile, one by one, others came back, and I couldn't help but hear the shame in them, too. The vulnerable little kids were certain they had been bad, and the breakdown was their punishment. They needed reassurance that even though they felt bad, they weren't bad. Some angry older kids and teens were out to prove their point: "Shit happened because those others were weak. It goes to show: don't trust anybody; don't depend on anybody. People will just hurt you." They needed to know that I understood where they were coming from. When I told Cynthia (with Sid's permission) that Sid was working on the shame she felt, Cynthia volunteered that a lot of her depression came from feeling shame about having a breakdown and not being able to face the people in her life afterwards.

Once this sea-change was underway, it became possible for the kids to revisit the scene of the therapist abuse, a scene defined by acute, searing shame. And I finally met Hilary in person. She confided that she still felt shame about her failure to recognize a fellow therapist as a predator, her failure to protect the kids. I haven't seen Hilary since. I'm told she's always busy with the kids, but I feel her watching me as the silent, powerful "quality control" she's been from the beginning. I feel now that if I make a mistake and she needs to talk to me about it, we'll have a discussion as colleagues who are on the same team, each doing our best.

What team are we on? What are we trying to do? Now and again, when Sid wonders about the point of therapy, I find myself saying something like, "What matters to me is that you all have a better life. It seems better when you can work together and help each other out." This is not the "integration" Sid fears and hates, believing it would be the loss of the only self she's ever known. Nevertheless, I think it's an important kind of integration, and not so different from the kind of integration we envision for our less dissociated clients or for ourselves.

The integration underway in Cynthia's group-life has many aspects. Since the breakdown, new memories of trauma have become available. In the telling, they have moved from bodily flashbacks to narrative memories. Most members of the group, not just the directly affected kids, can hold these memories "in mind" and can feel both the past and present emotions that they arouse. Just as important, if not more so, is the new narrative Cynthia and Sid have discovered together about their relationship with Cynthia's mother. "It was there in plain sight," Sid said. "We just couldn't see it."

Cynthia and her mom had always been very close, largely because Cynthia worked hard to please her mom. Things began to unravel after the breakdown, when she felt her mom's disgust at her for being "sick," and she realized this had happened every time she'd been depressed before. After a while she connected these hurt feelings with memories of being secretly, sadistically bullied by one of her brothers when she was little. She had tried to tell her mom about it, but her mom always told her she was too sensitive or she was exaggerating. She'd come to believe that the bullying was somehow her fault. I was present when the penny dropped for Sid: "That's when we started!"

I didn't get it. "When you started what?"

"When we started to *be*. When we knew: Nobody's going to look after us, so we have to look after ourselves. That was the beginning of me. It wasn't all that other crap abuse that did it; I was already there by then."

Cynthia and Sid have come to see that the mother's vision is limited to what she wants to see. They are learning how to spend "friendly enough" time with her while protecting themselves—even pushing back a bit—against her judgments. During this process, Cynthia has needed time to grieve for the mother she tried so hard to have and who wasn't really there. Sometimes she is also deeply sad about being multiple. Along with Sid, she now believes that multiplicity isn't going away, but she also knows what it costs her. She believes that she will never have close friends and certainly not another lover with whom she can be completely herself, all parts free to be out and known. Other members of the group, even the kids, seem to be able to share in this sadness, a grief that is consolidating a clearer, stronger sense of self for Cynthia.

Overall, during this time of integration, specific emotions and their embodiments have become less isolated within specific identities. The kids who from the beginning told me "I'm just bad!" aren't alone with shame now. The rejecting adolescents do blustery verbal sparring with me that feels like playful contact. Cynthia, a self-effacing pleaser, can feel angry sometimes. "I guess I have a voice now," she says, sitting up straight, looking me in the eye. In a heated moment, however, Sid will still be the one to step up and say what needs saying. That's okay with Cynthia. When there's a question about clothes and nail polish at the office Christmas party, Sid will listen to her and accept a deal they both can live with. And Sid doesn't embarrass her anymore with one-night flings.

Cooperation has become the norm within the system; conflicts can be addressed and worked through. Sid and Hilary work together to look after the kids. I hear that Hilary is far less stressed now that she isn't doing crisis management all the time. She seems content to do the inner nurturing of the kids, while Sid brings them out close to the world, where they can hear the laughter of other kids in the park and feel the wind in their face while Sid cycles. For a "tough guy," Sid is remarkably empathic with all the others, even Cynthia, now that she can stick up for herself a bit. (Sid still calls her a prude about sex, but affectionately.)

Sometimes, when Sid feels scared or sad, she says, "I can't believe this is me." She wonders how she can continue to exist if she's so completely different from the Sid she was for so long. "If I don't stay tough, my reason for being here disappears. Right?"

I get her point. And what do we really know about how this multiplicity works? "Well," I say, "Seems you're still here." We have to laugh. I tell her I think she hasn't changed, she's just become a deeper, stronger version of the Sid she always was. I tell her I think it's true what they say: Real men cry. She snorts and tells me her dad didn't, but she hears me. I don't use the word "integration." But I do believe a kind of integration is happening that decreases the conflict and emotional pain in the group's self-system.

What has happened to make this integration possible? Fostering right-brain connection was my first intention. I met Cynthia (and the rest) in a spirit of open acceptance, with curious empathy. Sid must have felt my willingness to be playful, too, because she took me up on it in a radical way when she invited me into her world of multiple selves. I found myself in a right-brain reality that was against logic yet real in a vital, compelling sense. I felt I was living a "primary process" with her, where emotional dynamics constructed reality. What kind of truth was this? I knew that even Winnicott would tell me not to ask the question.[18] As with any client, what mattered was to be there and to be with.

And so I lean in to attune, making myself emotionally available to anyone who turns up. Using what multiple-self resources I can muster, I am a supportive, containing trauma therapist, but I am also a reassuring, storybook-reading mom for an eight-year-old, an imaginary playmate for a five-year-old, a "let's cut the shit" worker with angry, acting-out adolescents, and a punch-in-the-arm kind of buddy to the tough guy/girl. It's no different, essentially, than attuning to any client's different states of self, and in fact easier, since here each "self" is so clearly delineated from the others.

In this right-brain world, I offer different kinds of right-brain connectivity. Reliability, consistency, and truth-telling have contributed to secure attachment. Mirroring—simple, direct understanding with no agenda—undergirds my selfobject connection with all of them. The kids calm down as they are able to connect in an idealizing way, the teens do well when they can be adversarial and still be welcomed, and kinship is vital to the connectedness Sid and I share. I'm aware that every time I talk or write about working with this group (right now, for example), I feel Hilary watching and listening. Impossible. But I think it's my alogical right-brain measure of what Geist would call mutual connectedness, permeable boundaries, and an interpenetration of selves.[19]

Our right-brain connectedness changes things. It allows us to co-create a lived, implicit narrative of how we can be together and who we are to each other. Within the safety of this story, Cynthia, Sid, and the others tell further stories. Each of them begins as an emotional, relational "knowing" not yet assimilated, and then it finds its place among a network of right-brain ways of understanding emotions, others, and self. In time, perhaps very quickly, this new knowing can become material for left-brain logical, linear narrative. But with this group, some of it doesn't get there. I imagine that this is true for all of our clients: connectedness facilitates some important right-brain changes in implicit relational knowing and implicit sense of self that never make it to a left-brain narrative. And that's not a problem, because our clients can feel more whole and strong just on the strength of right-brain integration.

It's a wonder that Cynthia's core shame ever saw the light of day, since her personality was constructed to make it disappear. For years Sid was dissociated vulnerability embodied, a walking, talking, grandiose "character solution" to the problem of shame. But then, against her better judgment, against history and pattern, Sid allowed herself to connect with me, and then she allowed herself to fall in love. As the furious adolescents knew, that was the mistake. *Don't connect. Don't trust. You will only get hurt.*

Sid's move toward vulnerable connection disrupted the precarious balance of a whole system built around vigorous shame management. Despite Sid's unflagging, extreme attempts to make the relationship work, her lover told her the breakup was her fault. That's when a lifetime of dissociated shame broke through, self-hatred wrapped around the core implicit knowing, "I'll never get what I need from the other person. It's my fault. *I'm wrong, bad, disgusting.*" A flood of shame shut the system down, blocking connection between all parts of self and leaving Cynthia deeply depressed.

To put it more accurately, Cynthia's system was shut down by an emergency response to a breakthrough of intense shame. Extreme measures were taken to get it all locked away again, no matter what the cost. Yet this time of emergency—hardly safe emergency!—was also a time when something could change. Could this excruciating emotional experience be shared somehow? Sid found a way to show me shame in her body. I was able to recognize it and invite it forward into the light. We named it and made it a "thing" to understand and explore. Sid needed a strong sense of connected "we-ness" to get through it. And then a lot began to change.

Causality is very hard to prove in psychotherapy, but this part of the story strongly suggests that a cascade of right-brain connectivity may follow the naming, feeling, and working through of "right-brain" shame, that is, the shame induced by early relational trauma. For Cynthia, this wordless shame, structured into the here-and-now essence of each part's being, needs to be named and felt throughout the system. At the same time, a new narrative is slowly coming into focus. I haven't suggested to Cynthia/Sid that her new knowledge about her mother—that she completely failed to respond to her early, sustained trauma, and in fact blamed her for it—has a lot to do with her chronic shame. It seems her system knows what it needs to know about that for now. But I will hold this left-brain explanation in mind for her, should she ever need it.[20]

DISSOCIATION AND CHARACTER SOLUTIONS FOR SHAME

I don't intend the case example I have just talked about to be a guide for working with DID. In fact, I intend it to show that the principles that guide DID work are the same as those that guide any other relational psychodynamic work with early relational trauma, dissociation, and shame. DID is special because, as Colin Ross says, everything is on the surface. You don't see it all at once, but you do see it all—played out in living color.[21] I hope that the vividness of the Cynthia story will help illuminate what's at stake, what's difficult, and what's possible in therapy with clients who suffer dissociation in much more subtle ways. The splits in their personalities, too, are engendered by relational trauma, and their splits have the same function: to protect the self from feeling unbearable emotional pain, and especially the pain of annihilating shame.

When dissociation is well-concealed within a personality style, the dissociation is as much a secret as what it hides. There are various theoretical ways to imagine what's behind the veils of personality styles that disown shame and vulnerability, styles often linked with narcissistic pathology. For a number of reasons, I like the understanding proposed by Jack Danielian and Patricia Gianotti. First among those reasons is their belief that shame compels the self-protections of "narcissism," and that shame is a likely and powerful response to a wide range of narcissistic injuries clients have suffered, from ruptures of attunement to flagrant abuse. Shame, they say, is the "critical missing piece" in the puzzle of developing humane understanding and effective, in-depth treatment for our narcissistically injured clients.[22]

Danielian and Gianotti define narcissisism not as a *DSM* diagnostic set of symptoms, but rather as "the often formidable residue of characterological damage that remains in the present due to varying degrees of trauma, deprivation, or the lack of adequate relational attunement from the past."[23] Our chronically shamed, narcissistically injured clients manage their suffering with what Danielian and Gianotti call, following Horney, "character solutions." The language of *solution* rather than *structure* allows us to see character as a moving, evolving dynamic; "it enables us to see our clients as making very *live* attempts to clinically dissociate from pain, self-loathing, and toxic shame."[24]

In other words, character solutions are performative. The interpersonal and the intrapsychic are an integrated system, performing self-in-relation in the here-and-now. We come to know our clients' past not through archeological retrieval but through the organization of our clients' performance of this self in relation with us.[25] This matches my understanding of how we and our clients meet on the playing field of psychotherapy.

I also identify with the experience-near, interactive form of practice that Danielian and Gianotti espouse. They train therapists in an effective use of self that begins with moment-to-moment immersion in their clients' subjective life. They believe that only experience-near listening will enable us to sense our clients' dissociated states operating in the dynamic present. Only from within our clients' subjective worlds of experience will we have a chance to recognize those permeable moments when clients both "know and don't know" what's dissociated. And it's from within this moment-to-moment intersubjective struggle to understand that our clients will access strength and authenticity.[26]

I agree with how Danielian and Gianotti "re-imagine" transference. With other relational theorists, they see it as the "interpersonalization" of a client's unconscious organizing principles. As a here-and-now enactment of material not yet in a client's conscious awareness, transference offers access to what is still dissociated but not too far away. It shows us how a client's self-protections operate. Working in the transference requires us to work in our own "subjective present," too. When we operate from an intersubjective perspective, it's not easy, Danielian and Gianotti admit, to tease apart transference and counter-transference. But that's not essential; what matters is a deeper, fuller appreciation of all that's happening between us and our clients.[27]

This description of transference and how to work with it is both familiar and thought-provoking. It paves the way for exploring how enactments of shame can take over client–therapist relationships. But before I discuss working with co-transference enactments, including enactments of dissociated shame, I will outline the four quadrant model Danielian and Gianotti offer to explain "character solutions" to the problem of shame.

THE EXPERIENCE-NEAR FOUR QUADRANT MODEL

Danielian and Gianotti call their model experience-near because they don't intend it to be a diagnostic tool or a guide to technique. They suggest we simply hold all four quadrants in mind in order to listen to clients more deeply in the moment. When we can hear the splits hidden in what they say, our experience-near responses will subtly communicate what we hear. Bit by bit and roaming all over the quadrants with us, clients will come to experience the workings of their own personal solution to the problem of shamed vulnerability. Their dissociative "knowing and not knowing" of self can slowly give way to more integrated, authentic knowing and being.

The four quadrants are a diagram of a personality with four aspects. Two of the aspects are in a client's awareness; top-left is quadrant one, *How I View Myself (Aspirations, Belief Systems, and Self-Imposed Standards)* and top-right is quadrant two, *Symptoms (Depressive, Behavioral, Anxiety, and Somatic Clusters)*. The givens of *How I View Myself* are ego-syntonic or "feel-good" for a client, and the *Symptoms* of quadrant two are ego-dystonic or "feel-bad."

Outside of the client's everyday awareness, in hidden, preconscious, or unconscious territory, there are two more quadrants, located bottom-left and bottom-right in the diagram. Quadrant three, bottom left and the mostly "feel-good" one of these two, is called *Loyal Waiting*—the client's dogged commitment to patterns of behavior and relationship that he believes will pay off in the end, despite all evidence to the contrary. The "feel-bad" one, quadrant four and bottom-right, is *Revenge Enactments*—the retaliation inflicted on self and other as loyal waiting fails again and again. At the dynamic center of the quadrants is *Shame*, which threatens to annihilate the personality if it is felt. The quadrants describe the territory of a life organized to keep shame out of sight and out of mind.

In fact, this four-quadrant structure exists only because of shame. When a child's vulnerable self is not met with safe nurturance, support, and appreciation, the child must neutralize the shame of this absence. He or she must "manufacture through fantasy and imagination an idealized version of self, one that is overdetermined, absolute in its standards, and compulsively driven."[28] The four quadrants describe the interactive subsystems of an over-idealized, shame-phobic organization of self. Danielian and Gianotti believe that we can map onto this grid all of the diverse character solutions that our narcissistically injured clients invent to shield their vulnerability.

Yet holding this grid in mind does not govern our empathic, curious, experience-near engagement with these clients. We continue to follow their lead, exploring their interests and concerns with them, co-creating with them, as with all our clients, a narrative of their self-experience. We will certainly have chances to hear how they view themselves (quadrant one). We can come to understand what they hope for and what drives them, whether it's a need to be perfect, special, invincible, recognized, or loved. We can clarify with them their belief systems and standards for themselves and others, helping them put words to how they value, judge, and criticize. We will also certainly hear about the symptoms of their malaise (quadrant two) such as depression, anxiety, addictions, self-neglect, or overworked exhaustion.

As each client's narrative gains substance and depth, we will begin to understand his or her particular version of quadrant three, *Loyal Waiting*. The whole story of loyal waiting may lie outside of conscious awareness, but bits of storylines are accessible because they are "ego-syntonic." They just make comfortable sense, and fit with quadrant one, *How I View Myself*. It's important to note that the term "loyal waiting" doesn't describe healthy loyalty based on relational mutuality; it refers to a person's private fantasy construction that puts into play unrequited childhood longings. It's a way of relating to others based on a deep unconscious wish that someone will in some way make up for deep relational needs that were never met and thus fill the emptiness at the core of self.[29]

For some clients "loyal waiting" means waiting for a perfect other who will make up for the attuned care they missed in childhood. Some wait by clinging to the hope that a current abusive partner will turn into that perfectly loving other. Some clients wait loyally for the day when their quiet, consistent self-sacrifice will finally be seen and rewarded. Others live messier, more desperate lives, never giving up the hope of rescue and salvation. Some mask their sense of entitlement to "something better" with cynicism about what life has to offer, as if stubborn petulance could force a change. "Loyal waiting" can look like bitterness or constant sad disappointment.

There are clients for whom "loyal waiting" means an unwavering commitment to the values of family or group, no matter how self-constricting. Others commit themselves to an ideal of personal perfection, working and waiting for the day when their strivings will come to fruition and their exceptional capabilities will be acknowledged. Sometimes "loyal waiting" looks like blindness to others' faults and failings, sometimes it looks like martyrdom, and sometimes it looks like disdain for others who can't live up to demanding ideals.

As we come to know this quadrant or sub-system of our clients' internal worlds, we can begin to understand the links between this sub-system and their sub-system of beliefs, self-concepts, and self-criticisms (quadrant one). These non-threatening links can be integrated quite easily into our clients' developing narrative of self. We may also begin to notice how the symptoms of quadrant two intensify when something goes wrong with loyal waiting—the client who falls apart with anxiety on being passed over for a promotion, for example, or the client who buys six more pairs of shoes she doesn't need when her husband is "in an angry phase."

Inevitably things go wrong for narcissistically injured clients as they live out the imperatives of quadrant three (loyal waiting), partly because their interactions with others are grounded in fantasy rather than in the reality of mutual interactions from which they could grow and learn. Misunderstandings and hurt feelings abound. Most fundamentally, however, their waiting comes to grief because they just don't get what they are waiting for. Their deep, early losses will not be made up to them. As we listen to their repetitive stories of impossible longing and striving met by disappointment, we can keep our impatience in check by remembering that this is their core story, even deeper than their story of shame: profound loss that has not been mourned. Then we may be able—slowly, gently—to weave with them a narrative of compassion for their longing, striving, disappointed self.

But we will be working around the subversive destruction inflicted by an invisible quadrant four, which holds their rage about their losses. It also holds contempt, the underside of their over-idealized solution to the problem of shame—an intense, disgusted contempt that may be directed at self or at others. If these clients need to keep themselves in the dark about the whole story of quadrant three, unable to face that their waiting is futile, they definitely need to put the emotional essence of quadrant four, *Revenge Enactments*, in a far-away, not-me place.

The only news we hear from quadrant four are events and emotions that are compatible with conscious quadrant one, *How I View Myself (Aspirations, Belief Systems, and Self-Imposed Standards)*. In some clients' self systems, there's value in punishing oneself for mistakes and failures. At a less conscious level, a quick, harsh retaliation at self reinforces their self-cohesion against the threat of shame. A cohesive sense of self is not put at risk by the contempt or punishment they direct at a self who "deserves it." For many such clients, it's also ego-syntonic to lash out at someone else with rage or contempt—when they feel that person has done them a real injustice and that therefore their retaliation is justified.

We may find it hard to listen with empathy and acceptance to stories of disappointment that are turned into stories of personal betrayal. We may want to question or challenge our clients' tendencies to demean themselves, to blame others for their hurt feelings, or to "get even" with contempt and devaluation. It's especially difficult to stay attuned to a client's subjectivity while blame and devaluation are coming our way. It's useful, then, to be able to remember that this revengeful sub-system lives in unconscious home-ostatic balance with all the other sub-systems, and that together they are organized to protect a shamed, vulnerable self. When a client actively hates self or others, something must have gone wrong somewhere, most likely in the relational quadrant of *Loyal Waiting*. Rather than question our client's logic or challenge the injustice done to *us*, we can understand the enactments of quadrant four to embody the rage of a self whose strivings have been thwarted, whose longings have been denied, or whose valid emotional needs have been overlooked or misunderstood.

We and our client may be able to make a conscious, narrative link between the disappointed longing of quadrant three and the contemptuous rage of quadrant four. If so, we will have been able to soften or thin out the splitness just a bit, creating slightly more connection and flexibility within the whole system and a little more space for some more authentic self-experience. But we won't have changed the system—and that's because a construction of self built around shame does not give way to linear interpretation.

Danielian and Gianotti maintain that the dismantling of shame requires not linear thinking, but rather, "patience and deep listening. . . . Adequate treatment of shame requires a holding of the complexity, connecting the parts [of the four quadrants] to the whole, which eventually allows for the neutralization and dismantling of the narcissistic defense structure."[30] Lest we be tempted to try to *make it happen*—this dismantling of narcissistic structure—we need to hear what Danielian tells a supervisee who has for the first time contacted authentic emotion with a chronically shamed, narcissistically vulnerable client.

> Don't put pressure on yourself trying to make sure you maintain the gains. Once something like this happens, there's no going back for the psyche. The power of doing this work lies in tracking the process. The process will take care of itself if we just keep tracking and connecting the parts to the whole.[31]

I can't help but think of what I have learned from Cynthia and Sid. Change comes from how we *be* together, not through understanding or explaining. Likewise, the four quadrants model will be useful insofar as it helps me get to know *and to befriend* the parts of self that my split/splitting clients keep incognito from one another. If I can be "cool" with angry adolescents telling me that trusting me is worth shit, maybe I can contain my reaction to the devaluation that comes at me from the disappointed parts of longing, over-idealized selves. If I can simply understand Cynthia's steadfast allegiance to her dismissive mom, I can understand the loyal waiting that keeps shame-prone clients feeling emotionally balanced. If I can enjoy Sid's outrageous arrogance and larger than life swagger, I can enjoy the big energies and grandiose fantasies of my most "overcompensating" clients. If I can feel how a little kid just knows she's all-the-way bad, I can keep my wounded clients' shame not just in mind, but also "in heart."

Befriending all the aspects of my clients' split experience means: No part of you has to change. I don't have an agenda here. I think that all the parts of you have very good reasons for being. I'm here to listen to whatever you want to say, any part of you. I won't freak out. I won't disappear. I won't make you bad for anything that you feel or think or want. I care about what hurts you, and I want to help you manage it so that it doesn't hurt so much. I'm not the boss of this relationship; you are. But I'll definitely be right here. I'll be as engaged and real with you as you want me to be.

This is the offer of an unconditionally responsive affect-regulating other. In other words, it is right-brain relational work for right-brain relational trauma, the trauma that creates dissociation and shame.

TRANSFERENCE ENACTMENTS

The right-brain process of ongoing therapy often reveals itself in what client and therapist feel in relation to each other. Psychoanalytic theory has always tried to isolate aspects of this fluctuating, complex emotional interaction by calling the client's part "transference" and the therapist's part "countertransference." I will borrow Donna Orange's useful term "cotransference" to capture the actively intersubjective nature of what goes on.[32] I use "cotransference" to refer only to those feelings between client and therapist that interrupt the flow of open communication, thus shrinking intersubjective space and preventing mutual understanding.

To track cotransference, we work from an intersubjective, experience-near position. We notice when the conversation feels forced or false. We sense when our client seems uncomfortable, self-protective, or aggressive. We pay attention to how we feel from moment to moment: competent or incompetent, idealized or devalued, invited in or kept out. We pay attention to the power dynamics implicit in our conversation. We ask ourselves: What kind of person does this client seem to believe I am? What dangers—and promises—might I embody? We ask the same questions about ourselves: What's the promise and danger for me in this relationship, the attraction and aversion I feel?

Danielian and Gianotti maintain that it's our responsibility to become conscious of our contributions to the cotransference, whether they come from our unthought reactions to certain provocations, our relational history, or the theories we hold dear.[33] We keep our side of the cotransference in consciousness so that we can attend as consciously and carefully as possible to what the client is communicating from his or her side. We pay such careful attention because this is likely the most valuable information that will come our way in the process of this therapy.

This is such valuable information for the same reason it's so difficult to grasp: We aren't getting a package of verbal, rational information; the information is hidden within non-verbal *enactments*. Transference enactments are our clients' organized, non-conscious knowings about how to relate to others, put into play with us.[34] Their formative emotional/relational experiences, which have been turned into unconscious self-organizing principles, are transmitted directly, through the *how* of interaction, from their emotional/relational right brains to ours, bypassing the construction and the filter of language.[35] Our right brains respond in kind, from our own implicit relational knowing, but we can hope that we can also make explicit, at least for ourselves, some of what's happening.

This non-verbal information is valuable precisely because these clients have no conscious verbal access to what's wrong for them. It allows us to connect with aspects of their experience that they dissociate. For example, if we can notice a client's unspoken, constant pressure that we rescue her with love (quadrant three) while we tolerate her bitter, vengeful disappointment (quadrant four) that we won't be "the one"—the white knight or the mother she never had—we will have understood the relational/emotional story embedded in her enactment. If in this process we neither rescue nor retaliate, but patiently explore her unrequited longing with empathy and acceptance, that relational theme may give way to forms of connection that allow her more satisfaction.

How will this come to be? Splits soften and barriers between parts of our client's self thin out *not* when we interpret what we come to understand, but when we don't participate in an interaction in the way our client's relational knowing would predict. We gently insist, instead, on interacting in a more present and authentic way. Authentic communication helps our client develop new forms of implicit relational knowing. Within these new possibilities for relating, split-off parts of her psyche can slowly come together into a more complex whole.[36] This change process is generated not by rational, verbal understanding, but by experience—experience the client doesn't expect.

Danielian and Gianotti explain how this happens with reference to non-linear systems theory, which describes how many parts of a system influence all other parts and the whole in recursive feedback loops. Change comes by way of "emergence," defined as "the coming together of elements to form new configurations with new functions."[37]

If the transferential dynamic can be seen as an opportunity to introduce a greater degree of complexity to the patient's projections and expectations of the "other," the emergent property in any given moment may be the unfolding of greater understanding, acceptance, and trust. This in turn may lead to the emergence of greater degrees of authenticity and spontaneity in the personality.[38]

It's important to notice that the "different experience" that generates emergent change is *heightened affective relational experience*. This is the genius of psychotherapy, at least in its relational, psychodynamic modes: it creates safe co-transference space for relational intensity to develop and then to be experienced with the heightened intensity of enactment. From this perspective, enactments are to be welcomed as an important context for therapeutic change.

Clients who dissociate their shamed vulnerability with a "character solution" keep their defensive system intact by keeping it out of their awareness. But they can't help but enact it, and when they do so with us, we gain some access to their self-enclosed world. When punishing themselves for failure, they assume that we will join them in their self-contempt. They won't speak of hurt or longing for fear of being seen as pathetic. They hide the positive ways they view themselves, anticipating our subtle derision. So much enactment driven by so much dissociated shame: what can we do with it that's helpful in any way?

We counter enactment with large empathy for our shamed clients' necessary defenses and with moment-to-moment authentic interactions that don't reinforce their transference-driven expectations of us. That may be "all." Members of the Boston Change Process Study Group think in terms of non-linear dynamic systems theory, too.[39] They point out that although enactment is often viewed as the vehicle for bringing dissociated content into consciousness, "reflection upon" is not a necessary ingredient in the change processes of the implicit relational domain. Change can occur in the process of the interaction itself.[40]

With these notes on how to work with our clients' enacted dissociation, we could bring this chapter to a close. However, we haven't yet fully explored the reality that we therapists are vulnerable to dissociation and enactment, too. In fraught relationships, including relationships with clients, we find ourselves doing things we don't even notice, much less understand. Sometimes we cope with the pressure of a client's relational enactment with an enactment of our own. For further insight into the sticky, shame-ridden problem of mutual enactment, I'll move on from Danielian, Gianotti, and the Boston Change Process Study Group to consider another body of theory.[41]

DISSOCIATION/ENACTMENT THEORY AND SHAME

Dissociation and enactment have been hot topics in the world of interpersonal and relational psychoanalytic theory, generating a body of literature that's beyond the scope of this chapter to review.[42] As an important contributor to that conversation, Donnel Stern has drawn together a number of his articles into a book that addresses the problem of mutually dissociated enactments within the therapy relationship.[43] It's noteworthy that mutual shame is never far away from the problem he describes, whether the shame is consciously experienced or dissociated and unconsciously enacted.

Not-Me

Stern identifies dissociation as a defense not against a feeling, thought, or memory, but against a state of *identity*. Dissociation is not the action of putting out of mind what we can't bear knowing, the disavowal of psychic conflict. Rather, it is "the subjectivity we never create, the experience we never have."[44] We never create this part of subjectivity because it is a self-state we cannot inhabit without (we believe) being psychologically annihilated. Stern refers to this dreaded state of being as *not-me*. "One *will* not, *can*not be this person, because when one was, life was not bearable; and yet, if *not-me* enters consciousness, one *is* that person."[45] (For Stern, this kind of dissociation doesn't require overt or abusive trauma; "unbearable experience" is any relational experience that a self cannot own.[46])

Since *not-me* has never been symbolized, it remains "a vaguely defined organization of experience; a primitive, global, nonideational affective state."[47] Yet although it has not been symbolized, *not-me* does have history; it is an affective-state response to unbearable fear or humiliation. In my view, this affective state could best be called primitive, global shame, the right-brain dysregulated fragmentation that precedes any recognizable shame emotion or formulated thought about shame. When Stern mentions affects associated with *not-me* states, we hear of fear and humiliation, and also about feeling terrified, immobilized, contemptible, shamed, and weak. But of course when *not-me* is dissociated, all of this intense (and unformulated) affect can be kept away as well.

Stern points out that a dissociated *not-me* is not accessible to other self-states; it is not part of the normal multiplicity and expectable dissociation Bromberg describes, where we can "stand in the spaces" of a permeable separation between self-states and understand one state from the perspective of another.[48] There is no knowing or contacting *not-me*. Stern makes a useful distinction, too, between *bad-me* and *not-me*. *Bad-me* is what we don't much like about ourselves—but if we can think about it, it's not in *not-me* territory. We simply don't know about *not-me* because we can't afford to know.[49] For me this distinction also marks the line between *bad-me* shame that can be brought out of dark psychic hiding places into the light, and *not-me* shame that must remain dissociated and unknowable.

Mutual Enactment

Since psychotherapy offers relational space in which a client can come to know unknown aspects of self, psychotherapy creates a dangerous if not impossible situation for *not-me*. As an unbearable *not-me* threatens to break into self-awareness, the client keeps from becoming this intolerable identity by turning the therapist into that shamed identity. "I am not contemptible; *you* are contemptible." The dissociation is interpersonalized.[50]

As co-inhabitant of this world of unconscious contempt, a therapist is likely to dissociate from her own vulnerability and fall into her own enacted defense against shame. The enactment is then mutual; it is an entrenched, rigid, mutual dissociation of both selves from *not-me* identities that threaten to break in. Both therapist and client are also disconnected from other aspects of themselves and their shared relationship. What's happening feels bad and alienating, but neither person recognizes an enactment at work or knows what's being enacted.

Stern won't blame "projective identification" for the therapist's part of this mutual enactment. He believes that a therapist's dissociation is as much a product of her own life as the client's dissociation is a product of his life, and so the negotiation of an enactment requires growth from the therapist as well as from the client. The therapist's gift to the situation is not invulnerability but rather "a special (though inconsistent) willingness, and a practiced (though imperfect) capacity, to accept and deal forthrightly with her vulnerability."[51]

During an enactment the co-creation of narrative grinds to a halt. Client and therapist are no longer partners in thought. Meaning cannot be made while it is being enacted. The transitional space of imagination and creativity collapses; experience, thought, and feeling can no longer be linked meta-phorically. The former flexible openness of the client–therapist relationship tightens into rigid repetition. Neither partner in the relationship is aware of the internal conflict the situation embodies for him or her because both have laid a troublesome half of their own (dissociated) internal conflict at the door of the other's mind.

How Does Enactment End?

Mutual enactment can be terribly painful in therapy (as elsewhere in life). Sometimes clients can't bear it or see the point, and they leave therapy. But often they can bear to stay if their therapist can bear it along with them, while sharing with them a conviction that what they are doing together matters deeply somehow. Stern's narratives of his own work show us how therapists can keep this faith alive even when they don't know what's happening.

Enactments end, Stern says, not through insight. Nothing rational or verbal dissolves dissociation. Client and therapist struggle on, committed to a difficult process with as much mutual collaboration as they can muster, sticking it out on memories of mutual trust. And then one day something happens. Stern describes it as a change in affect and relatedness between partners, provoking an ever-so-slight change in each partner's perceptions of the other and of self. Insight about the change comes later and can be helpful.

But therapeutic action lies in becoming a different person, usually in a small way, in the here and now. The expansion of the self takes place in the present, in small increments. As enactment recedes, the treatment moves back into continuous productive unfolding, and new narratives once again begin to appear unbidden in the analytic space.[52]

Stern suggests that we think about the self-narratives of psychotherapy as non-linear, self-organizing systems. It is the therapist's responsibility not to guide the narratives, but to be a partner in the process that creates them. The power of these refashioned stories rests in the teller's expanded sense of self and newfound freedom to experience self with other openly and recipro-cally. Even as enactment resolves into narrative, "It is not so much that we learn the truth, but that we become more than we were."[53]

When enactment recedes, dissociated shame has been held long enough within the intention of human connection for it to have been touched in some way. Someone looks more softly at someone, and someone smiles back just a bit. Stern describes such a process between himself and a shamed/shaming cli-ent to show that shifts in relatedness precede shifts in mentalization.[54] Rather than recount Stern's story, I will share a similar story of my own. What I see in his story, as in mine, is how even a fleeting, guarded "I see you" holds the promise of recognition. Mutual recognition is what allows us all to "become more than we were," more than our shame allowed us to be.

A Case Example of Mutual Enactment

As a young therapist, I specialized in work with adult survivors of childhood trauma and abuse. Erin was a survivor, referred to me by the psychotherapy unit of the hospital that was discharging her. Throughout adolescence and young adulthood, Erin had pushed through recurrent deep depression to get an education and a solid professional career. She finally sought help when she realized she was planning to kill herself. She was given help in the form of medication, hospitalization, electro-convulsive therapy, and—finally— psychotherapy. By the time Erin came to me, she wanted no part of any treatment that, in her words, "wants to *do* something to me!" I was happy to hear that. I was reading self psychology and self-in-relation theory; I trusted empathic immersion and mutual connection to be forces for healing.

Our relationship began well. Erin pushed herself to express feelings in sessions, a skill her previous therapist had emphasized. I let her know that I didn't have benchmarks for doing "good therapy." She could be however she wanted to be in our time together. She seemed to relax, talk more easily, and start to trust me. Then slowly the truth began to emerge—in the form of colossal stuckness. I had no idea what was going on. I knew she had begun to dread coming to therapy, and I was dreading the hours with her, too. She could tell me only that she could not feel safe in therapy with me, that I was making her feel unsafe.

I asked how I could be different. She told me, "Don't ask for anything more than I say. Don't *tell* me anything. Don't put *your* ideas in, *your* curiosity, what *you* think I should feel or do. Just say things so I know you understand my feelings. Nothing more." I got it. I thought that was how I practiced therapy— absolutely non-intrusively. I was sure I could do what Erin needed.

But it seemed the harder I tried, the more often Erin got hurt and scared by little mistakes I kept making. She felt no safer. In fact, she felt worse, because if I said I was going to be safe and then I wasn't, how could she trust even my intentions? Yet she didn't threaten to leave therapy. And I just kept trying and trying to do better. Both of us were stuck for three hours a week doing something that made us feel awful, and neither of us could stop.

Why did I wait so long to share this impossible situation with my self psychologist supervisor? It was shame, of course. At the time I thought I was ashamed of doing empathic therapy badly. Now, through the dual lens of enactment theory and shame theory, I understand much better what was happening between Erin and me. I understand the deeper levels of shame that were at play. But before I explain our mutual enactment, let me describe how it ended.

When I told my supervisor the story, he said, "What a hard way to try to do therapy—like trying to work with your hands tied behind your back!"

I remember thinking, "Exactly!" and then, "Oh, so I'm not just incompetent!" I began to wonder what I might do if my hands were untied.

I decided to say to Erin, "I want to tell you about something I'm feeling because I think it's coming from somewhere bigger than us. I feel like I'll never get it right for you. It's like my hands are tied behind my back. I have to keep trying, but I'll never be good enough. That's how I feel. It reminds me of how you felt with your mom, trying so hard to be perfect, never being good enough. I wonder if somehow she's gotten here in the room with us."

Erin wasn't impressed with my interpretation of a projected-mother process, nor am I, looking back. Nevertheless, that was the day when the tension between us began to ease. I think it eased just because I told Erin what I was feeling, and she could, indeed, imagine what that felt like, trying so hard and failing. I shared my vulnerability; this was the small shift for me. When she could see me vulnerable and still trying to connect, she could make a small shift herself, seeing me as more of a whole person, fallible but on her side. She could feel that I was no longer just a threat, and I could feel that I wasn't completely failing her. That's how the softening between us happened, just a little bit at a time.

What was the nature of the mutual enactment that had immobilized us for so long? We were each warding off becoming a self we could not bear to be. Later in our work together, I came to understand that Erin could not be that self whose need for connection once left her open to profound misrecognition and violation. If she had not needed, she would never have become just a pawn of the other's need, an unbearable experience for her. Her needing self thus became a place of deep, wordless shame, a *not-me*. In order not to be that self, she closed off all possibilities for further need, misrecognition, and violation. My need to be a good therapist spelled deep danger. And yet the project of therapy asked her to need my understanding and open herself up to my knowing.

What about my *not-me*? I could not bear to be that self whose deep desire for connection had once been rebuffed, that self who had felt pushed away because of shameful longings to know and to be known, that self whose vitality the other experienced as trouble and imposition. I was still years away from having to feel that *not-me*. In retrospect, though, I can see how our mutually dissociated enactment was as much a product of my relational history as it was of Erin's. The project of therapy asked me to keep offering connection even when my approach felt to the other like threat, a misrecognition I knew in my bones, one that created a self I could not bear to feel.

Since neither of us could bear being our own *not-me*, we each laid our problem at the other's door. We each unconsciously believed that if only the other would be different, we would be safe from the relational trauma that spawns the primitive global affect—the shame—of *not-me*. Erin: "If only you would respond to my need for connection by seeing who I am, not what you need!" Me: "If only you would accept my reaching out as good, not dangerous!" Each of us believing: "If only you would . . . then *I* would not be contemptible."

Locked into this impossible, unconscious mutual necessity, we lost our capacity to talk with each other, or even to see each other except as a threat.

But then something happened, because in spite of the *not-me* shame we couldn't own, we meant well. Our dissociated shame was held long enough within the intention of human connection for it to be touched and eased. I spoke of a vulnerability that Erin understood. Ever so slightly, I could be fallible, she could be fragile, and we could be in connection. As we emerged from our mutual enactment, our mutual warding off of *not-me* shame, we couldn't say what had happened, but in small ways we had become different persons.

And then therapy continued. Narratives unfolded and changed—her story and our story together. We have never talked about the *not-me* shame experiences that once troubled our work together, but maybe we will now, when I ask her permission to use this material.[55] Twenty years later, Erin still comes to see me once a month. She comes for the kind of conversation she doesn't have with other people in her life. She says our conversations help her feel more whole and in touch with who she is. I like to think of them as right-brain conversations.

Right-Brain Coda

Stern identifies *not-me* as a primitive, global, non-ideational affective state so distressful it can't be held in consciousness. As I've said, this sounds to me like the right-brain, primitive, global shame experience of a self fragmenting in relation to a dysregulating other. From this perspective, a dysregulated state wrapped in shame-affect becomes *not-me* when the other fails to find me and be with me in that state, when that state persists without repair. *Not-me* is a failure of other-with-me, a deep, core failure of affect regulation.

If this is the case, it makes sense that *not-me* can be brought back into self only through enactment, that is, only through an experience of other-with-me *when I am in that very state of not-me*. And in fact, this is Schore's argument about enactments—that they represent "essential therapeutic contexts that potentially allow for the revelation of parts of the self that are not fully known (dissociated 'not-me states')."[56] A therapy that welcomes enactments welcomes what can't be verbalized, what is unconsciously avoided, and what has been dissociated. It does so with attuned, affective "right-brain" presence, which is ultimately what makes possible the shifts out of enactment and toward freedom that Stern describes.

Schore locates the healing effect of working with enactments within the right brain. It's very interesting that even without reference to the right brain, Stern now proposes that formulated meanings are not limited to the "verbal register." In his own words, "I now take the position that both verbal *and* nonverbal meanings can be formulated. I refer to the formulation of verbal meaning as *articulation* and that of nonverbal meaning as *realization*."[57] Realization is a powerful form of knowing; for example, the very perception of the other and of oneself that Stern believes will lead one out of enactment is a nonverbal perception. Its efficacy is in its non-verbal formulation, not in the insights that may flow from it later.

For Stern, not even new narrative is driven by new insight, but rather by new and unexpected relational experience. What we are seeking isn't insight, but freedom to be different than we were. In Schore's less existential, more scientific language, we move "from a constriction to an expansion of adaptive right brain affective functions."[58]

The convergence of right brain theory and relational psychoanalytic theory is unambiguous in the Foreword Schore wrote for Philip Bromberg's book on working through enactments with relationally traumatized patients.[59] Schore lays claim to deep agreement between Bromberg's ideas and his own. In his brain-science idiom, Schore describes enactments as implicit right brain to right brain non-verbal communications of emotional states between client and therapist.[60] When regulated, these conversations between limbic systems facilitate the top-down and bottom-up integration of the right brain.[61] Bromberg tells this very same story with narratives of contact, emotion, and relational movement. In his metaphorical, imagistic, right-brain idiom, the relational mind finds healing and growth within the experience of "the nearness of you."[62]

When as therapists we sustain this personal, emotional nearness as best we can—and in hard times sustain at least the offer and intention of nearness—we give our shamed clients a chance to soften their self-protections, even those who have locked their *not-me* shamed selves into dissociative closets. We have reason to hope that as they reach out to parts of themselves that have never been touched and as they allow themselves to be comforted by the presence of another, the shame that has kept them split from others and from themselves will be significantly eased. We have reason to expect that they will indeed be able to tell their stories, perhaps even their stories of longing and shame, with the freedom to become more than they were.

NOTES

1. See Karen Horney, *Our Inner Conflicts: A Constructive Theory of Neurosis* (New York: Norton, 1945) and *Neurosis and Human Growth: The Struggle towards Self-Realization* (New York: Norton, 1950). Jack Danielian and Patricia Gianotti, in *Listening with Purpose: Entry Points into Shame and Narcissistic Vulnerability* (New York: Jason Aronson, 2012), draw inspiration from Horney in developing a contemporary approach to treating chronic shame, described more fully later in this chapter.

2. Allan Schore, *The Science of the Art of Psychotherapy* (New York: Norton, 2012), 277.

3. Jon G. Allen, D.A. Console, and L. Lewis, "Dissociative Detachment and Memory Impairment: Reversible Amnesia or Encoding Failure?" *Comprehensive Psychiatry* 40 (1999): 165, quoted in Schore, *Science of the Art*, 277, Schore's italics.

4. Schore, *Science of the Art*, 291.

5. Schore, *Science of the Art*, 190.

6. Schore, *Science of the Art*, 126.

7. Bessel A. van der Kolk and Rita Fisler, "Dissociation and the Fragmentary Nature of Traumatic Memories: Overview and Exploratory Study," *Journal of Traumatic Stress* 8 (1995): 505–25.

8. Judith Lewis Herman, *Trauma and Recovery* (New York: Basic Books, 1992).

9. Jody Messler Davies and Mary Gail Frawley, *Treating the Adult Survivor of Childhood Sexual Abuse: A Psychoanalytic Perspective* (New York: Basic Books, 1994), 64.

10. Davies and Frawley, *Treating the Adult Survivor*, 62–85.

11. Davies and Frawley, *Treating the Adult Survivor*, 167.

12. *American Psychiatric Association, Diagnostic and Statistical Manual of Mental Disorders, Fifth Edition (DSM-5)* (Arlington, VA: American Psychiatric Association, 2013). "Multiple Personality Disorder" was the language of the DSM-III; the DSM-IV (1994) replaced the term with "Dissociative Identity Disorder," which continues in the DSM-5.

13. See, for example, Eugene L. Bliss, *Multiple Personality, Allied Disorders, and Hypnosis* (New York: Oxford University Press, 1986).

14. See, for example, Philip Bromberg, *Standing in the Spaces: Essays on Clinical Process, Trauma, and Dissociation* (Hillsdale, NJ: Analytic Press, 1998) and Donnel Stern, *Partners in Thought: Working with Unformulated Experience, Dissociation, and Enactment* (New York: Routledge, 2010).

15. Boston Change Process Study Group, "The Foundational Level of Psychodynamic Meaning: Implicit Process in Relation to Conflict, Defense, and Dynamic Unconscious," in *Change in Psychotherapy: A Unifying Paradigm* (New York: Norton, 2010), 143–60.

16. Robert Stolorow and George Atwood, "Three Realms of the Unconscious," in *Contexts of Being: The Intersubjective Foundations of Psychological Life* (Hillsdale, NJ: Analytic Press, 1992), 29–40.

17. Donnel Stern, *Unformulated Experience: From Dissociation to Imagination in Psychoanalysis* (Hillsdale, NJ: Analytic Press, 1997).

18. In Winnicott's classic explication of transitional objects and transitional phenomena, the experience which is intermediary between inner and outer experience—including the transitional space/experience belonging to play, imagination, art, and psychoanalysis—is to remain unchallenged with respect to its belonging to inner or external (shared) reality. In his words, "The transitional object and the transitional phenomena start each human being off with what will always be important for them, i.e. a neutral area of experience which will not be challenged. Of the transitional object it can be said that it is a matter of agreement between us and the baby that we will never ask the question: 'Did you conceive of this or was it presented to you from without?' The important point is that no decision on this point is expected. The question is not to be formulated." Donald W. Winnicott, *Playing and Reality* (London: Tavistock, 1971, Penguin Education reprint, 1982), 14 (page reference to the reprint edition), Winnicott's italics.

19. Richard Geist, "Connectedness, Permeable Boundaries, and the Development of the Self: Therapeutic Implications," *International Journal of Psychoanalytic Self Psychology* 3 (2008): 133–36.

20. Cynthia, Sid, and Hilary each read this account of our work and gave me kind permission to use it.

21. "In the treatment of MPD it is important to be as shallow as possible. There is no need for 'deep' exploration because the most important material is immediately available on the surface, though the surface is dissociated into separate compartments." Colin Ross, *Multiple Personality Disorder: Diagnosis, Clinical Features, and Treatment* (New York: Wiley & Sons, 1989), 217.

22. Danielian and Gianotti, *Listening with Purpose*, xii.

23. Danielian and Gianotti, *Listening with Purpose*, 21.

24. Danielian and Gianotti, *Listening with Purpose*, 5.

25. Danielian and Gianotti, *Listening with Purpose*, 10–11.

26. Danielian and Gianotti, *Listening with Purpose*, 4–5.

27. Danielian and Gianotti, *Listening with Purpose*, 221–31.

28. Danielian and Gianotti, *Listening with Purpose*, 80.

29. Danielian and Gianotti, *Listening with Purpose*, 44–47.

30. Danielian and Gianotti, *Listening with Purpose*, 173.

31. Danielian and Gianotti, *Listening with Purpose*, 179.

32. Donna Orange, *Emotional Understanding: Studies in Psychoanalytic Epistemology*, (New York: Guilford, 1995), 63–74.

33. Danielian and Gianotti, *Listening with Purpose*, 225–26.

34. See Boston Change Process Study Group, *Change in Psychotherapy*, 188–90.

35. See Schore, "Therapeutic Enactments: Working in Right Brain Windows of Affect Tolerance," in *Science of the Art*, 152–219.

36. Danielian and Gianotti, *Listening with Purpose*, 224.

37. Danielian and Gianotti, *Listening with Purpose*, 227–28.

38. Danielian and Gianotti, *Listening with Purpose*, 230.

39. Boston Change Process Study Group, *Change in Psychotherapy*, 70–74, 90.

40. Boston Change Process Study Group, *Change in Psychotherapy*, 190.

41. Danielian and Gianotti lean toward the position that mutual enactments can be avoided by paying careful attention to countertransference and should be avoided whenever possible. Relational/Interpersonal theorists such as Donnell Stern do not believe it is possible for therapists actually to have that much "knowing" about what is in unconsciousness or that much control over interpersonal process. They believe that mutual enactment is often the only route to the formulation of dissociated material, and so, although the experience of mutual enactment is difficult, they welcome it into their practice as inevitable and useful and write about it extensively.

42. For example, Stern, *Unformulated Experience*; Jodie Messler Davies, "Dissociation and Therapeutic Enactment," *Gender and Psychoanalysis* 2 (1997): 241–57; Karen Maroda, "Enactment: When the Patient's and Analyst's Pasts Converge," *Psychoanalytic Psychology* 15 (1998): 517–35; Stuart Pizer, *Building Bridges: Negotiating Paradox in Psychoanalysis* (Hillsdale, NJ: Analytic Press, 1998); Lewis Aron, "The Paradoxical Place of Enactment in Psychoanalysis: Introduction," *Psychoanalytic Dialogues* 13 (2003): 273–87; Philip Bromberg, *Awakening the Dreamer: Clinical Journeys* (Mahwah, NJ: Analytic Press, 2006), *The Shadow of the Tsunami and the Growth of the Relational Mind* (New York: Routledge, 2011), and *Standing in the Spaces*.

43. Stern, *Partners in Thought*.

44. Stern, *Partners in Thought*, 95.

45. Stern, *Partners in Thought*, 120.

46. Stern, *Partners in Thought*, 19–20.

47. Stern, *Partners in Thought*, 119.

48. Stern, *Partners in Thought*, 50.

49. Stern, *Partners in Thought*, 88.

50. Stern, *Partners in Thought*, 121.

51. Stern, *Partners in Thought*, 89.

52. Stern, *Partners in Thought*, 124.

53. Stern, *Partners in Thought*, 128.

54. Stern, *Partners in Thought*, 174–80.

55. Erin read my account and graciously gave me permission to use it here.

56. Schore, *Science of the Art*, 164–65.

57. Stern, *Partners in Thought*, xv.

58. Schore, *Science of the Art*, 165.

59. Bromberg, *Shadow of the Tsunami*.

60. Allan Schore, foreword to *Shadow of the Tsunami*, by Bromberg, xxvii.

61. Schore, foreword to *Shadow of the Tsunami*, xxxiv.

62. Bromberg, *Shadow of the Tsunami*, 7.

CHAPTER 11

Lifetime Shame Reduction

Is there a cure for chronic shame? As a psychotherapist, I would like to say to my clients, *Yes, absolutely. We can beat this thing!* As a person who has struggled to understand and integrate my own chronic shame, I would love to answer, *Yes, I'm over it.* To be honest, however, I have to say, *No, I don't think chronic shame can be cured.* Long-term relational trauma leaves our psyches indelibly marked. Even with the best psychotherapy, we don't just get over a lifetime of wondering whether we really matter to those closest to us or whether we can be enough for those to whom we do matter. We don't radically reconfigure a personality built around anxious self-protection.

On the other hand, coming to terms with chronic shame can make life far more bearable than if we just try to soldier on, oblivious. "Bearable" is putting it cautiously. I've seen people emerge from chronic states of shame into states of consistent well-being that include pleasure and even joy. That's because although shame can't be cured, the painful effects of shame can be reduced in our daily lives. Such shame reduction happens both inside and outside of therapy.

How to ease shame within the process of therapy is the gist of this book. The key is a relationship between client and therapist that's the antithesis of a shaming relationship. Our attuned responsiveness encourages clients to reconnect with relational needs and intensities of feelings long denied. Our empathic curiosity invites them to open up to the emotional story of their relational lives with others. Our compassionate acceptance of all of their experience makes space where even shame itself can be given light and air. And perhaps the most powerful antidote we offer our clients is our willingness to acknowledge and work through the shame that comes up between us and them in therapy.

If our clients lead lives of chronic shame, our relationship with them is our point of leverage against their suffering. But they see us for only an hour or two a week, and the rest of the time they live their lives in the world, outside of therapy. Will they feel less shame out there, too? When therapy ends, as it must, their lives will go on. Will their shame continue to be eased?

Our clients leave the therapy room with new memories, having had new experiences. When therapy works, they take with them expanded capacities to be in relationship with us and with themselves. We hope that the changes begun with us will spread organically to new growth outside of therapy. And in fact, often we do more than hope. To extend the metaphor, we don't just trust the wind and rain; we plant some chosen seeds and nurture them. Though it may seem outside the purview of a psychodynamic practice, we give our chronically shamed clients certain kinds of practical help so that they can have a better chance at lifetime shame reduction.

ON SHAME REDUCTION

Many of our chronically shamed clients have been disappointed by previous therapy, and for good reason: the therapy didn't help them with their shame. Therapists and clients often side-step the shame they enact with each other. No one wants to feel the relational devastation that lies at the heart of shame. Instead, therapists encourage shamed clients to work on their internal feelings of being wrong, ugly, inadequate, or worthless—on the effects, not the cause, of what's wrong. The relational essence of shame is not addressed. Sadly, when such "working on shame" fails to produce lasting change, a client may feel shame about this failure, too.

We intend to get to the root of shame with our clients. Yet we still need to talk with them about "shame reduction" instead of "cure." We know that even when our clients have been able to connect with the relational pain of the shame they have suffered, they won't find themselves pain-free or shame-free. This will disappoint them. Even as they come to feel more connected with us and more solid in themselves, these clients will still long for a more transformative therapy, and they may protest bitterly the difficult feelings that still plague them, the bad thoughts that come back to haunt them on vulnerable days.

We understand their anger as part of their grief about irrevocable losses. They will never know the naïve well-being of secure attachment; they can't go back in time to change what happened. We also understand that their idea of cure has been constructed by their shame. From the perspective of a chronically shamed self, cure looks like knowing at last that there's nothing wrong with you. When cured, you will be finally perfect, and perfectly loved. Shame-prone people wouldn't say that fantasy out loud. They "know" better. But, as they may tell you if you're the latest in a series of therapists they've seen, shame-prone people are easy marks for promises of transformation. They really do hope that there's a beautiful authentic self hidden inside, and that when they find that self, they will be able to dump their shame-riddled inauthentic self at the side of the road.

To keep from playing into this fantasy, I don't talk with clients about transformation through therapy. I know that it's not in our best interests, my clients' and mine, to imagine that our work will result in total transformative healing or the realization of a finally authentic self. For all of us, the changes we experience in therapy—as in life—are genuine and they matter. Yet, as we continue to change, we also remain the same persons that we were, if older, wiser, less troubled, and more connected with ourselves and others.

We hope not for cure but for shame reduction because shame is not only tenacious, it has become part of our being. Even if we manage to get the help we need to be able to face and feel our shame, we can't dump our shame-riddled self at the side of the road. Like it or not, that self remains an essential part of who we are. In the language of multiple selves, that enduring self needs not to be ostracized but to be understood and befriended. In the language of interpersonal neurobiology: we can ameliorate the effects of relational trauma on the brain, but we can't erase them.[1]

Neural plasticity means that new information, new neural firing, can help the brain heal itself. But as the literature on recovery from stroke and traumatic brain injury illustrates, building new neural pathways and networks takes long, hard work.[2] In the case of relational trauma, the new pathways don't replace networks that have been destroyed. Instead, new pathways connect what's been dissociated and open up what's been blocked or stunted. Then inner and interpersonal connection and comfort become possible, soothing even old hurts. Instead of experiencing the shame of disintegrating in relation to dysregulating others, one can experience integration—even of one's shamed self—within empathic relationships with others and with oneself. But even for these changes to become possible, neurons need to fire together many times before they begin to wire together, and new capacities need to be used consistently to keep them viable.

For many clients this may be the image that best explains why "there ain't no cure for shame." We can't wipe clean our internal operating system and start over. But we can keep giving the emotional/relational side of our brains chances to take in new information and process it differently. I may say just that to a client who knows what shame has cost him and wonders, "Where do I go from here?" He needs experiences that will continually create new synaptic connections that supersede and reconfigure the old.

In more relational language, he needs ongoing repetitions of interpersonal contact that feel much more safe, responsive, and validating than what his early wiring leads him to expect. And he needs just as many novel, positive experiences of being with himself. In this context, the context of relationship, "authentic" is a helpful word: he needs to learn how to be in authentic relationships with others and with himself. That sums up the two categories of practical help our chronically shamed clients need most from us as they attempt to reduce the power of shame in their daily lives.

AUTHENTIC CONNECTION WITH OTHERS

All of our chronically shamed clients have trouble where self meets other. For some the trouble is obvious, whether they come off as self-effacing or arrogant. For others, who hide their shame behind perfection or who live a psychologically split existence, the trouble between self and the world is far from obvious. But for all of them, whatever their protective self-organizations, their shame comes from the same basic experience: something went badly and consistently wrong in their early connection with others. And so right at the point where self and other might connect, the problem persists. In Judith

Jordan's words, "Shame is most importantly a felt sense of unworthiness to be in connection, a deep sense of unlovability, with the ongoing awareness of how very much one wants to connect with others."[3]

As clients become able to face their deep sense of unlovability and to link it with their unmet longings to be in connection, they will also begin to feel their loneliness here and now. As I said in the very first chapter, this is the one thing that chronically shamed clients have in common: they lead a profoundly lonely existence, often more lonely than they know, since it's all they have ever known.

Clients who believe they are unlovable are lonely not because there are no people in their lives (we rarely see hermits in therapy), but because their relationships with others are inauthentic. These clients may *seem* to be present, they may even seem to have many friends, but in the relational paradox the Stone Center theorists highlight, they stay in a semblance of connection by keeping most of who they are out of connection. We can help them notice this pattern, and we can also help them learn to do connection differently—not only with us, but also with the "real people" in their lives.

Sharing Emotions

For many of our clients, a first step in becoming more authentic in relationships is learning how to share their emotions with someone close to them. We can help that process along in simple, direct ways. For example, a client may have figured out that when her best friend Jane goes on and on about next summer's wedding plans, she feels envious at first and then hurt and distant. When we're confident our client feels our empathy with her, we might ask, "Have you ever thought about talking to Jane about that? What do you think might happen if you did?" That's when we hear our client's conviction that her feelings will only cause trouble in the relationship. She needs to keep her hurt to herself if she wants to keep Jane as a friend.

We can agree with our client that maybe Jane can't listen. Some friends can't. "On the other hand," we might say, "it seems possible—given how much you like Jane and given your history of not being heard as a kid—that you're putting some convictions from your past on your present. We all do that; it's a natural thing to do. But when those old beliefs make you sad and shut you down, it seems worth it to wonder if maybe they don't really fit. What if Jane could actually understand how you feel? What if your brain is doing an old thing with a new situation, and it could do something new? Do you think, with Jane, it's worth trying something new?"

Of course, we don't say all that at once; we remember and wonder together; we pause and listen and have a conversation. When we can keep ourselves in the mode of playful, curious exploration, accepting whatever gets uncovered, very often clients will decide, yes, they would like to try something new.

But they also quickly feel lost about how to proceed and may ask for input. Then we have a chance to talk about how to make space for two people to hear each other's feelings. We suggest that our client might begin by telling Jane she understands her excitement about the wedding, and her need to talk about it. We explain, "That makes it easier for Jane to hear what's bothering you. Especially if you can say it's just about something she *does* sometimes, not about who she is to you, and how when she does that one thing, you end up feeling like you don't matter." We ask our client how she'd feel if a friend talked with her like that. Would she get defensive and angry? Might she be able to listen?

Far more often than not, if clients follow through on a careful plan to share emotion with someone they feel they can probably trust, they come away pleasantly surprised by their new experience, if not downright shocked and exhilarated. This is *not* what they know in their bones: in a shamed client's inner world, affective attunement did not happen, and so, where empathic connection could be, there's shut-down self-protection. There's not even a felt sense of empathic *possibility*.

As Jordan explains, relational therapy brings a person back into connection in which empathic possibility exists. We can help our clients explore empathic possibility outside of therapy, too. Within any connected relationship, as empathy for self and other increases, shame decreases.[4] Then a more robust mutual empathy makes possible deeper, richer connection. This *connected* sense of authenticity is what our clients need to experience—over and over again, in as many contexts as possible, until it's no longer a surprise. This is not assertiveness training. Authentic connection is sharing emotion within "I-see-you-seeing-me" intersubjective space: I will tell you what I feel because we each hear and care about how the other feels.

Negotiating Needs

The language of "getting my needs met" bothers me. Even though I often say that the suffering of chronic shame has its roots in a person's early unmet needs for emotional connection, I don't make it a project with clients that they try to get their emotional needs met from the people in their lives. The project feels to me like the opposite of authentic connection. It seems to reduce moments of interpersonal mutuality—of desire and risk, hope and disappointment, giving and receiving—to a list of needs managed by a series of transactions. What a left-brain way to try to get emotional connection!

But the language of "getting needs met" does seem to appeal to many shame-prone clients, perhaps because a project organized by the left brain creates a sense of safety for them. For shamed people, needing is indeed dangerous territory. If they had never needed attuned, engaged responsiveness (and then failed to get it), they never would have fallen so far into shame. Needing is the original "something wrong with me."

It's small wonder that persons once deeply shamed by emotional need might jump at the chance to make their needs "all good." I suspect, though, that this nifty reversal simply bypasses relational shame. Insisting on "getting my needs met" puts my needs in the third person and distances them from myself. I'm not looking you in the eye and saying, "I would like this from you," nor am I inviting you to tell me how that is for you, or what you might like from me, too. Ironically, talking about my needs lets me escape the relational moment of being a needing self with you. I don't risk being thrown into relational shame all over again—but I also fail to make genuine contact with you.

If clients of mine want to discuss getting their emotional needs met, I don't, however, quibble with their language. I do ask them to tell me more about those needs in their relational contexts: What's happening with somebody when a need comes up? What do they feel and want in that moment? I try to help them imagine details of conversations they could have. How will they tell their partner (for example) exactly what they would like? Do they think they will be heard? What can they do to increase the likelihood of mutual listening? How will they feel if their partner wants something in response, or in kind?

What my clients need from others matters, of course. But I'm attuned to another kind of need, one they gave up feeling a long time ago. They need to be able to have safe, real conversations about what they want and don't want from people close to them. If their shame is truly to diminish, what their needing, desiring, vulnerable self needs most of all is to make authentic reciprocal connection with others. In the process, some of their needs will get met, but what matters most is the negotiation. As in the dance of continual miss/repair attunement between mother and infant, the negotiation *is* the authentic connection, the place where the self finds safe freedom to work through desire and emotion with another.

Stopping Shame/Blame Cycles

At the beginning of therapy with chronically shamed clients, we may notice how susceptible they are to feeling unreasonably responsible for anything that goes wrong in any of their relationships. These are moments to be curious, and also, perhaps, to say, "I don't think that just because someone feels bad, that means you're at fault." This may be a new and intriguing idea for them. There may be a chance, then, to talk about how blame and shame affect relationships, perhaps with a link to the family system in which they grew up.

Nobody—and especially not somebody prone to shame—wants to see himself or herself as a person who inflicts blame or shame on others. That's why places where clients are the target of blame are the best places to help them learn how blaming works: "She believes that the only way for her to feel better is to 'make you bad.' I guess she can't be vulnerable enough to talk about her own feelings. It takes some real courage to do that, to own what you feel."

When clients come to understand the shame/blame dynamic, they want out of it. They want family members and friends to be more vulnerable and emotionally responsible with them. Then they find that if they want changes in their relationships, they'll likely have to take the lead. Instead of responding to blame with blame, they'll have to respond with their own feelings and experience. That's when they look to us for guidance in how to be more vulnerable and responsible.

The groundwork will have been laid. By now clients will have spent many hours with us, developing new neural networks about being understood and accepted. They know we won't "make them bad" for their feelings or thoughts. They don't need splits and defenses as much as they did before. In this more relaxed, connected state of self, clients know what empathic possibility feels like. And so they can explore how to keep empathic possibility open in their difficult conversations—empathy for themselves and for others—even imagining that others might have empathy for them, given a chance.

Our clients will look to us to model vulnerability, authenticity, and empathy—the alternatives to blame. Therefore, when our feelings are present in the therapy room, we acknowledge them. When we make mistakes, we say we're sorry, and if a mistake, such as a double booking, has consequences for a client, we make amends. If there's a misunderstanding between us, we don't blame our clients, but try to see both sides of what happened.

If our clients are angry with us in a blaming way, we feel the blame, of course, but we don't retaliate with defense or with counter-accusations. Instead, we try to understand what they feel about what we did. We show them it's possible to take responsibility for our own actions, to understand and care about how the other person feels in response, and at the same time not to take the blame for how the other feels. This kind of emotional/relational learning is a right brain experience. Even without being explained, it can generate major change in our clients' capacity to exit shame/blame cycles and to relate to others more openly and authentically.

Guilt and Remorse as Authentic Connection

If we are a lucky kind of unlucky, we will have chances to share with our clients the relational sequence of injury, guilt, remorse, and forgiveness within the client–therapist relationship. Important new experience can happen whether we or our clients cause the injury. For the sake of example, let's say that we have injured a client. And let's put this uncomfortable story in the first person; I'll wear the guilt for the sake of the learning.

Let's say that after a night of broken sleep, I'm not at my best. Having mustered the adrenalin to bring some calm and focus to a couple in crisis, I take ten minutes for quick notes, and then I welcome my client into her weekly session. She looks tense, and she tells me she's had a terrible week, therapy isn't working, it never has worked, and it probably never will. I know this is a state that overwhelms her regularly. I know I need to bring curious empathy to the emotional reality behind her statements. I also know she'll say that she isn't angry, she's just hopeless, and can't I see that she has every reason to feel hopeless.

I do my best to squash my rising frustration, trying to enact "good therapist." But of course she knows (her right brain knows) that I'm not really there in my stabs at curious empathy, that really I'm fed up and angry myself. Eventually, as nothing shifts between us, I happen on an idea. I don't think it through, and it feels like a relief. I say in a calm, good-therapist voice,

"You know, you may be right. Maybe this therapy isn't working for you. We've struggled with it for quite a while. Maybe what you need is something more intensive, maybe psychoanalysis two or three times a week. Maybe that would keep you from falling into these states between sessions that feel so awful. And then your life would be more bearable."

It's as if she hasn't heard me. We go on to other details of her life that aren't working out, and then the session ends uneventfully. But by the time she returns a week later, she knows that she is feeling terribly hurt and mis-understood. She also feels like she's too much for me and I'm trying to get rid of her.

Then I have to face that I have done something that has caused my client injury. It's true: in the previous session, my stressed state of self could not manage her disruptively anxious affect, and yes, I wanted to be rid of her, at least in those moments. Now I have to access quickly everything I know about the uselessness of falling into shame about my failure, and about the value of owning up to making a mistake that has caused injury.

I tell her that I understand what she's saying and that I remember what I did. I ask her to tell me more about what that was like for her. As I listen, I also have time to assess my guilt and consider the best way to speak of it. I decide not to speak of my stressed state last week (defensive), or about how her hopelessness wears me down (blaming). Instead I decide to tell her simply that she's right about what I was feeling and what I did.

I say: "In that session, I wasn't feeling very capable, and what I said was to make *me* feel better, not to help you. I tried to make it *look* like help. But I know that what I said was hurtful, and I'm sorry that I hurt you. I'm sure it felt like I was getting back at you for being angry. I think I had some angry feelings, but I didn't let myself know about them. I knew that I didn't want to keep on doing what I was doing, feeling what I was feeling. So in some way I *was* trying to get rid of you—and that's why it felt that way."

I check that so far I'm hearing her feelings accurately and making sense. She says that I am, and so I go on: "I know that our deal here is that you bring whatever you're feeling, and it's my responsibility to help you explore and make sense of it—*not to react to it*. So I failed on my side. I made a serious mistake. I appreciate that you're holding up your end by telling me how you feel about what I did. I do owe you an apology, so let me say again that I'm sorry, and that I'll do my best not to fail you in that way again."

My client is looking at me, undistracted. Her eyes are clear; her face is no longer tight with anger. She says, "Thank you for saying that." I nod, accept-ing her thanks. She adds, "I needed to hear that." I nod again, feeling mostly forgiven and sensing more connection between us than I have sensed for a long while. I feel grateful for what I've learned about aspiring to guilt instead of falling into shame. If I can be a good therapist who did a bad thing, I don't have to cut myself off from my client in abject shame; I can move toward her with remorse appropriate to the size and meaning of the bad thing done. Then we might have an affectively potent opportunity—just like this—to find out that the sequence of injury, guilt, remorse, and forgiveness can create connection that feels authentic and meaningful.

When I think about this event in the weeks following, I realize that this client, with her intense, painful shame, has always tried desperately never to be in the wrong with anyone. But now she has begun to talk about times in her life when she wishes she had been "nicer." She wonders if she's making some mistakes with her anger, and we wonder together whether mistakes are tolerable and fixable. I talk about the goodness of guilt as opposed to shame—about how sometimes saying you're sorry from a place of remorse, not shame, can bring you closer to the other person. We even talk a bit about the awful angst of shame.

All of this is about her life "out there." Since my client doesn't mention what happened between us, I don't bring it up. She may not see the connection consciously; perhaps a shift is happening in her right-brain neural networks that register implicit relational knowing. I hope she can begin to give up the isolation of shame for the authentic connectedness of guilt, remorse, and forgiveness. I'm happy that, whether or not she remembers, I have "walked the walk" with her.

AUTHENTIC CONNECTION WITH SELF

According to relational theories of psychoanalysis and psychotherapy, our sense of self comes into being through connection with others.[5] Not only is a core sense of self created by our early relationships, our current sense of self is an ongoing, fluctuating product of relatedness.[6] Our self-experience may in any moment be altered by the here-and-now quality of a particular connection with another person.

In analogous ways, our felt sense of self is also the product of the relationship of self-with-self. This internal relatedness-in-motion is created by a part of our brain that constantly synchronizes internal cognitions, emotions, body feelings, memories, and fantasies into patterns recognized as the self's own. Even if the multiplicity of our selves or self-states barely registers with us, what holds us in coherence is the moment-to-moment connection we experience among our various parts of self.

Therefore it's important that we talk with our clients, not about uncovering their one true, authentic self, but rather about finding connection with and among their diverse experiences of self. This goal meshes well with a simple explanation of how relational psychotherapy works, one that makes good sense to most clients: In relational therapy you take the time to have a genuine, meaningful relationship with another person so that you can have a genuine, meaningful relationship with yourself.

Clients who suffer from chronic shame find relating to others and to self equally difficult. Just as we can help them learn to be in more authentic connection with us and with the other people in their lives, so too we can help them begin lifelong habits (develop new neural networks) of connecting more authentically with themselves. Three habits of connecting with self are particularly useful in countering the effects of chronic shame: *self-compassion*, *mindfulness*, and *self-expression*.

Self-Compassion

Shame theorists note that shamed clients have an especially destructive, non-empathic self-to-self relationship. Paul Gilbert summarizes studies that find self-criticism to be the major link between relational trauma and depression and anxiety. He concludes, "It is the way in which difficult, stressful, and traumatic experiences influence self-to-self relating that is key to vulnerability to psychopathology."[7] Changing this damaging self-to-self relationship is far from easy, however, since high-shame people have little experience of compassion from others or from self. Gilbert concludes that we can't just hope that our clients will grow into self-empathy; we need to teach our high-shame clients self-compassion, and to that end he suggests Compassion Focused Therapy.

Gilbert begins, as all relational therapists do, by demonstrating non-judgmental, caring curiosity in interactions with shamed clients, showing them how they can think about troubling feelings, be "mindful" about them, and simply accept them. He mixes this right-brain modeling with left-brain teaching, taking psycho-educational opportunities to normalize or "de-shame" negative emotions, internal conflict, and ambivalent feelings. He validates shame experience as painful and understandable, given the client's history and life circumstances.

Gilbert shares with clients his understanding that they may have learned to blame themselves in order to keep themselves safe in dangerous relationships, and he helps them consider what they might risk in relationship if they stopped being so self-critical. He helps clients learn the difference between shame-based self-criticizing (with its emotions of anger, contempt, and disappointment) and compassionate self-correction, in which clients can recognize errors as guides to growth and improvement. Not surprisingly, Gilbert also suggests guidelines to help clients distinguish between feelings of shame and feelings of guilt.[8]

Since all of these left-brain interventions offer clients an attuned, validating experience, they also speak subliminally to a client's right-brain shame. But how might we speak more directly to it? Gilbert explains that our most compassionate efforts may not touch a client's shame when the client has never experienced positive emotional regulation. Clients who grew up deprived of empathy or compassion can't access an endorphin/oxytocin emotional regulation system, which, in contrast to the dopamine excitement system, generates soothing, calming feelings and creates a sense of closeness and connectedness. Thus Gilbert arrives at this critical question: "Can we teach people how to practice and generate a particular type of self-to-self relationship that is based on self-compassion . . . with the aim of stimulating the soothing system?"[9]

Gilbert's answer is, "Yes," and the kind of "teaching" his answer describes is highly right-brain/experiential. He suggests that we help clients feel into the *attributes* of compassion, first of all helping them experience self-compassion as desirable instead of weak. We invite them to be as sympathetic to their own feelings and needs as they would be to the feelings of others. We stay close to their experiences of pain and fear, letting them see that we are touched by their trouble, and inviting them to be moved by their own distress. We support them to tolerate unpleasant negative emotions and frightening positive emotions. In a mentalizing way, we gently understand the "safety strategies" they learned early in life. Again and again we bring *compassionate nonjudgment* to the therapy conversation we share with them.[10]

Gilbert also tells us to teach the *skills* of compassion. We do so by helping clients pay attention to problems in ways that are useful and forward-looking instead of self-critical and self-limiting. Helping them develop these skills takes much kind, supportive repetition, and we have to remember that what matters most is that our clients learn to hear and feel the emotional tone of each self-to-self conversation they have. Gilbert admits that helping shamed clients feel warmth, kindness, and encouragement for themselves can be very difficult. And yet developing a positive self-to-self emotional tone is so important to the success of their therapy that it should be an explicit focus of our work with them.

To boost this right-brain learning that can be so difficult, Gilbert suggests exercises that heighten the experience of self-compassion. An exercise might begin with a focus on self-quieting breathing. Then a client is invited to imagine being a compassionate person. She is asked, while being this compassionate person, to pay attention to the expression on her face, the tone of her voice if she were to speak, and the feeling-quality of her thoughts. While securely in the role of compassionate self, she is invited to watch as if on video replay the anxious, fearful self she has stepped away from for a moment. The point of the exercise is simply that she feels compassion for that self. If self-criticism begins to break through, the video fades to black, and the client re-focuses on inhabiting the role of compassionate self.

The details of such an exercise matter far less than the overall idea: "to create experiences in which clients can engage with problematic aspects of themselves, but through the eyes of the compassionate self."[11] This compassionate self can become a center from which chronically shamed clients can explore memories and feelings that would otherwise be highly likely to stimulate self-blame and self-criticism. Gilbert notes that the compassionate self can be understood as one of a number of other possible selves (for example, an angry self, an anxious self, a lonely self), and that with practice the compassionate self can find a significant place in a client's diverse self-system.

In my practice, I have never (yet) used such an explicit exercise to bring to life a client's compassionate self. I'm more likely to nudge a client toward compassion from within our conversation, in much the same way as I speak of parts of a client's self that have just "turned up." I certainly recognize and affirm a client's compassionate self whenever he or she appears, however fleetingly. Gilbert's clarity about how shamed clients deeply need—and don't have—self-compassion helps me understand better what makes authentic connection with self so difficult for them. I become more alert for moments when I can help clients ease into a compassionate mind toward themselves. Sometimes being more helpful means just holding my clients' need for a compassionate self in mind, hoping that some mentalization of self-compassion will happen subliminally.

Mindfulness

The habit of mindfulness, understood in its simple, secular sense as reflective awareness of the present moment, is good for anyone's mental well-being. So says attachment-trained and neurobiologically-informed psychiatrist/ psychotherapist Daniel Siegel, as do many proponents of mindfulness practice.[12] Many shame theorists suggest that the habit of mindfulness can be especially useful for clients who want to experience changes in their shame-constricted neural networking.[13] Practicing mindfulness is a good way for them to give themselves a better chance at lifetime shame reduction.

As Siegel describes mindfulness, it's more than neutral reflective awareness of the present moment; it's a way of approaching each moment of our here-and-now experience with curiosity, openness, acceptance, and love.[14] Mindfulness is the intentional, focused practice of putting aside preconceptions and judgments in order to be present to our own experience with kindness and respect. Put very simply, it *is* self-compassion, and as a daily repetitive practice it lays down neural networking, including access to an endorphin/oxytocin emotional regulation system, that supports the experience of connected well-being.

If we practice therapy from a developmental/relational perspective, we believe that our clients internalize the capacities for emotional regulation, mentalization, and compassion that are embedded in how we relate to them. We don't re-parent them, and yet our clients take in these right-brain "goods" in much the same way that children internalize their parents' emotional capacities and intentions. The practice of mindfulness allows our clients to give themselves more of the same goods they receive from us, and on a daily basis. The guiding hypothesis of Siegel's book on mindfulness is that the practice of mindfulness promotes well-being because it is an attunement to self that works (fires neurons) very much as interpersonal empathic attunement works, and with many of the same effects.[15]

Siegel proposes that the attachment experiences of childhood can be replicated to a significant degree in adulthood by the practice of attunement to self. Mindfulness can be one of many relational experiences that promote the development of self-regulation in the brain. If we think of mindfulness as a secure relationship with ourselves, we can understand how this internal attunement would support capacities such as affective body-regulation, emotional balance and flexibility, attuned communication, empathy, self-awareness, and fear modulation.[16] (We also note that these capacities would be on Schore's "right-brain" list.) Siegel acknowledges that brain research does not yet validate this correspondence between interpersonal attunement and personal mindfulness, but he cites some studies that move in that direction.

Siegel also hypothesizes that self-attunement involves the creation of highly complex functioning in the brain that has the quality of neural synchrony, that is, "the harmonious firing of extended neural groups when they become linked in a state of neural integration."[17] Neural synchrony is felt subjectively as a state of coherence. Hard evidence for this synchrony is also elusive. But Siegel believes that first person accounts of the well-being and harmony that emerge with mindful awareness practices give substantial evidence (if not from brain research) to support his belief that self-attunement creates coherence in the mind.

In a full circle most interesting to a relational psychotherapist, Siegel brings his argument for self-attunement back around to interpersonal connectedness. He names three basic, interdependent aspects of mental well-being—neural integration, mental coherence, and empathic relationships. Each is necessary and they are irreducible to one another. Self-attunement leads to neural integration and mental coherence, which enhance interpersonal empathy. The interpersonal attunement of secure relationships interacts with personal mindfulness to produce even more neural integration, which is felt subjectively as coherence, harmony, and well-being.[18]

If mindfulness and empathy go hand in hand, neither we nor our clients need fear that a commitment to mindfulness will reinforce their anxious, narcissistic preoccupations. On the contrary, their commitment to openness and acceptance will naturally embrace others as well as self. We can also expect that as our clients gain a secure, empathic relationship with self that is something like a child's mutually empathic relationship with a parent, they will use their security as a base from which to explore the world with curiosity, passion, and self-expression.

The benefits of mindfulness are not reserved just for those dedicated persons who are able to sustain a daily practice of meditation. Some of our chronically shamed clients will find it very helpful to learn a formal mindfulness practice, and it's worth mentioning the possibility of such learning to all of them. However, we can also remember that in a very significant way, the process of open-ended, curious, empathic, and accepting psychotherapy is itself a process of mindfulness. As Siegel emphasizes, interpersonal and intrapersonal attunement are very closely related. Within the ambience of our compassionate, nonjudgmental interest, clients are "induced" into taking that same kind of interest in themselves. We can expect that after absorbing many hours of kind, respectful interest during therapy, our clients may be able to learn to give some of that attentive kindness and respect to themselves.

Self-Expression

It's evident that self-compassion and mindfulness are modes of authentic connection with self, and it's also easy to see how, as kind habits of mind, they counteract the effects of chronic shame. But how is self-expression an authentic connection with self, and how is it an antidote to shame? I can answer these questions only by first saying that I have in mind a very particular kind of "self-expression," one most clearly defined as *not* the performance of self that a client's shame-defenses have always demanded.

Chronically shamed clients enter therapy with unconscious commitments to performances of self that protect their vulnerability. As we have seen, these performances range from helpless rage to aloof self-sufficiency, to complex "split" character solutions to the problem of shame. To call them performances is not to demean the performers. In every case, our clients are doing what they have learned to do to make necessary contact with the world while avoiding the contact that they know will leave them alone, once again, with a needing, empty, humiliated self. But all the energy they spend on managing a dangerous relational world is energy not available for them to explore what actually moves and excites them in life.

Psychotherapy creates interpersonal space in which, over time, shamed lonely selves can come to be known and understood, and in that process, self-protective performances of self become less necessary. In brand-new ways, our clients can afford to know who they are and what they feel, and their process of coming-to-know is intimately and reciprocally connected with their process of coming-to-say.

This emergence of self-expression begins slowly, with the expression of feelings that have been denied. Clients allow that they feel anger and envy. They remember anguish from the past, and they acknowledge pain in the present. They make emotional contact with hidden longings, and they grieve their losses with deep sadness. They feel both the kindness and the trouble in their relationships, and they make choices to interact more authentically with those close to them. They take comfort in being understood, and they use support to make necessary changes in their lives. All of this is the expression of an emotional/relational self in the world, a self gaining enough strength and self-awareness to face shame, too.

Brené Brown and others suggest that in order to develop shame resilience, shame-prone people need to reach out and speak their shame.[19] I agree that shame loses power when people are able to put it out where light and air and the acceptance of others can get at it. I also agree that the process of speaking shame makes way for more authentic expressions of self. For Brown, authenticity has to do with accepting imperfection, limitations, and vulnerability. Authenticity exercises compassion in the face of struggle, and it nurtures resilience and connection. Authenticity, for Brown, is about being *enough*, and it's not an achievement; it's a practice, a series of conscious daily choices about how to live.[20] In other words, authenticity, self-compassion, and mindfulness belong together.

Therapy is a training ground not only for self-compassion and mindfulness, but also for authentic self-expression. In the interactions of therapy, the neural networks of *I feel*, *I want*, *I choose*, *I intend*, *I enjoy*, and *I will do* are laid down well enough to begin to override networks based on shame and fear, and also to begin to override the compensatory networks of performance and perfection. For our chronically shamed clients, the emergence of this ordinary, daily, grounded self-expression is both compelling and fragile. It deserves and needs our direct encouragement.

We help our clients develop shame-reducing neural pathways of self-expression when we respond to their emergent self-discovery with genuine pleasure. As the power of their past diminishes and the future beckons, we let them know that talking about exciting "good stuff" is just as important as talking about painful stuff. We understand how scary it is for them to try to do something that might not turn out well, and we help them focus on the doing of it, whether it's joining a running group, building a garden, or writing a poem. *What does it feel like to do this? How is it a part of who you are? What does it mean to you to do this?* As our clients' new initiatives emerge, we speak these questions gently, with playful, empathic curiosity.

It's our privilege to help our clients master their fears of making mistakes, supporting them to "goof bravely." We help them accept the bruises their self-esteem suffers as they take more chances in the world. After a while, we notice with them that their dreams are no longer escape fantasies, no longer compensatory illusions to make up for hidden self-loathing. What they want is possible, and we back them up as they go after it.

Somewhere in this process of learning how to be an imperfect, vulnerable self capable of compassion and creativity, our clients come to realize that they are the persons they always were—and yet there is something new. What's emerging isn't a brand-new authentic self, but on the other hand, it's more than just a reduction in the intensity and frequency of their feelings of shame. Underneath this movement toward lifetime shame reduction, there is something transformative after all. Their relationships with others and with themselves are changing profoundly, and at the center of this transformation is a new relationship with their own shame.

Our clients are no longer at the mercy of a disintegrative power they don't understand. They can tell a story about what happened to make them feel so bad. They feel better when they reach out to us and others for comfort or reassurance. They can calm and soothe themselves. Shame no longer owns them; they own it. They know where their shame hides out, when it attacks, and how to limit the damage it does.

As our clients accept the challenges of lifetime shame reduction, they become ever more aware that there are no perfect families, no perfect lives, and no perfect endings. That's often when they start to think about ending therapy. Imperfection, finitude, mortality—it's all part of life, they tell us now. But it's sad to see them go. With their acceptance of the limits of therapy and the limits of life, they have found humor and wisdom, too. Our connection feels warm and infused with mutual understanding. But that's not a good enough reason to keep doing therapy. And so we say good-bye . . . at least for now. They may be back, they say. If they need to see us, they'll call. They know and we know that there would be no shame in that. Because being vulnerable and needing others is the human condition, and we're in it together.

NOTES

1. Some brain-aware therapists believe that implicit relational learning can be erased. In *Unlocking the Emotional Brain: Eliminating Symptoms at Their Roots Using Memory Reconsolidation* (New York: Routledge, 2012), Bruce Ecker, Robin Ticic, and Laurel Hulley teach therapists to induce emotional experiences that reactivate specific old learnings and then to hold them open in the presence of new emotional learnings that do not match the old. With good planning and timing, such an "erasure sequence" can eliminate symptoms rapidly, effortlessly, and permanently, they maintain.

2. See, for example, Norman Doidge, *The Brain that Changes Itself* (New York: Viking, 2007).

3. Judith Jordan, "Relational Development: Therapeutic Implications of Empathy and Shame," in *Women's Growth in Diversity: More Writings from the Stone Center,* ed. Judith Jordan (New York: Guilford, 1997), 138–61.

4. Jordan, "Relational Development," 152–53.

5. For example, self psychologists maintain that a cohesive sense of self emerges from self-object experiences that are grounded in affect attunement. Mentalization theory tells us that a child comes to know his own mind (or self) as his mind is held within the mind of another. In affect regulation theory, a sense of self emerges as a right brain experience when a child's affect finds the consistent regulation from another that's necessary for optimal right brain development. Stone Center self-in-relation theorists believe that empathy for oneself becomes possible only as one experiences another person's empathic understanding.

6. My thinking here aligns more with theorists of the Interpersonal/Relational school of psychoanalysis who, along with Stone Center self-in-relation theorists, de-emphasize the existence of an ontologically defined singular self; self psychology and other developmentally oriented theories still seem to count somewhat on the notion of an individual, historically constructed, essential self.

7. Paul Gilbert, "Shame in Psychotherapy and the Role of Compassion Focused Therapy," in *Shame in the Therapy Hour,* eds. Ronda L. Dearing and June Price Tangney, (Washington, DC: American Psychological Association, 2011), 330.

8. Gilbert, "Compassion Focused Therapy," 331–38.

9. Gilbert, "Compassion Focused Therapy," 341.

10. Gilbert, "Compassion Focused Therapy," 341–43.

11. Gilbert, "Compassion Focused Therapy," 345.

12. Daniel Siegel, *The Mindful Brain: Reflection and Attunement in the Cultivation of Well-Being* (New York: Norton, 2007); see also Jon Kabat-Zinn, *Full Catastrophe Living: Using the Wisdom of Your Body and Mind to Face Stress, Pain, and Illness* (New York: Dell, 1990) and *Coming to Our Senses: Healing Ourselves and the World Through Mindfulness* (New York: Hyperion, 2003).

13. For example, Gilbert, "Compassion Focused Therapy," 343; Leslie Greenberg and Shigeru Iwakabe, "Emotion-Focused Therapy and Shame," in *Shame in the Therapy Hour,* eds. Dearing and Tangney, 77; Brené Brown, Virginia Hernandez, and Yolanda Villarreal, "Connections: A 12-Session Psychoeducational Shame Resilience Curriculum," in *Shame in the Therapy Hour,* eds. Dearing and Tangney, 364; Shireen Rizvi et al., "The Role of Shame in the Development and Treatment of Borderline Personality Disorder," in *Shame in the Therapy Hour,* eds. Dearing and Tangney, 249.

14. Siegel, *Mindful Brain,* 15.

15. Siegel, *Mindful Brain,* 17.

16. Siegel, *Mindful Brain,* 191.

17. Siegel, *Mindful Brain,* 193.

18. Siegel, *Mindful Brain,* 198–201.

19. Brown, Hernandez, and Villarreal, "Connections," 368.

20. Brené Brown, *The Gifts of Imperfection: Let Go of Who You Think You're Supposed to Be and Embrace Who You Are* (Minneapolis, MN: Hazelden, 2010), 49–50.

REFERENCES

Ainsworth, Mary. 1978. *Patterns of Attachment: A Psychological Study of the Strange Situation*. Hillsdale, NJ: Erlbaum.

Ainsworth, Mary, and John Bowlby. 1965. *Child Care and the Growth of Love*. London: Penguin Books.

Allen, Jon G., D.A. Console, and L. Lewis. 1999. "Dissociative Detachment and Memory Impairment: Reversible Amnesia or Encoding Failure?" *Comprehensive Psychiatry* 40 (1999): 160–71.

Allen, Jon G., Peter Fonagy, and Anthony W. Bateman. 2008. *Mentalizing in Clinical Practice*. Washington, DC: American Psychiatric Press.

American Psychiatric Association. *Diagnostic and Statistical Manual of Mental Disorders, Fifth Edition (DSM-5)*. 2013. Arlington, VA: American Psychiatric Association.

Aron, Lewis. *A Meeting of Minds: Mutuality in Psychoanalysis*. 1996. Hillsdale, NJ: Analytic Press.

————. 2003. "The Paradoxical Place of Enactment in Psychoanalysis: Introduction." *Psychoanalytic Dialogues*, 13: 273–87.

Bacal, Howard. "Shame – the Affect of Discrepancy."1997. In *The Widening Scope of Shame*, edited by Melvin Lansky and Andrew Morrison, 99–104. Hillsdale, NJ: Analytic Press.

Badenoch, Bonnie. 2008. *Being a Brain-Wise Therapist: A Practical Guide to Interpersonal Neurobiology*. New York: Norton.

Bliss, Eugene. 1986. *Multiple Personality, Allied Disorders, and Hypnosis*. New York: Oxford University Press.

Boston Change Process Study Group. 2010. *Change in Psychotherapy: A Unifying Paradigm*. New York: Norton.

Bowlby, John. 1988. *A Secure Base: Parent-Child Attachment and Healthy Human Development*. New York: Basic Books.

Bradshaw, John. 1988. *Healing the Shame that Binds You*. Deerfield Beach, FL: Health Communications.

Bromberg, Philip. 1998. *Standing in the Spaces: Essays on Clinical Process, Trauma, and Dissociation*. Hillsdale, NJ: Analytic Press.

————. 2006. *Awakening the Dreamer: Clinical Journeys*. Mahwah, NJ: Analytic Press.

————. 2011. *The Shadow of the Tsunami and the Growth of the Relational Mind*. New York: Routledge.

Broucek, Francis. 1991. *Shame and the Self*. New York: Guilford.

Brown, Brené. 2007. *I Thought It Was Just Me (but it isn't): Making the Journey from "What Will People Think?" to "I Am Enough."* New York: Gotham.

_____. 2010. *The Gifts of Imperfection: Let Go of Who You Think You're Supposed to Be and Embrace Who You Are.* Minneapolis, MN: Hazeldon.

_____. 2012. *Daring Greatly.* New York: Gotham.

Cloitre, Marylene, Lisa R. Cohen, and Karestan C. Koenen. 2006. *Treating Survivors of Childhood Sexual Abuse: Psychotherapy for the Interrupted Life.* New York: Guilford.

Cozolino, Louis. 2012. *The Neuroscience of Psychotherapy: Healing the Social Brain,* 2nd edn. New York: Norton.

Danielian, Jack and Patricia Gianotti. 2012. *Listening with Purpose: Entry Points into Shame and Narcissistic Vulnerability.* New York: Jason Aronson.

Davies, Jodie Messler. 1997. "Dissociation and Therapeutic Enactment." *Gender and Psychoanalysis,* 2, : 241–57.

Davies, Jodie Messler, and Mary Gail Frawley. 1994. *Treating the Adult Survivor of Childhood Sexual Abuse: A Psychoanalytic Perspective.* New York: Basic Books.

Dearing, Ronda L., and June Price Tangney, editor. 2011. *Shame in the Therapy Hour.* Washington, DC: American Psychological Association.

DeYoung, Patricia. 2003. *Relational Psychotherapy: A Primer.* New York: Routledge.

Doidge, Norman. 2007. *The Brain that Changes Itself.* New York: Viking.

Donald-Pressman, Stephanie, and Robert Pressman. 1994. *The Narcissistic Family: Diagnosis and Treatment.* New York: Macmillan.

Dutra, L., K. Callahan, E. Forman, M. Mendelsohn, and J.L. Herman. 2008. "Core Schemas and Suicidality in a Chronically Traumatized Population." *Journal of Nervous and Mental Disease* 196: 71–74.

Ecker, Bruce, Robin Ticic, and Laurel Hulley. 2012. *Unlocking the Emotional Brain: Eliminating Symptoms at Their Roots Using Memory Reconsolidation.* New York: Routledge.

Fonagy, Peter, Gyorgy Gergely, Elliot Jurist, and Mary Target. 2002. *Affect Regulation, Mentalization, and the Development of the Self.* New York: Other Press.

Fonagy, Peter, Miriam Steele, Howard Steele, George Moran, and Anna Higgitt. 1991. "The Capacity to Understand Mental States: The Reflective Self in Parent and Child and Its Significance for Security of Attachment." *Infant Mental Health Journal* 12: 201–18.

Fosha, Diana. 2009. "Emotion and Recognition at Work: Energy, Vitality, Pleasure, Truth, Desire, and the Emergent Phenomenology of Transformational Experience." In *The Healing Power of Emotion: Affective Neuroscience, Development and Clinical Practice,* edited by Diana Fosha, Daniel Siegel, and Marion Solomon, 172–203. New York: Norton.

Fossum, Merle, and Marilyn Mason. 1986. *Facing Shame: Families in Recovery.* New York: Norton.

Geist, Richard. 2008. "Connectedness, Permeable Boundaries, and the Development of the Self: Therapeutic Implications." *International Journal of Psychoanalytic Self Psychology* 3: 129–51.

_____. 2011. "The Forward Edge, Connectedness, and the Therapeutic Process." *International Journal of Psychoanalytic Self Psychology* 6: 235–50.

George, Carol, Nancy Kaplan, and Mary Main. 1985. The Adult Attachment Interview. Berkeley, CA: University of California at Berkeley, unpublished manuscript.

Goldberg, Arnold. 1999. *Being of Two Minds: the Vertical Split in Psychoanalysis and Psychotherapy*. Hillsdale, NJ: Analytic Press.

Guntrip, Harry. *Schizoid Phenomena, Object Relations, and the Self*. 1969. New York: International Universities Press.

Harper, James, and Margaret Hoopes. 1990. *Uncovering Shame: An Approach Integrating Individuals and Their Family Systems*. New York: Norton.

Herman, Judith Lewis. 1992. *Trauma and Recovery*. New York: Basic Books.

————. 2012. "Shattered Shame States and Their Repair." In *Shattered States: Disorganized Attachment and Its Repair*, John Bowlby Memorial Conference Monograph 2007, edited by Judy Yellin and Kate White, 157–70. London: Karnac.

Horney, Karen. 1945. *Our Inner Conflicts: A Constructive Theory of Neurosis*. New York: Norton.

————. 1950. *Neurosis and Human Growth: The Struggle toward Self-Realization*. New York: Norton.

Hughes, Daniel. 2007. *Attachment Focused Family Therapy*. New York: Norton.

Jordan, Judith. 1997. "Relational Development: Therapeutic Implications of Empathy and Shame." In *Women's Growth in Diversity: More Writings from the Stone Center*, edited by Judith Jordan, 138–61. New York: Guilford.

Jordan, Judith, Alexandra Kaplan, Jean Baker Miller, Irene Pierce Stiver, and Janet Surrey. 1991. *Women's Growth in Connection: Writings from the Stone Center*. New York: Guilford.

Kabat-Zinn, Jon. 1990. *Full-Catastrophe Living: Using the Wisdom of Your Body and Mind to Face Stress, Pain, and Illness*. New York: Dell.

————. 2003. *Coming to Our Senses: Healing Ourselves and the World Through Mindfulness*. New York: Hyperion.

Kahn, Michael. 1997. *Between Therapist and Client: The New Relationship*, 2nd edn. New York: Freeman.

Kaufman, Gershen. (1980) 1992. *Shame, the Power of Caring*. Rochester, VT: Schenkman Books, 1980. 3rd edn.

Kohut, Heinz. 1971. *The Analysis of the Self: A Systematic Approach to the Psychoanalytic Treatment of Personality Disorders*. New York: International Universities Press.

————. 1984. *How Does Analysis Cure?* Chicago: University of Chicago Press.

Lee, Ronald, and J. Colby Martin. 1991. *Psychotherapy after Kohut: A Textbook of Self Psychology*. Hillsdale, NJ: Analytic Press.

Lewis, Helen Block. 1971. *Shame and Guilt in Neurosis*. New York: International Universities Press.

————ed. 1987. *The Role of Shame in Symptom Formation*. Hillsdale, NJ: Erlbaum.

Lichtenberg, Joseph. 1989. *Psychoanalysis and Motivation*. Hillsdale, NJ: Analytic Press.

————. 2007. *Sensuality and Sexuality across the Divide of Shame*. New York: Routledge.

Luborsky, Lester, Barton Singer, and Lise Luborsky. 1975. "Comparative Studies of Psychotherapies." *Archives of General Psychiatry* 32: 995–1008.

Main, Mary "Adult Attachment Interview Protocol." http://www.psychology.sunysb.edu/attachment/measures/content/aai_interview.pdf. Accessed January 18, 2014.

Main, Mary, and Ruth Goldwyn. 1998. *Adult Attachment Scoring and Classification System.* University of California at Berkeley: unpublished manuscript.

Main, Mary, and Judith Solomon. 1990. "Procedures for Identifying Infants as Disorganized/Disoriented during the Ainsworth Strange Situation." In *Attachment in the Preschool Years: Theory, Research, and Intervention*, edited by Mark T. Greenberg, Dante Cicchetti, and E. Mark Cummings, 121–60. Chicago: University of Chicago Press.

Main, Mary, Nancy Kaplan, and Jude Cassidy. 1985. "Security in Infancy, Childhood, and Adulthood: A Move to the Level of Representation." In *Growing Points of Attachment Theory and Research*, edited by Inge Bretherton and Everett Waters, 64–104.

Maroda, Karen. 1998. "Enactment: When the Patient's and Analyst's Pasts Converge." *Psychoanalytic Psychology*, 15: 517–35.

Maté, Gabor. 2008. *In the Realm of Hungry Ghosts: Close Encounters with Addiction.* Toronto: Knopf.

Miller, Jean Baker, and Irene Pierce Stiver. 1997. *The Healing Connection: How Women Form Relationships in Therapy and in Life.* Boston: Beacon Press.

Miller, Susan. 1985. *The Shame Experience.* Hillsdale, NJ: Analytic Press.

Morrison, Andrew. 1987. "The Eye Turned Inward: Shame and the Self." In *The Many Faces of Shame*, edited by. Donald Nathanson, 271–91. New York: Guilford.

_____. 1989. *Shame, the Underside of Narcissism.* Hillsdale, NJ: Analytic Press.

_____. 2011. "The Psychodynamics of Shame." In *Shame in the Therapy Hour*, edited by Ronda L. Dearing and June Price Tangney, 23–43. Washington, DC: American Psychological Association.

Nathanson, Donald, ed. 1987. *The Many Faces of Shame.* New York: Guilford.

_____. 1992. *Shame and Pride.* New York: Norton.

Orange, Donna. 1995. *Emotional Understanding: Studies in Psychoanalytic Epistemology.* New York: Guilford.

_____. 2008. "Whose Shame Is It Anyway? Lifeworlds of Humiliation and Systems of Restoration." *Contemporary Psychoanalysis* 44: 83–100.

Perls, Frederick S., Ralph F. Hefferline, and Paul Goodman. (1951) 1994. *Gestalt Therapy: Excitement and Growth in the Human Personality.* New York: Julian. Reprint, Goldsboro, ME: Gestalt Journal Press.

Pizer, Stuart. 1998. *Building Bridges: Negotiating Paradox in Psychoanalysis.* Hillsdale, NJ: Analytic Press.

Potter-Effron, Ronald. 2002. *Shame, Guilt, and Alcoholism*, 2nd edn. New York: Haworth.

Rogers, Carl. 1951. *Client-Centered Therapy: Its Current Practice, Implications, and Theory.* London: Constable.

_____. 1961. *On Becoming a Person: A Therapist's View of Psychotherapy.* London: Constable.

Ross, Colin. 1989. *Multiple Personality Disorder: Diagnosis, Clinical Features, and Treatment.* New York: Wiley & Sons.

Rusch, Nicolas, Klaus Lieb, Ines Gottler, Christiane Hermann, Elisabeth Schramm, and Harald Richter. 2007. "Shame and Implicit Self-Concept in Women with Borderline Personality Disorder." *American Journal of Psychiatry* 164: 500–508.

Rusch, Nicolas, Daniela Schulz, Gabi Valerius, Regina Steil, Martin Bohus, and Christian Schmal. 2011. "Disgust and Implicit Self-Concept in Women with Borderline Personality Disorder and Posttraumatic Stress Disorder." *European Archives of Psychiatry and Clinical Neuroscience* 261: 369–76.

Schore, Allan. 1994. *Affect Regulation and the Origin of the Self*. Mahwah, NJ: Erlbaum.

———. 2003a. *Affect Dysregulation and Disorders of the Self*. New York: Norton.

———. 2003b. *Affect Regulation and the Repair of the Self*. New York: Norton.

———. 2011. Foreword to *The Shadow of the Tsunami and the Growth of the Relational Mind*, by Philip Bromberg. New York: Routledge.

———. 2012. *The Science of the Art of Psychotherapy*. New York: Norton.

Schwartz, Richard. 1995. *Internal Family Systems Therapy*. New York: Guilford.

Shane, Morton, Estelle Shane, and Mary Gales. 1997. *Intimate Attachments: Toward a New Self Psychology*. New York: Guilford.

Siegel, Daniel. 1999. *The Developing Mind: How Relationships and the Brain Interact to Shape Who We Are*. New York: Guilford.

———. 2007. *The Mindful Brain: Reflection and Attunement in the Cultivation of Well-Being*. New York: Norton.

Stern, Daniel. 1985. *The Interpersonal World of the Infant: A View from Psychoanalysis and Developmental Psychology*. New York: Basic Books.

Stern, Donnel. 1997. *Unformulated Experience: From Dissociation to Imagination in Psychoanalysis*. Hillsdale, NJ: Analytic Press.

———. 2010. *Partners in Thought: Working with Unformulated Experience, Dissociation, and Enactment*. New York: Routledge.

Stolorow, Robert, and George Atwood. 1992. *Contexts of Being: The Intersubjective Foundations of Psychological Life*. Hillsdale, NJ: Analytic Press.

Stuss, Donald, and Michael Alexander. 1999. "Affectively Burnt-In: One Role of the Right Frontal Lobe?" In *Memory, Consciousness, and the Brain: The Talin Conference*, edited by Endel Tulving, 215–27. Philadelphia, PA: Psychology Press.

Talbot, Jean, Nancy Talbot, and Xin Tu. 2004. "Shame-Proneness as a Diathesis for Dissociation in Women with Histories of Childhood Sexual Abuse. *Journal of Traumatic Stress* 17: 445–48.

Tangney, June Price, and Ronda L. Dearing. 2002. *Shame and Guilt*. New York: Guilford.

Tomkins, Silvan. 1963. *Affect, Imagery, Consciousness*. Vol. 2, *The Negative Affects*. New York: Springer.

Tronick, Edward, Heidelise Als, Lauren Adamson, Susan Wise, and T. Berry Brazelton. 1978. "The Infant's Response to Entrapment between Contradictory Messages in Face-to-Face Interaction." *Journal of Child Psychiatry* 17: 1–13.

van der Kolk, Bessel A., and Rita Fisler. 1995. "Dissociation and the Fragmentary Nature of Traumatic Memories: Overview and Exploratory Study." *Journal of Traumatic Stress* 8: 505–25.

Wallin, David. 2007. *Attachment in Psychotherapy*. New York: Guilford.

Wampold, Bruce E. 2001. *The Great Psychotherapy Debate: Models, Methods, and Findings*. Mahwah, NJ: Erlbaum.

Winnicott, Donald W. (1971) 1982. *Playing and Reality*. London: Tavistock. Reprint, Harmondsworth, Middlesex, England: Penguin Education.

Wolf, Ernest. 1988. *Treating the Self: Elements of Clinical Self Psychology*. New York: Guilford.

Young-Eisendrath, Polly. 2008. *The Self-Esteem Trap: Raising Confident and Compassionate Kids in an Age of Self-Importance*. New York: Little, Brown.

INDEX

abuse 67–8; childhood *see* childhood abuse
abusive shaming other 62
acceptance 83
achievement 128–9
adaptive shame 58
addiction 7, 8, 11–12, 16, 84–5; assessing for shame 71–3
Adult Attachment Interview (AAI) 106–7
affect, shame as 22–3
affect attunement *see* attunement
affect regulation theory (ART) xii, xiv, 20–1, 22–3, 55–6; attachment theory, affect regulation and shame 48–50; dissociation and shame 68–9; dysregulation and the right brain 36–7; family shame narratives 125–6; objectification 44–5; self psychology, affect regulation and shame 50–1 thoughts on shame from 39–42; vertical splitting as affect regulation 70
affect theory xiii–xiv, 22
affective resonance 38
agency 132
aggression 63
Ainsworth, M. 36
Alexander, M. 104
alienation 9–11
ambition 52–3, 93
ambivalent attachment 48–9, 97–8, 110–11
anger 13–15, 31, 65–6, 94
anxiety 3, 14–15, 105
archaic selfobject experience 91

Aron, L. 84
art of psychotherapy 55–6
articulation 158
assessing for shame xiv, 58–74; addiction 71–3; dissociation 68–71; family-of-origin patterns 64–7; feelings of therapist with a client 59–60; from the right brain 73; performance, perfection and control 60; self-with-other patterns 60–1; self-with-self patterns 61–4; trauma 67–8
attachment 36–7, 37–8, 118; affect regulation, shame and attachment theory 48–50; and the capacity for right-brain narrative 106–8; insecure 48–50, 106; and narrative style 106–11; providing attachment experience 97–8; secure 48, 106, 107, 113–14; to the therapist 132
attunement xiii, 21, 66, 72, 98, 102, 113; empathic 19, 35, 36; misattunement 24, 34, 39, 40–1; self-attunement 173–4
Atwood, G. 51, 67
authentic connection 164–76; with others 164–70; with self 170–6
avoidant attachment 48, 49, 97, 108–10

Bacal, H. 24
bad self (bad-me) 27, 46–8, 127, 154
Badenoch, B. 35, 103, 131, 132
beauty, cultural ideal of 71–2
befriending parts of split clients 150–1
binge-and-purge cycle 71

blame 31; stopping shame/blame cycles 167–8
body image 71–2
borderline personality disorder 45
Boston Change Process Study Group 32, 36, 134, 153
Bowlby, J. 36
brain injury 164
Bromberg, P. 135, 154, 159
Broucek, F. 25–6, 29, 44
Brown, B. 3, 175
bulimia 71–2

calmness 93–4, 97, 98
case examples: angry kind of split (Ellen) 8–9; dissociated shame (Cynthia, Sid and Hilary) 140–5; double life (Gary) 6–8; feeling unbearably alone (Susie) 9–11; giving up on love (Andrea) 11–13; mutual enactment (Erin) 156–8; narrative of avoidant/dismissing client (Martha) 108–10; raging couple (Trevor and Megan) 13–15; stellar performance (Clare) 4–6
categorical affect 89
central relational paradox 61
character solutions 136, 146–53
childhood abuse 67–8; sexual 138–9, 141
chronic shame xiii, 3–17, 58; clients' stories 4–15; common features 15–17; defining shame 18–22
co-created narratives 111–14, 133
coherence, mental 174
coherent narrative 103
coherent self 19, 20, 44–5, 66
cohesive narrative 103
collapse 41
communication 132
compassion 132
Compassion Focused Therapy 171–2
conflict 66; eliciting family shame narratives 127–8
connectedness 118–22
connection: authentic *see* authentic connection; intersubjective 64–7, 118; lack of between client and therapist 59–60; non-verbal 87–9,

158–9; right-brain *see* right-brain connection
conscience 40
contempt 59
control 60
conversations, family 124–5
co-transference 139, 151–3
couples' repetitive fight cycles 13–15
Cozolino, L. 32, 35, 89, 101, 102, 105, 107
cure 162, 163–4; *see also* shame reduction
curiosity 65; therapeutic stance 83–4
curious empathy 168

Danielian, J. 146–53, 161
Davies, J. 138–9
Dearing, R.L. 4, 30–1, 32, 80
definition of shame 18–22
dependency 96
depression 3, 14–15, 65–6
despair 9–11, 18, 125
difference 127–8
dignity 122
diplomacy 122–3
direct shaming other 62
disconnection 61; right-brain 90–1
discrepancy 24
disgrace 30
disgust 45–6
disintegration xiii, 18–20, 25, 26, 29–30, 35, 41
dismissing narrative style 106–7, 108–10
disorganized attachment 49–50, 98, 107, 110–11
dissociation xv–xvi, 41–2, 63, 136–61; assessing for shame 68–71; character solutions 136, 146–53; dissociation/enactment theory and shame xvi, 153–9, 161; four quadrant model 147–51; and the right brain 137; and shame 140–5; transference enactments 147, 151–3; and trauma theory 137–9; and the unconscious 139–40
dissociative identity disorder (DID) 139, 146; case example 140–5
double life case example 6–8

dysregulating other xiii, 18–19, 20–2, 29–30, 63
dysregulation 36–7, 38, 41, 42

eating disorders 71–2
Ecker, B. 176
efficacy 51
ego ideal 40, 95; troubles with 53–4
embarrassment 29
emergent change 152
Emotion-Focused Therapy (EFT) 58
emotional regulation *see* attunement
emotional sensitivity 78
emotions: eliciting family shame narratives 125–6; linking to events 98–101; linking words to 105; as problem in family-of-origin 65; shame as emotion 23–5; sharing and shame reduction 165–6
empathic attunement 19, 35, 36
empathic immersion 117, 118
empathic possibility 18, 166, 168
empathy: large 90, 136; mindfulness and 174; mutual 118–19; therapeutic stance 80, 83–4
enactment: end of 155–6; mutual xvi, 153–9, 161; transference enactments 147, 151–3
ending therapy 176
engagement with how stories are told 108–11
enmeshed narrative style 107
erasure sequence 176
escape from self 29
evaluation 44–5, 46
events, linking emotions and 98–101
exiles 130–1
experience-near approach 146–53; four quadrant model 147–51; transference enactments 147, 151–3

failure: ideas of 25; of treatment 24
faith in narrative process 108
family history 78
family-of-origin patterns 64–7
family shame narratives 124–9
fight cycles 13–15
firefighters 130–1
Fonagy, P. 81
forgiveness 168–70

Fosha, D. 118
fostering right-brain connection *see* right-brain connection
four quadrant model 147–51
Frawley, M. 138–9
free, autonomous adults 106

Gales, M. 134
gaze 25–6
Geist, R. 118–19, 120, 121
Gestalt therapy 131–2
Gianotti, P. 146–53, 161
gifted child 52–3
Gilbert, P. 171–2
Goldberg, A. 70
good self 46–8
grandiose shaming other 62
grandiosity 52–3, 93
guilt 29, 30, 124, 127, 171; as authentic connection 168–70; difference from shame 30–2

hara-kiri 19–20
heightened affective relational experience 152
here-and-now relational patterns 99–100, 101
Herman, J. 67–8, 122, 138
historical relational patterns 100–1
honesty 122–3
horizontal integration 44–5, 102–3
Horney, K. 61, 136
How I View Myself quadrant 147–8, 149
Hughes, D. 64, 82
Hulley, L. 176
humiliation 29, 52, 122
humor 83
hyperarousal 62–3

ideal self 47
idealizing selfobject experiences 28, 50–1; failure of 28, 53–4; fostering right-brain connection 93–5
ideals, commitment to 95
images 133
implicit relational knowing 32, 100, 134
implosion 41
indignity 30

indirect shaming other 62
inefficacy 25
inferiority, feelings of 29, 30
injury-guilt-remorse-forgiveness
    sequence 168–70
insecure attachment 48–50, 106
integrated self 19, 20, 44–5, 66
integration 138; horizontal 44–5,
    102–3; narrative as right-brain
    integration *see* right-brain narrative;
    neural 173–4; vertical 102–3
interest 65
inter-hemispheric narratives 104–5
internal community model 131
Internal Family Systems Therapy
    130–1
internal others 62–4
interpreting from inside the client's
    world 119–21
intersubjective connection 64–7, 118
isolation 9–11, 16–17, 18, 48, 61,
    125, 165

Jordan, J. 18, 164–5, 166

Kaufman, G. 74
kinship 96; *see also* twinship
Kohut, H. 22, 27, 51

labeling effect 105
large empathy 90, 136
left brain 102
left-right integration 44–5, 102–3
Lewis, H.B. 22, 23–4, 25, 26, 27, 30
Lichtenberg, J. 51, 56–7
lifetime shame reduction *see* shame
    reduction
light and air metaphor 116–17; *see
    also* speaking of shame
listening 108–11
loneliness 9–11, 16–17, 18, 48, 61,
    125, 165
long-term intensive psychotherapy 77–8
love 16–17; giving up on 11–13;
    unlovability 165
low-arousal state 41–2
Loyal Waiting quadrant 147–9, 150

Main, M. 107
maladaptive shame 58

managers 130–1
Maté, G. 72
mental coherence 174
mentalizing 38–9, 90–1, 93; stance
    81–2; the teller in the story 111–12
merger selfobject experience 51
metaphors 133
Miller, S. 29
mindfulness: shame reduction 170,
    173–4, 175; stance 82
mirror-hunger 93
mirroring selfobject experiences 28,
    50–1; failure of 52–3; fostering
    right-brain connection 92–3
misattunement 24, 34, 39, 40–1
mistakes 127
moments of meeting 129, 134
Morrison, A. 27–8, 29, 53
mortification 30
mother-child relationship 6, 143; *see
    also* parenting
motivational systems 51, 56–7
movement schemes 61
multiple personality disorder *see*
    dissociative identity disorder (DID)
mutual empathy 118–19
mutual enactment xvi, 153–9, 161
mutual recognition 66, 155–6, 158
mutuality 117–18

narcissism 27–9, 146, 149–50
narrative 90; attachment theory,
    affect regulation and shame 48–50;
    disgust 45–6; eliciting family shame
    narratives 124–9; end of enactment
    155; good self/bad self 46–8; linking
    events and emotions 98–101;
    narratives of shame xiv, 44–57;
    objectification 44–5; parts of self
    work and 133; right-brain *see* right-
    brain narrative; self psychology,
    affect regulation and shame 50–1;
    selfobject failure and pathways to
    shame 51–6
Nathanson, D. 22, 23, 27, 61
needs: eliciting family shame narratives
    126–7; negotiating in shame
    reduction 166–7
neglect 6, 11–12
neglectful shaming other 62

negotiation of needs 166–7
neural integration 173–4
neural plasticity 164
neural synchrony 173–4
non-linear systems theory 152–3
non-verbal connection 87–9, 158–9
not-me 70, 153–4, 157, 158
now moments 36, 69, 134

object relations theory 62–4
objectification 25–6, 44–5
optimal stress 89
Orange, D. 23, 151
other: authentic connection with
    others 164–70; dysregulating xi,
    18–19, 20–2, 29–30, 63; internal
    others 62–4; regulating 21; self-
    with-other patterns 60–1
other-directed mindset 26

PACE stance 82–4
parent/child dyads, internal 131
parental gaze 25–6
parenting: affect regulation theory and
    shame 39–40; child misbehaviour,
    disintegration and 20; failure of
    idealizing selfobject experience 28,
    53–4; family-of-origin patterns
    64–7; family shame narratives
    124–9; mother-child relationship
    6, 143; normal 26; reflective self-
    functioning and secure attachment
    113–14
parts of self: befriending parts of
    split clients 150–1; working with
    129–33, 135
passivity 54
pathways to shame 51–6
perfection 60
performance 4–6, 18, 26, 49, 60, 120,
    174–5
Perls, F.S. 101
personality style 146
phenomenological approach 29
playfulness 82–3, 97
post-traumatic stress disorder (PTSD)
    45, 68, 137–8
Potter-Effron, R. 71, 84–5
Powers, T. 116
practicing 39

praise 128–9
preoccupied narrative style 107, 110
prerequisites for working with shame
    xiv–xv, 77–86; motivation for
    working with shame 84–5; reading
    shame theory 78–9; shame-free
    frame for therapy 79–80; stance
    80–4; therapist's knowledge of own
    shame 77–8
presence 123
present moments 36, 69, 134
primary communion with others 26
protectors 131
psychodynamic theory 22–32

rage 13–15, 31, 65–6, 94
rapprochement crisis 40
reading shame theory 78–9
realization 158
recognition, mutual 66, 155–6, 158
reduction of shame see shame
    reduction
reductionism 23
regulating other 21
regulation see attunement
relational neurobiological narratives
    see narrative
relational theory xiii–xiv,
    18–33; defining shame 18–22;
    disintegration 18–20, 25, 26, 29–30;
    dysregulating other 18–19, 20–2,
    29–30; guilt 29, 30–2; shame as
    affect 22–3; shame as emotion 23–5;
    shame as self-image 27–9; shame
    as thought 25–7; varieties of shame
    experience 29–30
relational trauma 3, 34, 38, 164
relational validation 80–1, 82–4
remorse 168–70
repair: interactive 39; of rupture
    121–2
resistance 119, 120
responsible power 127
Revenge Enactments quadrant 147–8,
    149–50
right brain xiv, 34–43; affect
    regulation, dysregulation and
    36–7; affect regulation theory and
    shame 39–42; assessing from 73;
    dissociation and 137; psychotherapy

and 37–9; working with enactments 158–9

right-brain connection xv, 87–101; dissociation and shame 144–5; family-of-origin patterns 64–7; linking events and emotions 98–101; non-verbal 87–9, 158–9; providing attachment experience 97–8; providing selfobject experience 91–6; selfobject transference as safe emergency 96–7; tolerating right-brain disconnection 90–1

right-brain insight 38–9

right-brain narrative xv, 102–15; attachment and the capacity for 106–8; engaging with how stories are told 108–11; faith in the process 108; linking emotion to words 105; mentalizing the teller in the story 111–12; process not content 112–13; role of the therapist 113–14

right-left integration 44–5, 102–3

Rodin, J. 71

Rogers, C. 36

Ross, C. 146

rupture 40–1, 120–1; repairing 121–2

safe emergencies 89, 91, 101; selfobject transference as 96–7

Schore, A. xii, xiv, 35, 36–7, 38; disgust 45; dissociation 69, 137; enactments 158–9; right-brain narrative 103–4, 105; shame 39–41; trouble with ego ideal 47

Schore, J. 37

Schwartz, R. 130–1, 132

secure attachment 48, 106, 107, 113–14

self: authentic connection with 170–6; escape from 29; ideal 47; integrated 19, 20, 44–5, 66; left brain 104; parts of see parts of self; right brain 103–4

self-acceptance 47–8

self-attunement 173–4

self-awareness xiv, 77–8

self-compassion 170, 171–2, 175

self-consciousness 29–30

self-delineating selfobject experience 51

self-denigration 34

self-disclosure 121–2

self-disintegration xiii, 18–20, 25, 26, 29–30, 35, 41

self-evaluation 45, 46

self-expression 170, 174–6

self-image, shame as 27–9

self-in-relation therapy 36, 117–18

self-loathing 9–11, 45, 47, 68

self-narrative 107

self psychology 19, 117, 118, 119; affect regulation, shame and 50–1

self-reflection 105, 107

self-reflexivity 113–14

self-regulation 38, 39

self-regulatory ego ideal 40

self-shaming other 62

self-with-other patterns 60–1

self-with-self patterns 61–4

selfobject experiences 50–1, 55, 56–7; fostering right-brain connection 91–6

selfobject failure 51–6

selfobject transferences 92–6; nurturing the tendrils of 118–19; as safe emergencies 96–7

sexual abuse 138–9, 141

shame, definition of 18–22

shame/blame cycles 167–8

shame-free frame for therapy 79–80

shame reduction xvi, 162–77; authentic connection with others 163–70; authentic connection with self 170–6; vs cure 162, 163–4

Shane, E. 134

Shane, M. 134

Shapiro, E. 116

Siegel, D. 35, 43, 102, 104, 173–4

Silberstein, L. 71

speaking of shame xv, 116–35; bringing shame into the light 117–22; eliciting family shame narratives 124–9; honesty and diplomacy 122–3; shame in a therapy session 129; teaching about shame 124; working with parts of self 129–33, 135

split existence clients 6–9

splitting see dissociation

Stadter, M. 62, 63

stance, therapeutic 80–4
Stern, D. 89, 153–6, 158–9
still-face experiments 12
Stolorow, R. 51, 67
strength 94
Striegel-Moore, R. 71
Stuss, D. 104
suicidality 10–11
superego 40
supervision 77
Symptoms quadrant 147–8

Tangney, J.P. 4, 30–1, 32, 80
teaching about shame 124
theory, reading 78–9
therapeutic stance 80–4
therapist: feelings when with a client
    59–60; knowing own shame xiv,
    77–8; motivation for working with
    shame 84–5; role in right-brain
    integration 113–14; self-disclosure
    121–2; shame in relation to 129
therapy contract 79
thought, shame as 25–7
Ticic, R. 176
Tomkins, S. 22, 23, 24, 39
transference-countertransference 77
transference enactments 147, 151–3
transitional objects 160
transitional phenomena 160

trauma 122–3, 140; assessing for
    shame 67–8; dissociation and
    trauma theory 137–9; relational 3,
    34, 38, 164
twinship 51; failure of 55; fostering
    right brain connection 95–6

unconscious, the 139–40
understanding 66
unlovability 165
unresolved/disorganized narrative style
    107
unworthiness 18

values 95
varieties of shame experience 29–30
vertical integration 102–3
vertical splitting 70–1
vitality affect 89
vulnerability 31

Wallin, D. 82
watchers 131
weakness 54
Winnicott, D.W. 144, 160
wisdom 94
Wolf, E. 51
words, linking to emotions 105
worthlessness 9–11, 15, 52
Wurmser, L. 26, 27